BATH

''tis a Valley of Pleasure, yet a sink of Iniquity; nor is there any Intrigue or Debauch acted in London but is mimick'd there.'

In the summer of 1702 the swashbuckling Beau Richard Nash, together with many of the fashionable men and women of quality, was drawn to Bath following the visit of Queen Anne. His aim was to supplement his meagre income with success at the gambling tables.

Yet from this unpropitious beginning Beau Nash and with him, Bath, were to increase in dignity, power and splendour. The Beau was to rule the city like an autocrat, controlling the taste and mores of the fashionable, instituting reforms whose unquestionable propriety and decency afforded them the force of law. Under his auspices the construction of the Pump Room and Assembly Rooms took place, and the creation of Bath as we now know it.

Edith Sitwell's delightful cameos – the dancers, the sparkling ladies and gentlemen, the quack doctors administering the 'waters', the perpetual shuffling of cards – evoke with great skill and charm the society of Bath from its beginnings through to the era of Jane Austen's *Northanger Abbey*.

'The Lag Minuet, as danced at Bath' by Bunbury

BATH

Edith Sitwell

Century in association with The National Trust
London Melbourne Auckland Johannesburg

First published in 1932 by Faber and Faber Ltd

This edition first published in 1987 by Century, an imprint of Century
Hutchinson Ltd by arrangement with The Redcliffe Press Ltd, and in
association with The National Trust for Places of Historic Interest or
Natural Beauty, 36 Queen Anne's Gate, London SW1H 9AS

Century Hutchinson Ltd, Brookmount House, 62–65 Chandos Place,
London WC2N 4NW

Century Hutchinson Australia (Pty) Ltd,
PO Box 496, 16–22 Church Street, Hawthorn, Melbourne, Victoria
3122

Century Hutchinson New Zealand Limited,
PO Box 40-086, 32–34 View Road, Glenfield, Auckland 10

Century Hutchinson South Africa (Pty) Ltd,
PO Box 337, Berglvei 2012, South Africa

ISBN 0 7126 1507 5

Published in association with the National Trust, this series is devoted
to reprinting books on artistic, architectural, social and cultural
heritage of Britain. The imprint will cover buildings and monuments,
arts and crafts, gardening and landscape in a variety of literary forms,
including histories, memoirs, biographies and letters.

The Century Classics also include the Travellers, Seafarers and Lives
and Letters series.

Printed in Great Britain by
Richard Clay Ltd, Bungay, Suffolk

To
My Father and Mother

Acknowledgements

The publishers wish to thank Miss Jill Knight, Keeper of Art at the Victoria Art Gallery, Bath, for her invaluable help in providing most of the illustrations for this edition and to the City Council for permission to use them. The portrait of Sarah Siddons is reproduced by courtesy of the National Portrait Gallery, London.

In an Author's Note to the first edition, Edith Sitwell acknowledged her debt to Barbeau's *Life and Letters at Bath in the Eighteenth Century*; Ashton's *Social Life in the Reign of Queen Anne*; Peach's *The Life and Times of Ralph Allen* and *Historic Houses in Bath*; and to Penley's *The Bath Stage*.

Author's Note

I N WRITING THIS BOOK, THE AUTHOR HAS BEEN much indebted to Monsieur Barbeau's *Life and Letters at Bath in the Eighteenth Century* (Messrs. William Heinemann, Limited), to Mr. John Ashton's *Social Life in the Reign of Queen Anne* (Messrs. Chatto and Windus), to Mr. R. E. M. Peach's *The Life and Times of Ralph Allen* (Messrs. D. Nutt), to the same author's *Historic Houses in Bath* (Messrs. Simpkin Marshall, Limited), and to *The Bath Stage* by Mr. Belville S. Penley (Messrs. William Lewis and Son, *Bath Herald* Office).

Whilst expressing her gratitude to these authors and publishers for the pleasure that their books have given her, the writer of this book would like to express her gratitude, also, to the learned and kind Mr. F. J. Cox, of the London Library, for the invaluable help he has given her.

Contents

BEAU NASH

From an engraving by M. Jackson

CHAPTER I

The Arrival of Beau Nash

IN THE SUMMER OF THE YEAR 1702, A YOUNG MAN OF
twenty-eight years of age, with a fine swashbuckling
appearance, which was carried out by his rather ancient,
but very gaudy finery—a young man with a brown wig,
beneath a tall white hat, a red heavy face with watery blue
eyes, and a rather clumsy figure, might have been seen
entering the city of Bath, on foot. He enjoyed walking, and
so had left the coach in which he had travelled from London,
before it approached the gates of the city. 'The gold voice
of the sunset was most clearly in the air', and the lovely
summer light, richening into evening, had deepened the
shades, until the shadow that Beau Richard Nash cast in the
fluttering, fawning white dust seemed bent and shrivelled
and frayed, as if it were already very old. Indeed the shadow
seemed thin and poor, as if, perhaps, it had not had much to
feed it. But the late sunlight flashed from the Beau's gilt
braid, from all his gauds, from the handle of his cane, until
you would have thought almost, that they were made of real
gold: and the Beau neither thought of, nor noticed, the
shadow. He was, as a matter of fact, wondering whether the
prospect of gambling, at Bath, now that the visit of Queen
Anne had drawn the fashionable young men, as well as the
ladies of quality, to that city, had made it worth while for
him to risk the very small amount of money which he had in
his pocket.

But he was soon to be interrupted, and removed from

these speculations; for a creeping figure, strangely like the bent, thin shadow which, all the time, had been walking in front of him—only a little way ahead of him—stopped, and in a voice which made scarcely more sound than the fluttering dust, begged him for help. The Beau stopped dead in the wake of his shadow: his face turned even redder than before, his eyes became more watery, and, putting his hand in his pocket, he withdrew a large part of the small sum which it had contained, and, pressing it into the beggar's hand, he tilted his white hat on one side, and walked on, with an even more swaggering gait than before.

When Beau Nash arrived in the city, his swaggering gait escaped unnoticed, because of the crowd, and of the terrific din which swirled down from the air, swirled up from the dust. All the bells were pealing, and all the people were shouting, trying to drown the noise of the bells, and all the dogs of the city were trying to drown the noise of both by barking. Though it was sunset, the noise was so cataclysmic that it seemed as if the city were being broken into bits by the noonday sun. The reason for this loyal uproar was that Queen Anne and the Prince Consort were driving round and round the city, followed by the Mayor and all the civic dignitaries, as well as by a strange procession, and that the occasion was one of no little delicacy and awkwardness, which was felt by everybody concerned. It is true that Queen Anne's face wore its usual stupid smile, and her vacant eyes reflected nothing, but the Prince Consort was looking watchful, and, perhaps, a little cross, and the Mayor's face was extremely red.

The fact was, that some years before, Queen Anne, who was then only the Princess Anne, had gone to Bath, and had been welcomed with fervour and civic honours. Whereupon her sister Queen Mary, who disliked her intensely, had reproved the civic dignitaries and had rebuked the civic honours, and had commanded that such a thing must never occur again. The civic dignitaries, terrified that Princess Anne might once more take it into her head to descend on the city, wrote to that lady and explained matters, with reverence but firmness. They were very sorry, they said, but they could not receive her. They had their duty to their Queen to consider, they had their Queen's express orders. . . . But when they had done this, Queen Mary died, and they had a new Queen whom they had just told they could not receive! However, Queen Anne had graciously overlooked the matter, and had chosen this moment in which to pay the city of Bath another visit, accompanied by the Prince Consort. And the Mayor and the other civic dignitaries, on their side, forgot the instructions of Queen Mary, and forgot her express wishes, and their duty towards her. For she was dead, and therefore could do nothing about the matter. So Queen Anne and the Prince Consort and their lords and ladies in waiting were received on the borders of Somersetshire by one hundred young men of the city 'uniformly clad and armed, and two hundred of its female inhabitants, dressed after the manner of Amazons'. This procession, headed by Her Majesty and her train, then proceeded to the West Gate of the City of Bath.

In this way was Queen Mary buried and forgotten, as far as Bath was concerned; and as far as Queen Anne was concerned. That lady, indeed, had shown a forgiving nature, for in returning to Bath, she had had to forget, not only the behaviour of the Mayor and the other civic dignitaries, but also the fact that on the occasion of her last visit, she had escaped, very narrowly, an exceedingly awkward accident. For, as the royal carriage was dragging her not inconsiderable weight up Lansdown Hill, the horses, suddenly overcome by this, staggered, straddling their legs wide apart, in an effort, both to bear the weight, and to recover their balance. Unsuccessful in these efforts, the horses' hooves gave way, and the carriage began to slide down the hill backwards,

The Arrival of Beau Nash

tilting the royal lady's feet in the air. Anxious and loyal observers, accompanied by footmen, flew to the rescue, darting at the royal carriage from behind, and impeding its retrogression down hill, until, at last, strengthened and fortified by this aid, the horses recovered their balance, and Princess Anne her normal position. The Princess, however, was so much shaken by the incident that she left the carriage until the horses had had time to reflect on their duty, when returning to it, she continued her progress up Lansdown Hill as serenely as if nothing had happened to interrupt it.

However, all these mishaps and awkwardnesses were, by now, forgotten by Queen Anne; and everything went well, until, in the following year, the Queen and the Prince Consort returned to Bath, and, most unfortunately, the Prince Consort died, some little time after, from one cause or another.

Queen Anne, remembering Doctor Radcliffe's warning to the Prince not to take the waters, never could forgive Bath for his death, although that city had nothing whatsoever to do with the matter.

Drawn by the presence of the Queen and the Prince Consort, immense flocks of ladies and gentlemen had fluttered down on the city, like so many highly-coloured birds, and Beau Nash hoped to win a little money from the latter at gambling. For this was, at the time, his profession, and he must go where other gamesters might be found. Bath was at the moment their headquarters, since 'Wherever people of fashion came', said Goldsmith, 'needy adventurers were generally found in waiting. With such Bath swarmed; and among this class Beau Nash was certainly to be numbered in the beginning, only with this difference, that he wanted the corrupt heart too commonly attending a life of expedients, for he was generous, humane, and honourable, even though by profession a gamester.'

In the splendid summer sunset, in the wide spaces that

seem haunted by some peaceful Roman ghost, the ladies and the gentlemen walking upon the parrot-green grass, had all the appearances of strange great birds in their splendid attire. The hoops of the ladies nearly hid their little feet, which had the movement of the feet of a bird. At moments, their gowns seemed made of plumage, and the ladies resembled the Bird of Paradise described by Ward in *The London Spy*, 'Beautiful with variety of Colours, having no discernible Body, but all Feathers, feeding when alive, upon nothing but Air, . . . as light as a Cobweb'.

Yet it was not the ladies, but the gentlemen, who, at this serious moment, engaged Beau Nash's attention, for it was with them that he must gamble, and from them that he hoped to win money. His whole career, indeed, had been a gamble until now.

Born on the 18th of October, 1674, the son of a gentleman who was a partner in a small glass manufactory, and of a lady whose uncle, Colonel John Poyce, after having commanded a company of Roundheads, changed sides of a sudden and, at the end of a year of fighting on the side of the Royalists, was captured and executed by Cromwell, Beau Richard Nash inherited none of the business capacity of his father, but much of the rashness of his great-uncle. He mentioned his father but rarely in later life, but, when asked by his friend Sarah Duchess of Marlborough if the reason for this was because he was ashamed of his birth, he replied, 'No, but his father had some little cause to be ashamed of him'.

We will look, for a while, at the dull chrysalis cocoon from which Beau Nash, that magnificent butterfly, emerged into the splendours and delights of Bath.

Educated at Carmarthen Grammar School, he went from there to Jesus College, Oxford. But studying bored him, whereas love-making did not. There were stolen meetings with a cherry-cheeked young girl—both the lovers were only seventeen years old—beneath those pyramids of fire the cherry trees; and a secret engagement was entered into. I wonder if Beau Nash, when he was very old, and lonely, and uncared for—if we except the ministrations of Mrs. Juliana Papjoy—remembered the young and romantic love that came into his life but once. There had been many sordid stolen meetings in that long life, but never one like those innocent meetings, so cruelly interrupted by his tutor, years ago. For that gentleman came to hear of the secret engagement, and interfered, so that it was broken off. Then, one of two things happened. Either Richard Nash was sent down from Oxford, as a punishment for the indiscretion of becoming engaged (and this was Goldsmith's belief), or he was withdrawn by his father, or (and this was the most likely reason of all) he left Oxford of his own accord because he was bored with studying, his love affair had been ruined, and he owed a small debt to his College, which, as Goldsmith tells us (a little morosely, against his will, and in the second edition only of his life of Nash) stands on their books to this day. As some compensation to the college, however, he left behind him a pair of boots, two plays, a tobacco box and a fiddle, though, on the other hand, he took with him his allowance, which had just been sent to him.

Beau Nash's father now wished him to become a lawyer, but the Beau imagined himself as an officer in the army, resplendent in a red coat, and swashbuckling in a sword. And, indeed, this life afforded plenty of opportunity for swashbuckling, though no opportunity for affording anything else, as we may see from the conversation between Sylvia and Scale in Farquhar's play *The Recruiting Officer*, in which Sylvia says:

' I'm called Captain, Sir, by all the Coffee men, Drawers, and Groom porters in London; for I wear a Red Coat, a Sword, a Hat bien troussé, a Martial Twist in my Cravat, a fierce knot on my Periwig, a Cane upon my Button, Picquet in my Head, and Dice in my Pocket.'

The Arrival of Beau Nash

Scale: 'Your name; pray Sir.'

Sylvia: 'Captain Pinch! I cock my Hat with a Pinch. I take snuff with a Pinch, in short I can do anything at a Pinch, but fight and fill my Belly.'

Mr. John Ashton tells us that 'In Bickerstaff's *Lottery for the London Ladies*' another class of officer is spoken of. 'Young spruce Beauish non-fighting officers, often to be seen at Man's Coffee House, Loaded with more Gold Lace than even worn by a thriving Hostess upon her Red Petticoat, all Ladies' Sons of a fine Barbary Shape, Dance admirably, Sing charmingly, speak French fluently, and are the Darlings of their Mothers, have little Pay for their Service, are kept at home by the Interest of their Friends, to oblige the Ladies, they are as much afraid of daubing their Cloaths as they are of venting their Carcases.'

Richard Nash, however, was not one of these fine gentlemen. He had, it is true, gold lace and a sword, but he had, as well, very small pay and precious little to eat. In addition to this his extravagance landed him in trouble, as usual, and he was bored by his duties, which took up all his time. So, after a while, he discovered that his father had been right after all, and, leaving the army, he settled down in the Temple as a student of law.

Here this poor and lovable creature, who knew pleasure, but no happiness save in relieving the poverty of others, underwent much misery, hidden under a smart coat, much carefully disguised hunger, in order to show a fine appearance to the world, and in order to have a chair in which to go to the play, that he might be seen there by the fashionable world—the Beau was always, I am afraid, a snob, but he was also a kindly and an innocent one, and this care for the opinion of the world was not due to snobbishness only, for through the opportunity offered by that world, he hoped eventually to earn his livelihood, in one manner or another. That fine coat hid but little underlinen, it was not warm

enough to make it a fit covering for the heart which, over-
hearing, at a later time, a poor man with a wife and large
family of children say that '£10 would make him happy',
could not resist giving him this sum, and charging it to the
Masters of the Temple, whilst hastening to explain that if
the Masters were unwilling to incur this expense, he, of the
smart coat, and little underlinen, would be willing to refund
the money. It seems strange that he was able to charge this
to the Masters of the Temple, but the reason is explained by
Steele, who told the story. 'I remember to have heard a
Bencher of the Temple tell a story of a tradition in their
house where they had formerly a custom of choosing kings
for such a reason, and allowing him his expenses at the charge
of the society; one of our kings [Beau Nash] carried his royal
inclinations a little too far, and there was a committee
ordered to look into the management of the treasure. Among
other things it appeared that His Majesty, walking incog. in
the cloisters, had overheard a poor man say to another, such
a small sum would make me the happiest man in the world.
The King, out of his royal compassion, privately enquired
into his character, and finding him a proper object for charity,
sent him the money. When the committee read their report,
the House passed his account with a plaudite without further
examination, upon the recital of this article in them:

'For making a Man Happy - - £10. 0. 0.'

Goldsmith adds that 'the Masters, struck with such an
uncommon instance of good nature, publically thanked him
for his benevolence, and desired that the sum might be
doubled, as a proof of their satisfaction'.

Here, then, in the Temple, Richard Nash developed those
qualities which were, in after life, to make him much loved,
and much envied, but not much esteemed. For, as Goldsmith
says of him in his beautiful and moving *Life of Richard Nash*,
'a cool biographer, unbiassed by resentment or regard, will
find probably nothing in the man either truly great, or

strongly vicious. His virtues were all amiable, and more
adapted to procure friends than admirers; they were more
capable of raising love than esteem. He was naturally en-
dued with good sense, but having long been accustomed to
pursue trifles, his mind shrank to the size of the little object
on which it was employed. His generosity was boundless,
because his tenderness and his vanity were in equal pro-
portion; the one impelling him to relieve misery, and the
other to make his benefactions known. In all his actions,
however virtuous, he was guided by sensation and not by
reason, so that the uppermost passion was ever sure to
prevail.' . . . 'He had pity for every creature's distress, but
wanted prudence in the application of his benefits. He had
generosity for the wretched in the highest degree, at a time
when his creditors complained of his justice. He often spoke
falsehoods, but never had any of his harmless tales tinctured
with malice.'

He was, I think, a sweet and lovable creature, though a
little rank in some ways, and one who has been infinitely
misjudged, though there were even at that early time some
to appreciate those better qualities, as we have seen from the
story of the £10.

Meanwhile his two investments—the fine coat, and the
fine manners, had been entirely successful . . . since they had
attracted the attention of various fashionable young men,
who took him up and made friends with him. As a result of
these friendships, Richard Nash, who was by now a member
of the Middle Temple, was put in charge of the pageant
produced by the Inns of Court to celebrate King William's
accession. The King, like the fashionable young men, was
much struck by him, and offered him a knighthood; but
the Beau refused this honour, for in spite of his vanity, he
would have preferred money, and said so, with some
frankness. 'Please, your Majesty', said Beau Nash, when the
offer was made him, 'if you intend to make me a knight, I

wish it to be one of your poor knights of Windsor, and then I shall have a fortune at least able to support my title.' But either King William did not hear, or he pretended not to hear; in any case, he took no notice of this remark, and Beau Nash was left as poor as he had ever been. This, then, was the man who, knowing all the fine world, but nobody from whom he could invoke aid, finely clothed, yet in want of a meal, walked into Bath on the day of Queen Anne's arrival.

But now that he had arrived, where was he to sleep? For the flocks of fine ladies and gentlemen who had descended on the city had so increased the costs of a lodging a hundredfold, that the price of a bed was a guinea.

CHAPTER II

The Rise to Fortune

ALL NIGHT LONG, THE GHOSTS AND SHADES OF a forgotten civilisation murmured in the leaves, chuckled in the water, creaked on the stair. They had scarcely melted away under the first rays of the sun, when Beau Nash awoke, in the small and humble room he had taken as a lodging. Those shadows of an ancient wisdom lay buried under the ruins of night, but here was the Beau, in a city whose origins were as strange, and as unfathomable, as these, whose legends lay in the dimmest and most remote dawn of time, since it was believed that the raising of the city was due to the British King Bladud, the son of King Hudibras, and the father of Lear.

'About thirty-five centuries ago', says the last and completed version of the legend, 'Lud Hudibras swayed the sceptre of Britain. Bladud was the heir-apparent of this monarch, a prince of the highest expectations, the darling of his parents, and the delight of a splendid court. This amiable personage became a leper, and the courtiers prevailed upon his reluctant father to banish him, lest he should contaminate their immediate circle with his horrible malady.

'Lud Hudibras, therefore, dismissed the Prince with tears and blessings, to which the Queen added a brilliant ring as a mark by which he might make himself known, should he get rid of his disease. Shut out from society, Bladud could now only aspire to the meanest employments; and having travelled as far as Keynsham, a village about six miles from

Bath, he offered himself to a man of that village, who dealt largely in pigs, to take charge of those respectable animals.

'Bladud soon discovered that he had communicated his disorder to the herd; and dreading the displeasure of his patron, he requested that he might drive his charge to the opposite side of the river, under the pretext that the acorns were finer there. The owner complied with his request, and Bladud, passing the river at a shallow since called Swineford, conducted his pigs to the hills which hung over the northern side of Bath. The health-dispensing springs of this place stole at that time unperceived and disregarded through the valley. The swine, however, led by instinct, soon discovered the treasure, and anxious to rid themselves of the disease, quitted their keeper, rushed violently down the hill, and plunged into the muddy morass below. The royal swineherd endeavoured in vain to entice his troop from the spot; but at length, having seduced them away by the sight of a bag of acorns, he led them back and settled them in their pens. No sooner, however, had he washed from them the mud and filth than he perceived that many of the animals had already shed the scabs of their disorder.

'Bladud wisely concluded that there could be no effect without an adequate cause. If the waters cured the hogs of the leprosy they would be equally beneficial to a man in a similar situation. He proceeded to bathe himself in them, and had the inexpressible happiness to find himself cleansed from the disease.

' Bladud marched back his pigs to his patron, returned to Court, was acknowledged with rapture, proceeded to the place where he had found his cure, cleansed the springs, erected baths, and built a splendid city on the spot. Here he lived and reigned for many years with great honour ; but getting foolish as he became old, and scorning any longer to tread the earth like a common mortal, he determined to tread the air on a pair of wings which he had constructed.

'On a certain day he sprang from the pinnacle of a temple

which he had founded to Minerva at Bath, tumbled instantly
to the ground, and at once put an end to his life.'

I must admit that although I try to avoid thinking about
the subject as much as possible, there are moments when I
cannot resist wondering what was the exact fate of the
'respectable animals' after they had been cured of their disorder. This aspect of the story, however, does not seem to
have disturbed certain citizens of Bath in the year 1741; for
they were content to add this footnote, in writing, without
comment (it is preserved in the British Museum) :

'We, whose names are herewith written, natives of the
city of Bath, having perused the above tradition, do think
it very truly and faithfully related, and there is but one
material circumstance omitted in the whole story, which is
the grateful acknowledgement Bladud made to his master;
for it is said Bladud richly arrayed him, made him a knight,
and gave him an estate to support all his dignity—as witness
our hands, this first day of November, 1741.'

It must, however, be said, that it was a common belief that
the baths could cure leprosy, and this was accepted as late
as the eighteenth century, for the Leper's Bath contained the
inscription: 'William Berry, of Galthorp, near Melton Mow-
bray, County of Leicester, cured of a dry leprosy by the help
of God and the Bath, 1737'. It is also possible that King
Bladud may have tried some flying experiment; it is believed,
also, that there once existed a British temple to Minerva, for
stones have been found upon which appear the helmet and
owl, emblems that were reserved for Minerva.

When Beau Nash awoke in this city haunted by many
legends, and by the dark shadows and glittering ghosts of
bygone powers, the sun had only risen an hour since, and
the streets seemed deserted, until, as the Beau sat by his
window of his lodging and drank his chocolate, there was a
sudden gust of wind, and two hundred sedan-chairs went
swirling by, carrying their burdens—young ladies, 'Egyp-

tian mummies, old musty skeletons, and other antiquated trumpery, abortives in pickle, and abundance of other memorandums of Mortality, that looked as ghostly as the pictures of Michael Angelo's "Resurrection"; as if they had collected their scattered bones into their original order, and were about to march in search after the rest of the appurtenances'.[1] These beauties and mummies were on their way to the Cross Bath and the King's Bath. Immediately afterwards the early morning was darkened, by what, at first, seemed to be a whole universe of ravens, black, cawing, and solemn, or by a whole universe of locusts—so dark and dense was the cloud. Leaning out of the window so that he might see more clearly, Beau Nash perceived that the cloud he had taken for a universe of ravens, or for locusts, was, in fact, a cloud of quack-doctors who had gathered together to pursue the invalids to the Baths.

These gentlemen were the descendants of such quacks as Dr. Seneschall, and of Dr. Anodyne, who lived in the time of King Charles the Second, and whose fame was not due, alone, to his habit of wearing a fur coat beneath the rays of the dog-star, in the very height of summer, but also to his skill in alchemy. Doctor Anodyne was the industrious gentleman who invented necklaces to cure children of teething troubles, and who, according to Bairns, 'informs us gratis, that all the woodcocks and cuckoos go annually to the moon'. Inexorable in their attentions as well as in their remedies, these quacks, his descendants, went so far as to have correspondents in London, who would inform them of the age, means, history, character, and illness of every patient who arrived at Bath—what kind of flattery the patient would prefer, and what subject must not be mentioned in his or her presence—together with the precise form taken by the spite and rancour felt by certain invalids towards the young, and what lady

[1] Ward, *London Spy*, the description is of a warehouse, Gresham College, then the home of the Royal Society.

was the object of another lady's jealousy. Both the rancour of the aged and the jealousy of the young (and middle-aged) were then fanned assiduously.

Steele tells us that the physicians 'are very numerous, but very good-natured. To these charitable gentlemen I owe that I was cured in a week's time of more distemper than I ever had in my life. They had almost killed me with their humanity. A learned fellow-lodger presented me with a little something at my first coming to keep up my spirits; and the next morning I was so much enlivened by another, as to have an order to bleed for my fever. I was procured a cure for the scurvy by a third, and had a recipe for the dropsy gratis before night. In vain did I modestly decline these favours, for I was awakened early in the morning by an apothecary, who brought me a dose from one of my well-wishers. I paid him, but withal told him severely that I never took physic. My land-lord hereupon took me for an Italian merchant that suspected poison; but the apothecary, with more sagacity, guessed that I was certainly a physician myself.' No matter how 'modestly'—and firmly—the invalid 'declined these favours' he might be, and was, given such restoratives and remedies as 'Live Hog Lice, Burnt Coke quenched in Aqua Vitæ, Red Coral, New Gathered Earth Worms, Live Toads, Black Tips of Crabs' Claws, Man's Skull, Elks' Hoofs, Leaves of Gold, Man's bones calcined, Inward Skin of a Capon's Gizzard, Goose Dung gather'd in the Spring Time, Dry'd in the Sun, the Stone of a Carp's Head, Unicorn's Horn, Boar's tooth, Jaw of a Pike, Sea Horse Tooth rasp'd, Frog's livers, white dung of a Peacock Dry'd, and Toads' and Vipers' flesh'. In such a manner was illness warned away, or, if it ignored the warning, expelled. To add to the other horrors attendant upon smallpox, the invalid was forced to take Pulver's 'Aethiopicus, the Black Powder'— which was compounded of thirty or forty toads, burnt in a new pot to black cinders or ashes, and made into a fine

27

powder. Jaundice, again, was no light matter, for the remedies in that case were either goose-dung gathered in the spring time, dried in the sun, finely powdered, and then mixed with the best saffron and some sugar candy, and taken twice a day in Rhenish wine for six days together—or else roots of tumerick, white tartar, earthworms and choice rhubarb, taken in a little glass of white wine. Indeed, one learned physician was in the habit of routing the illness by mixing these preparations together, so that the invalid got the benefit of both!

But worst of all, Intemperance, that favourite pastime of the day, was not merely a disgrace, it was a positive danger; while lowness of spirits, whether resulting from this intemperance, or from some other cause, was not encouraged either, as we shall see from this advertisement: 'Whereas the Viper has been a Medicine approv'd by the Physicians of all nations; there is now prepar'd the Volatile Spirit Compound of it, a Preparation altogether new, not only exceeding all Volatiles and Cordials whatsoever, but all the Preparations of the Viper itself, being the Receipt of a late eminent Physician, and prepar'd only by a Relation. It is the most Sovereign Remedy against all Faintings, Sweatings, Lowness of Spirits, etc.—as in all Habits of Body, or Disorders proceeding from Intemperance, eating of Fruit, drinking of bad Wine, or any other poysonous or crude Liquors, and is good to take off the ill effects or Remains of the Bath of Jesuits Powder'.

In short, the intemperate not only *saw* snakes—they were forced to swallow them!

It was, then, a menacing cloud of this sort of physicians, bearing about them the faint aura and aroma of the remedies I have mentioned, that darkened the early morning as they pursued the invalids to the Baths. These were, at the time of Beau Nash's arrival in Bath, in a primitive state, and the sense of hygiene does not seem to have been improved in any very remarkable manner since the time of King Bladud.

The Baths were five in number, including the Leper's

The Rise to Fortune

Bath; but, of these, only two were fashionable and frequented by the society of the time—the King's Bath and the Cross Bath. These had no roofs, they were exceedingly dirty, and they were, as well, surrounded by buildings, so that anybody was at liberty to watch the bathers. The passages leading to the baths were very narrow and dark, and Dr. Sutherland in his *Attempts to Revive Ancient Medical Doctrines*, complains that 'The Slips resemble rather cells for the Dead than dressing-rooms for the living. Their walls and floors are composed of the same materials, cold stone, and eternally sweating with the steam of the baths, dark as dungeons, and in their present condition incapable of being warmed. From these dressing-rooms we descend by narrow steps into open unseemly ponds.'

The only shelter that the invalids could hope to find, when returning from the baths, on hot summer days, was the shadow cast, in the centre of one of the baths, by an octagonal tower with seats for the bathers, a stone balustrade, and a seated statue of King Bladud in a hollow of the wall—a statue bearing the inscription:

BLADUD
SON OF LUD HUDIBRAS
EIGHTH KING OF THE BRITONS
FROM BRUTE
A GREAT PHILOSOPHER AND MATHEMATICIAN
BRED AT ATHENS
AND RECORDED THE FIRST DISCOVERER AND
FOUNDER OF THESE BATHS,
EIGHT HUNDRED AND SIXTY-THREE YEARS
BEFORE CHRIST,
THAT IS
TWO THOUSAND FIVE HUNDRED AND SIXTY-TWO
YEARS,
TO THE PRESENT YEAR
ONE THOUSAND SIX HUNDRED AND NINETY-NINE.

In the other bath, a shadow was cast by a small monument with colours, erected in memory of Queen Mary of Modena, on which bathers whose paralysis had disappeared owing to the benefit of the waters, hung their crutches.

One of the favourite, and most inexplicable amusements of the idlers at Bath, was to watch the bathing from the galleries. And I admit this pleasure must have held endless possibilities, if we may believe an anonymous brochure which is thought by Mr. John Ashton to have been written by Ward. (The name of the pamphlet is *A Step to the Bath, with a Character of the Place*.)

'The First [Bath] we went to is call'd the King's; and to it joins the Queen's, both running in one; and the most famous for Cures. In this Bath was at least fifty of both Sexes, with a score or two of Guides, who by their Scorbutic Carcases, and Lacquered Hides, you would think that they had lain Pickling a Century of years in the Stygian Lake; some had those Infernal Emissaries to support their Impotent Limbs; others to Scrub their Putrify'd Carcasses, like a Race Horse. . . . At the Pump was several a Drenching their Gullets, and Gormandizing the Reaking Liquor by wholesale.

'From thence we went to the Cross Bath, where most of the Quality resorts, more fam'd for its Pleasure than Cures. Here is perform'd all the Wanton Dalliances imaginable; Celebrated Beauties, Panting Breasts, and Curious Shapes, almost expos'd to Public View; Languishing Eyes, Darting Killing Glances, Tempting Amorous Postures, attended by soft Musick, enough to provoke a Vestal to forbidden Pleasures, Captivate a Saint, or charm a Jove. Here were also different Sexes, from Quality to the Honourable Knights, Country Put, and City Madams . . . the ladies with their floating Jappan Bowles, freighted with Confectionary, Knick-knacks, Essences, and Perfumes, Wade about like Neptune's Courtiers, supplying their Industrious Joynts; the

Vigorous Sparks, presenting them with several Antick Postures, as Sailing on their Backs, then Embracing the Element, sink in Rapture! . . .' and he ends the pamphlet by an even more displeasing picture: 'The Baths I can compare to nothing but the boilers in Fleet Street or Old Bedlam, for they have a Reaking Steam all the Year. In a word, tis a Valley of Pleasure, yet a Sink of Iniquity; nor is there any Intrigues or Debauch acted in London but is mimick'd there'.

Nevertheless, Bath and the baths seem to have improved since the sixteenth century, when John Leland records 'that the Cross Bath is much frequented of People diseased with Lepre, Pokkes, Scabbes, and great Aches, and is temperate and *pleasant*' [the italic is mine]. 'Many', he continues with delightful *naïveté*, 'be help by this Bath for Scabbes and Aches'; but he does not tell us the subsequent history of those who were cured of the Aches—and if that cure brought other, and worse, ailments in its train.

The city itself cannot have been in a much more pleasing state than the Baths, for Queen Elizabeth, when she was visiting Sir John Harrington at Kelston, in 1591, drove to Bath, and, almost immediately afterwards, drove out again. The smell of the city proved too much for her. But she did not drive out again before she had frightened the sewer away altogether. We do not know what the Queen said on this subject, but whatever she *did* say, had remarkable, and not altogether happy results, which astonished Sir John, who, writing to Lord Burleigh in the same year, remarked . . . 'The sewer, which stood before in an ill place, stands now in no place, for they have not any at all.'

Nor was the state of Bath in the time of King Charles the First any more pleasing, as we shall see from John Wood's description. For after complaining that 'all kinds of disorders were grown to their highest pitch in Bath; insomuch that the streets and public ways of the city were become like so many dunghills, slaughter house, and pig-styes: for soil of all sorts, and even carrion, were cast and laid in the streets, and the pigs turned out by day to feed and rout among it; butchers killed and dressed their cattle at their own doors; people washed every kind of thing they had to make clean at the common conduits in the open streets; and nothing was more common than small racks and mangers at almost every door for the baiting of horses'—he goes on to say: 'the baths were like so many bear gardens; and modesty was entirely shut out of them; people of both sexes bathing by day and night naked; and dogs, cats, and pigs, even human creatures, were hurl'd over the rails into the water, while people were bathing in it'.

I do not think that, after we have read John Leland's description of the invalids, and Sir John Harrington's description of the results of Queen Elizabeth's curtailed visit, and John Wood's complaints about the city, we can be surprised at the phenomena which so terrified Queen Anne of Denmark, the consort of James the First, when she bathed in the King's Bath in 1615. 'As the Queen was bathing', says Warner in his *History of Bath*, 'there arose from the bottom of the cistern, just by the side of Her Majesty, a flame of fire like a candle, which had no sooner ascended to the top of the water, then it spread itself upon the surface with a large circle of light, and then became extinct. This so frightened the Queen, that notwithstanding the physicians assured her that the light proceeded from a natural cause, yet she would bath no more in the King's Bath, but betook herself to the New Bath, where there were no springs to cause the like phenomena; and from thence the cistern was called the Queen's Bath.'

No wonder that Doctor Jordan, in 1636, was 'sorry he could not recommend the water for personal use, as they could not be procured clean enough for drinking'. No wonder that the Corporation, in September, 1646, formed these Bye-Laws (which were promptly, and completely, disregarded!), in which it was ordered:

'That no person shall presume to cast or throw any dog, bitch, or other live beast into any of the said Baths, under the penalty of three shillings and fourpence.'

'That no person shall thrust, cast, or throw another into any of the said Baths, with his or her clothes on, under a penalty of six shillings and eightpence.'

'That no person or persons shall disorderly or uncivilly demean themselves in the said Baths, on pain of forfeiting five shillings.'

The only touch of brightness to be found amongst this otherwise unmitigated gloom, is contained in the rules, formed many years later, including the orders that:

'A Sergeant shall not demand more than threepence for each time of bathing.

'A guide shall not demand more than one shilling for each time of bathing.

'A cloth-woman shall not demand more than three pence for each time of bathing.'

And if we were a servant or a person in low circumstances we were not even obliged to pay that. We were allowed to bathe for sixpence only, and this fee included the hire of a guide and of bath-cloths.

Although the state of the baths was, to say the least of it, displeasing, there was nothing else to be done in the early morning, except to bathe; and the lodgings were so intolerable that the visitors to Bath were in the habit of bathing early, so as to escape from the discomforts by which they were surrounded—the uncleanliness of the rooms, though this cannot have compared with the filth of the baths, the rush-bottomed chairs, and the carpetless floors over which the plumage-like hoops of the ladies must sweep.

The earlier, the better. Indeed, Mr. Pepys, three reigns earlier, had risen at four o'clock in order to keep an appointment at the Cross Bath. Some fine ladies had appeared, but had been, finally, carried away, wrapped in a sheet, 'and in a chair, home'. And Mr. Pepys had dawdled about for two hours or so, and then had gone home, also, and had returned to his uncomfortable bed.

We cannot be surprised that Mr. Pepys *did* go home to bed, after waiting and watching, because the costume of the ladies, although they were fine ladies, was scarcely attractive. Celia Fiennes, writing about twelve years later, says: 'The Ladyes go into the bath with garments made of a fine yellow canvas, which is stiff and made large with sleeves like a parson's gown; the water fills it up so that its borne off that your shape is not seen, it does not cling close as other linning, which looks sadly on the other sort which goes in their own linning. The gentlemen have drawers and waistcoats of the same sort of canvas, this is the best linning, for the bath water will change any into yellow'.[1] So, although the ladies and gentlemen floated like water-lilies among the waters of the baths, Mr. Pepys, thirty-four years before the arrival of Beau Nash in Bath, had thought it best to go home to bed—at six o'clock in the morning. For, added to the usual disappointment of the scene, there had been a great deal of noise, because musicians insisted upon serenading the ladies as they floated like yellow water-lilies, and, in reply, the gentlemen bathers had burst into song—as a result of which, in the end, the Mayor and Council refused to allow music of any sort.

These conditions remained at Bath, when the Beau, whose title was not regarded as an insult, as it would be now, but as a compliment, made his first appearance in that city. Not only the hygiene, but the pleasures in Bath, until the Beau reigned over and reformed these, were of the most elementary kind. Thirty-two years before, there had been no place in which to hold an assembly, until my maternal ancestor,

[1]Celia Fiennes' *Diary*, page 13.

the Duke of Beaufort, 'took upon him to conduct the company to the Town Hall'.[1] And even then, ten couples were thought to make a fine rout. Before this happy inspiration about the Town Hall, there was no place but the bowling-green on which to form country dances (not Sir Roger de Coverley—that was to come later—but other dances of much the same kind). These dances had, for an accompaniment, only a fiddle and a hautbois, and, if it were night-time, a few dying torches. For other occupations, there were strolls among the flowered walks round the city, like those walks among whose trees the Beau had hidden only ten years ago—but how many centuries those ten years held—with his beloved, the young girl of the wide eyes and cherried cheeks. How small, how unripe, was the budding world of fashion in which the Beau made his appearance.

By nine o'clock, the invalids had all returned from the baths, and the quack-doctors had tired of pursuing them, and there was a hush and a lull in the city, during which Beau Nash made his plans. He must be seen wherever the fashionable world was to be seen; he must meet the young men of fashion, and the professional gamblers, at the coffee-houses (such as existed), on the bowling-green, at the baths, and in the flowered walks—which were still in a very primitive state. Or he could meet them again as they walked up and down outside the shops of a little fair—shops where they could buy ribbons and gloves, or fans for the ladies, or that powdered coral which was used as tooth-paste—or as they loitered in the 'several little cake houses where you have fruit-lulibubs and some liquors to entertain the company that walk there'—or, again, where 'Hydromel and Spanish wines are served in the Arbours'.[2]

It was in one of these meeting-places that the Beau made,

[1]Fleming, *Life of T. Ginnadrake*, Vol. III., pp. 6-7.
[2]Celia Fiennes' *Diary*.

in some manner, the acquaintance of Captain Webster, who was, at this time, Master of the Ceremonies in Bath, and who was a gamester like himself. Mr. R. E. M. Peach, who wrote many books about Bath, gives this portrait of the Captain— a portrait which, though imaginary, probably bears a good deal of likeness to the original:

'You see that middle-sized man at the end of the tent (in the Bowling Green), on a slight elevation, under a canopy of common material; he is dressed in a square-cut coat, a vast neckerchief, tied in a vast bow, much frilled in the centre; his legs are encased in breeches or pantaloons of a dark material; over which are drawn top-boots. That gentleman is Captain Webster. As he moves, you perceive he falters a little—yes, he has been drinking, but he swaggers and brings his feet down as if all his enemies were there, and he is resolved to crush them by the concentrated vigour of his boot-heels. He arranged his forces—men and women— the former arrayed very much like himself, their features being painted evidently by the same artist who has done such justice to their leader—the brandy bottle; the latter resemble that licentious queen whose reputation was immoral, and whose evil deeds brought her where it will bring many of those exalted painted beauties—to the dogs.'

Captain Webster, recognising in the Beau some kind of mirror of himself, treated him with great politeness; an intimate friendship was begun between them, and before long, the Beau became the Captain's aide-de-camp.

The aide-de-camp soon attracted attention—partly by his swagger, partly by his advice about the organisation of the few ceremonies, but most of all by his way of dealing with a threat uttered by Doctor John Radcliffe.

Doctor Radcliffe, it seems, had not only warned Prince George of Denmark not to take the waters, but he had also (according to a letter from a citizen of Bath to the Doctor) said, first, that he would put a Toad in the Waters; secondly, that he would spoil the Trade of the Bath Waters, by G—d, he would; and thirdly, that he would bring the lodgings down to half-a-crown a week.

Nash, at once, comforted the alarmed citizens. He would, he said, were he allowed to do so, counteract the poison of the toad as that of the tarantula is counteracted, by music. And he started a subscription for an orchestra, the popularity of which was so great that floods of fresh visitors appeared in the city.

I do not know if the Beau and the Doctor were ever brought face to face, but if they were, the encounter must have been exciting, for the Doctor's eccentricity was very great (though this eccentricity had, at moments, admirable results, as in the case when Alexander Pope was taken seriously ill, at the age of sixteen, from overstudy, and Doctor Radcliffe, who was called in as a last resource, ordered neither earth-worms nor vipers, but fresh air and exercise as a cure). At the moment when the Doctor threatened the city of Bath, and the waters of Bath—I cannot help feeling that this last eccentricity was another proof of his sound commonsense and understanding of hygiene—he was fifty-two years of age, and had not, as yet, given full proof of his originality. He had, however, when summoned to deal with the case of Queen Anne's unhappy, overworked, misunderstood little son, the Duke of Gloucester—too late for any eccentricity, or kindness, to help him—comforted himself, for he was a kind-hearted man, by reproaching the two famous physicians, Sir E. Hannes and Sir Richard Blackmore. But even this did not retain for him the position of court physician, for, unfortunately, he was addicted to speaking the truth, not only to the right people, but also to the wrong people. When, for instance, Queen Anne languished, after the death of her sister Queen Mary—who had always hated her, and who had forbidden the citizens of Bath to receive her with honours—when Queen Anne pined for the sister of whose hatred she had been very well aware, and sent for Doctor Radcliffe, saying that she was ill, that firm-minded man—who was at the moment enjoying a bottle of Tokay at his favourite tavern in St. James, and who was not going to be disturbed by any lady, however eminent—replied that there was nothing whatsoever the matter with the Queen, and that she was as well as anybody else! This statement, though true, was not tactful. Queen Anne flew into one of her rare rages, and when Doctor Radcliffe arrived at the Palace next day, he was told that he had been dismissed, and that his place had been filled by Doctor Gibbons. This fact was unfortunate, since it deprived him, a few years later, of an opportunity; for, at the age of sixty, Doctor Radcliffe made himself a general laughing stock by falling in love with Miss Tempest, a maid of honour to Queen Anne, and by trying to impress her by the splendour of his equip-age. Even the kind-hearted Steele could not resist poking a little gentle fun (in the *Tatler*, No. 44) at the carriage and its owner.

'This day, passing through Covent Garden, I was stopped in the piazza by Pacolet, to observe what he called the triumph of Love-and-Youth. I turned to the object he point-ed to, and there I saw a gay gilt chariot, drawn by fresh prancing horses; the Coachman with a new cockade, and the lacqueys with insolence and plenty in their countenances. I asked immediately "What young heir or lover owned that glittering equipage?" But my companion interrupted, "Do you not see there the mourning Aesculapius?" "The mourn-ing?" said I. "Yes, Isaac", said Pacolet, "he's in deep mourn-ing, and is the languishing, hopeless lover of the divine Hebe, the emblem of youth and beauty".'

Indeed, Doctor Radcliffe had more than one cause for languishing, for he, who was, as a rule, more than a little disinclined to spend money, had been drawn, by his infatua-tion for Miss Tempest, into spending a small fortune on the gay gilt chariot, and on the fresh prancing horses, and on the lacqueys with insolence in their countenances—and all for nothing, since Queen Anne would not forgive him, and allow him to come to Court.

But Doctor Radcliffe had the best of the battle in the end, for when the Queen *did* forgive him, she was on her death-bed, and sent for him in desperation; and then Doctor Radcliffe, who had not been allowed at Court for so long, would not come to Court, but sent a message saying that he was prevented, because he had taken physic.

So Queen Anne died, and the populace was enraged against Doctor Radcliffe, and said that it was his fault. But he did not care.

But although he did not care about this, there were other battles in which he met with a very decided defeat. There was, for instance, the defeat which ended the minor guerilla warfare between Doctor Radcliffe and his next-door neighbour, Sir Godfrey Kneller. The *casus belli* was the door which connected Sir Godfrey's garden with that of the Doctor, whose servants were in the habit of stealing through that door into the painter's garden, picking as many of the painter's flowers as they could carry, and then rushing home again with a loud titter. Sir Godfrey was, not unnaturally, annoyed by this behaviour and sent a message to Doctor Radcliffe saying that in future he would keep the communicating door locked. Doctor Radcliffe, who was, always, delighted to have the chance of beginning a battle, answered that Sir Godfrey might do anything with the door but paint it, to which Sir Godfrey replied that he would take anything from Doctor Radcliffe but his physic. And there the matter seems to have ended.

There was, too, another occasion when Doctor Radcliffe's wits were put to rout by an adversary of a very different kind; and this defeat came about because the Doctor never could, never would, pay a bill without squabbling over the details. On the occasion in question, a paver had been repairing the pavement in front of Doctor Radcliffe's house, and when the paver asked for his money, he was told that he had spoiled the pavement, and then covered it with earth to hide his bad work. 'Doctor', was the reply, 'mine is not the only bad work the earth hides.'

This, then, was the adversary with whom Beau Nash had to deal, and on whose crazy shoulders he rose to a fresh eminence—the eminence from which he stepped into the position of the uncrowned King of Bath. For soon after this time, Captain Webster was challenged to a duel by a man who had lost while playing cards with him; the Captain was killed; and the Beau stepped, very naturally, into his place.

CHAPTER III

The Rules of Bath

'WE ARE NOW', SAID GOLDSMITH, IN HIS *Life of Richard Nash,* 'to behold this gentleman as arrived at a new dignity, for which nature seemed to have formed him: we are to see him directing pleasures, which none had better learned to share; placed over rebellious and refractory subjects, that were to be ruled only by the force of his address, and governing such as had long been accustomed to govern others. We see a kingdom beginning with him, and sending off Tonbridge as one of its colonies'. And he continues: 'His [Beau Nash's] former intercourse among people of fashion in town had led him into most of the characters of the nobility; and he was acquainted with many of their private intrigues. He understood rank and precedence, with the utmost exactness; was fond of show and finery himself, and generally set a pattern of it to others. These were his private talents, and he was the favourite of such as had no other.'

Beau Nash and the city of Bath increased in dignity, splendour and power side by side; and the indispensability of the Beau was realised so soon, that even 'the magistrates of the city found he was necessary and useful, and took every opportunity of paying the same respect to his fictitious royalty that is generally paid to or claimed by real power'.[1] Understanding that, in the then existing state of the roads, and the

[1]Fleming, *Life of T. Ginnadrake,* Vol. III., p. 61.

primitive nature of the pleasures, Bath could not become a watering-place of the first standing, Beau Nash, as soon as he became Master of the Ceremonies, enforced a regular tariff for lodgings—for he remembered the guinea he had been obliged to pay for his bed on the night of his arrival at Bath. It was useless for the harpies and the birds of prey to weep and to groan, his word was law, and that law was carried out. He hired an orchestra from London, and although the players were, at that time, only six in number, the six were infinitely superior to the five painstaking but painful musicians who performed under the reign of Captain Webster. A row of new houses was built, fine pavements were laid down, and as much as £1,700 or £1,800 was raised by subscription in 1705, and early in 1706, and was spent in levelling the Alps and filling up the craters of the roads outside Bath. The houses and the streets became splendid in appearance, and, in short, Bath would have been unrecognisable to a visitor returning there after an absence of twenty years.

There were, too, minor reforms, such as that enforcing the proper lighting of the streets. For whereas, before the time of Beau Nash, the lighting of the town had been left entirely to chance and to the choice of the inhabitants, these latter were now forced, by a bye-law, to hang out lanthorns between the 14th of September and March the 25th, 'as it shall grow dark, until 12 o'clock at night, upon pain of forfeiting two shillings for default'. Not content with this, Beau Nash, after considerable trouble, induced the Corporation, which had announced with some firmness that it found it 'impracticable to keep the streets and public ways of the city clean and in good order by their own authority', to apply to Parliament for permission to force the inhabitants to take on this 'impracticable' duty also, and, as well, for permission to institute a night watch, and to punish beggars and loiterers. As for the chairmen, who had made the streets of Bath a menace and a peril, their highwaymen-like conduct was put a stop to. In the past, it had been disgraceful. We find in Celia Fiennes' *Diary*, some years before this time, that 'There are chairs as in London to carry the better sort of people, but no control was exercised over them, so that they imposed what fares they chose, and when these were disputed they would not let their customers out of the chair—though if it was raining they would open the top and let him or her— often an invalid—be exposed to the wet, until in despair the charge was met'. Indeed, it was due as much to the disgraceful behaviour of the chairmen as to duels between gamblers, that Beau Nash, eventually, forbade the wearing of swords in Bath; for 'it having been usual with these turbulent people to provoke gentlemen to draw their swords upon them, and then to defend themselves with their chairpoles, the danger of murder affrighted the ladies to such a degree that the public assemblies for diversion seldom ended without the utmost confusion'.

Under Beau Nash's rule, however, such behaviour was discouraged, to say the least of it; but as the chairmen were unused to being controlled, and were very turbulent, trouble broke out again from time to time; and on one occasion, in 1743, when a certain Duke and his company decided to walk home after a ball, instead of hiring the chairs, the disappointed and aggrieved chairmen came into conflict with the authorities. The result was the following advertisement:

'*Bath, May* 18*th*, 1743.

'Whereas on the 12th instant, between hours of twelve and one o'clock, several gentlemen and ladies were greatly insulted by having dirt thrown upon them, by some persons unknown, in, and near, the churchyard, and Mr. Nash having promised a reward of Two Guineas, for the discovery of such person or persons, so as he or they may be thereof convicted:

The Rules of Bath

The Corporation of the City,

to show their resentment of such insufferable insolence, do hereby promise a reward of Twenty Guineas, to any person or persons who shall make such a discovery, as aforesaid: And as a further encouragement for a discovery, the Corporation will not only apply for a pardon for any person concerned, who shall inform against their accomplices, but will give to such person so informing, on the conviction of the others, the reward of Twenty Guineas.

ROBERTS.

By Order of the Corporation.'

Beau Nash, and the Corporation, then decided that it would be worth their while to provide a proper shelter for the bathers and for those who had come to Bath in order to drink the waters, so that they need not be reduced to remaining in their lodgings if the weather was bad, or to sitting under the meagre and tattered shadow cast by King Bladud's statue, if the weather was sultry. A Pump Room was built, therefore, on the south side of the Abbey, was rented by Beau Nash from the Corporation, and was placed under the charge of an officer called the Pumper. Opened in 1706, with all the pomp of a procession and a festival which included music (a song in honour of the mythical King Bladud was specially written for the occasion), this Pump Room was sufficient for the needs of the time, but as the number of visitors grew, it was obvious that a larger one must be built; in 1732, therefore, the old Pump Room was pulled down and a room which would be adequate to the large company that, by now, flooded the entertainments, was built on its site. Meanwhile, a certain Thomas Harrison had built a room for dancing on the east side of the Grove, close to the bowling-green—this again being at the instigation of the Beau, who paid him three guineas a week for the Assembly Room and Candles. This Assembly Room was built in 1708, and was enlarged several times. But after a while, Harrison became so exorbitant in his prices that the visitors to Bath complained to Beau Nash, and asked that another Assembly Room might be built where the charges would be regulated. A certain Thayer, under the Beau's instructions, built a new set of Assembly Rooms on the lower end of Borough Walls, from the design of John Wood. These rooms were opened in the autumn of 1729, or the spring of 1730, and from that time, the balls on Tuesdays took place at Harrison's Rooms, the balls on Friday at Thayer's. The rivalry between the two sets of Rooms was very great. The Lower Rooms were named after their successive owners— Harrison, Mrs. Hayes, afterwards Lady Hawley, Gyde, Simpson; and the Upper Rooms bore the names of *their* successive owners—Thayer, Mrs. Lindsay, Wiltshire. But in the end, the Lower Rooms, declining slowly, were vanquished, and finally, in 1820, were burnt down.

Mrs. Lindsey, or Lindsay, an opera singer, was the manager of Thayer's; and this lady seems to have behaved herself, and to have kept her charges moderate enough, until the death of Harrison. She was then seized with the idea of persuading Nash to give Harrison's vacant place to her sister, Mrs. Hayes. This was done, with disastrous results. For the two ladies played into each others' hands with regard to charges, to such a degree that the company found themselves subjected to worse exactions than before the second Assembly Rooms were built. Once more, Beau Nash received a complaint, and intervened; and Mrs. Hayes and her sister found themselves obliged to refrain from further extortions. Eventually Mrs. Hayes, who had been much enriched by the extortions in question, married Lord Hawley, who, having run through his own fortune, was glad enough to acquire hers.

Meanwhile, in order to afford the expenses of the Pump Room, and Harrison's Assembly Rooms (this was before the building of Thayer's), Beau Nash had raised the subscription for music from one to two guineas; but the subscribers to this were but few and far between, so that by the time Christmas came, the subscription money was generally spent, and another subscription of a guinea a head had to be raised in order to continue the balls until about the middle of January 'without Pump music', and during this time the expense of the rooms was reduced from five guineas a night to three. Then, from the middle of January until Easter, the music died down, the ghosts of the last visitors faded away, and the great rooms were filled with nothing but echoes of the music and the voices, floating like little cold airs round the deserted rooms, and those thinner, drier echoes of the sound made by the ladies' hooped skirts as they swept the floors, a sound like that of thin and drifting leaves.

These, then, were the first foundations of Bath in the reign of Beau Nash; and with every year the city grew in size, in beauty, and in splendour, whilst the fact that the Beau was an arbiter of elegance, and that he knew all, or most of, the rich young men about town, brought new visitors, of greater grandeur, to the city, until Bath became as much a centre of fashion as London.

Beau Nash was caused but little trouble, in his character of Master of the Ceremonies, by these visitors; in fact, the only serious trouble arose from the refusal of certain of the nobility to treat the country squires and their wives and daughters as equals—and the refusal of the latter to mix with tradesmen and *their* wives and daughters. Beau Nash dealt with this situation in a characteristic manner. According to Goldsmith, he told the story, continuously, and to audience after audience, of a certain unnamed market town, in which the principal inhabitants organised a monthly Assembly 'in order to encourage that harmony which ought to subsist in society, and to promote a mutual intercourse between the sexes, so desirable to both, and so necessary for all. The agreeable character of the reunion became known, the families of the surrounding gentry attended, and eventually the great nobleman of the district came with his wife and children. Gradually, the number of the members of the upper classes present at these functions increased.' . . . But then came a darker note; for that harmony which was so desirable for both sexes and so necessary for all, was disturbed; and although the sexes might indulge in mutual intercourse, the classes refused to, with firmness and decision. 'All went on agreeably enough', as Goldsmith remarks, somewhat gloomily, 'until a foolish lady of rank issued a decree that her friends should not dance with the tradesmen's daughters. Now, the tradesmen of that town included many well-to-do men who could afford to be independent, and they promptly retaliated upon those who had offended them by announcing that henceforth they would give no credit to anyone living beyond the boundaries of the town, and that all outstanding accounts must be immediately discharged. Writs were issued, and all sorts of unpleasantness happened, before the affair was settled, but the Assembly was ruined.'

By means of this ample warning, issued without comment, and, as well, by the use of a mixture of firmness and tact, Beau Nash succeeded in quelling the rising snobbishness of his subjects. Any sign of rudeness arising from a feeling of social superiority was reproved immediately. If, for instance, Beau Nash noticed a lady of quality touching the back of the hand of the social inferior with whom she was dancing, instead of clasping it, he walked up to the offender and reproved her, telling her, in no measured terms, that if she could not behave with ordinary politeness, she must leave the room. After some time, this course of conduct on the part of Beau Nash produced its effect. But although the nobility consented to mingle with the 'private gentlemen' and their families whilst they were in Bath, it was a very different matter when they returned to London, and were no longer under Beau Nash's rule. 'A maxim universally prevails among the English people'—according to Smollett in *Ferdinand Count Fathom*—'to overlook and wholly neglect, on their return to the Metropolis, all the connections they have chanced to acquire during their residence at any of the medical wells. And this social disposition is so scrupulously maintained, that two persons who live in the most intimate correspondence at Bath and Tonbridge shall, in four and twenty hours, so totally forget their friendship, as to meet in St. James's Park without betraying the least token of recognition; so that one would imagine those mineral waters were so many streams issuing from the river Lethe, so famed of old for washing out all traces of memory and recollection.' This state of affairs and of forgetfulness was convenient enough for the great ladies and gentlemen, and the young men of fashion whose memories were affected; but many hopes and innocent ambitions must have been crushed in the breasts of certain young unmarried ladies, mothers of young unmarried ladies, and in the breasts of young married women, whose lower social position did not permit them to afford a loss of memory. How surprising and sad it was, for instance, to find that old Lady Hectick, who had been so condescending at Bath, had no recollection of her friends, now that they were in London. She looked at them as though she had never seen them before. How different was the gay and easy life in Bath, to this formal dull life in London. For, as Scott remarked a century later, 'the society of such places' [watering places] 'is regulated by their very nature, upon a scheme much more indulgent than that which rules the world of fashion, and the narrow circles of rank in the Metropolis. The titles of birth, rank, or fortune are received at a watering place without any very strict investigation, as adequate to the purpose for which they are preferred: and as the situation infers a certain degree of in-

The Rules of Bath

timacy and sociability for the time, so to whatever heights it may have been carried, it is not understood to imply any duration beyond the length of the season. No intimacy can be supposed to be more close for the time, and more transitory in its endurance, than that which is attached to a watering place.'

So fashionable Mrs. Millamant, and old Lady Hectick, continued to forget countrified Mrs. Meadows and her daughters, to whom they had been most condescending whilst in Bath, so much so that Lady Hectick had invited them to a tea party, whose gaiety might, in part, be ascribed to the fact that, as the Abbé le Blanc rather spitefully remarked, in his *Lettres d'un Français*, 'Their tea is made with arrack, lemon and sugar. This is what *they* call Arrack Tea, and is known everywhere else as Punch.' But worse still, sadder than the desertion of old Lady Hectick, and Mrs. Millamant, was the forgetfulness of Lord Loveworth, and Mr. Reynard, and Captain Cormorant, who had been so attentive in Bath. How could Mrs. Meadows and her daughters know that Lord Loveworth and Mr. Reynard and Captain Cormorant had believed the young ladies to be heiresses—and that Captain Cormorant was not a Captain at all? And now these gentlemen had found out that the young ladies were not as rich as they had supposed—and as for Mrs. Millamant and Lady Hectick, they continued to forget their rustic acquaintances, for their lives and occupations were totally different to those of these countrified misses, whose lives were composed of syllabub-making and cream-churning, with evenings spent in playing 'hot cockles', 'questions and commands', 'mottoes', 'similes', 'cross purposes', 'blindman's buff', 'parsons has lost his cloak', 'Lady Queen Anne', 'Honey Pots', 'Mr. Pope and his Lady', 'the Shepherd and the Wolf', with a few other young ladies of the neighbourhood and the curate. Mr. Addison, in the *Spectator* (No. 323), gives a picture of the very different kind of life led by Mrs.

The Rules of Bath

Millamant, Lady Hectick, and their friends and acquaintances, in a quotation from the supposed Diary of a lady of fashion:

'*Wednesday. From eight till ten.* Drank two dishes of chocolate in bed, and fell asleep after 'em.

From ten to eleven. Eat a slice of bread and butter. Drank a dish of Bohea, read the *Spectator*.

From eleven to one. At my toilet. Try'd a new head. Gave orders for Veney to be combed and washed. *Mem:* I look best in blue.

From one till half an hour after two. Drove to the change, cheapened a couple of fans.

Till four. At dinner. *Mem:* Mr. Froth passed by in his new liveries.

From four to six. Dressed, paid a visit to old Lady Blithe and her sister, having heard that they were gone out of town that day.

From six to eleven. At basset. *Mem:* Never set again upon the ace of diamonds.

Thursday. From eleven at night till eight in the morning. Dream'd that I punted to Mr. Froth.

From eight to ten. Chocolate. Read two acts of *Aurengzebe* abed.

From ten to eleven. Tea table. Sent to borrow Lady Faddle's Cupid for Veney. Read the play bills. Receiv'd a letter from Mr. Froth. *Mem:* Locked it up in my strong-box.

Rest of the morning. Fontange, the tire-woman, her account of my Lady Blithe's wash. Broke a tooth in my little tortoiseshell comb. Sent Frank to know how my Lady Hectick rested after her monkey's leaping out of window. Looked pale. Fontange tells me my glass is not true. Dressed by three.

From three to four. Dinner cold before I sat down.

From four to eleven. Saw company. Mr. Froth's opinion of Milton. His account of the Mohocks. His fancy for a pincushion. Picture in the lid of his snuff-box. Old Lady Faddle promises me her woman to cut my hair. Lost five guineas at Crimp.

Twelve o'clock at night. Went to bed.

Friday. Eight in the morning. Abed. Read over all Mr. Froth's letters. Cupid and Veney.

Ten o'clock. Stay'd within all day—not at home.

From ten to twelve. In conference with my Mantua maker. Sorted a suit of ribbonds. Broke my blue china cup.

From twelve to one. Shut myself up in my chamber. Practised Lady Betty Modely's skuttle.

One in the afternoon. Called for my flowered handkerchief. Worked half a violet leaf in it. Eyes ached and head out of order. Threw by my work, and read over the remaining part of *Aurengzebe.*

From three to four. Dined.

From four to twelve. Changed my mind, dressed, went abroad, and played at Crimp till midnight. Found Mrs. Spiteley at home. Conversation: Mrs. Brilliant's necklace false stones. Old Lady Loveday going to be married to a young fellow that is not worth a groat. Miss Prue gone into the country. Tom Towneley has red hair. *Mem:* Mrs. Spiteley whispered in my ear that she had something to tell me about Mr. Froth. I am sure it is not true.

Between twelve and one. Dreamed that Mr. Froth lay at my feet and called me Indamora.[1]

Saturday. Rose at eight o'clock in the morning. Sat down to my toilet.

From eight to nine. Shifted a patch for half an hour before I could determine it. Fixed it above my left eyebrow.

From nine to twelve. Drank my tea and dressed.

From twelve to two. At chapel. A great deal of good company. *Mem:* the third air in the new opera. Lady Blithe dressed frightfully.

---

[1]The heroine of *Aurengzebe.*

The Rules of Bath

From three to four. Dined. Miss Kitty called upon me to go to the opera before I was risen from table.

From dinner to six. Drank tea. Turned off a footman for being rude to Veney.

Six o'clock. Went to the Opera. I did not see Mr. Froth till the beginning of the second act. Mr. Froth talked to a gentleman in a black wig. Bowed to a lady in the front box. Mr. Froth and his friend clapped Nicolini in the third act. Mr. Froth cried out 'Ancora'. Mr. Froth led me to my chair. I think he squeezed my hand.

Eleven at night. Went to bed. Melancholy dreams. Methought Nicolini said he was Mr. Froth.

Sunday. Indisposed.

Monday. Eight o'clock. Waked by Miss Kitty, *Aurengzebe* lay upon the chair by me. Kitty repeated without book the eight best lines in the play. Went in our mobbs to the Dumb Man[1] according to appointment. Told me that my lover's name began with a G. *Mem:* The Conjuror was within a letter of Mr. Froth's name.'

And so on, through an eternity of triviality. No wonder that Beau Nash, faced with the problem of dealing with the airs of such feather-witted impertinents as Lady Hectick and Mrs. Millamant, Lady Blithe and Mrs. Spiteley, Mr. Froth, Lord Loveworth, Mr. Reynard, and Captain Cormorant, and with the rustic woodenness of worthy creatures like Mrs. Meadows and her daughters, thought it well to formulate his famous Code of Behaviour, which was posted in the Pump Room, and in all other public places, in 1742, according to Monsieur Barbeau.

BY GENERAL CONSENT DETERMIN'D

1. That a Visit of Ceremony at coming to Bath and another at going away, is all that is expected or desired, by Ladies of Quality and Fashion;—except Impertinents.

[1]Duncan Campbell, a fortune-teller.

The Rules of Bath

2. That Ladies coming to the Ball appoint a Time for their Footmen coming to wait on them Home, to prevent Disturbances and Inconveniences to Themselves and Others.

3. That Gentlemen of Fashion never appear in a Morning before the Ladies in Gowns and Caps, shew Breeding and Respect.

4. That no Person takes it ill that any one goes to another's Play, or Breakfast, and not theirs;—except Captious by Nature.

5. That no Gentleman gives his ticket for the Balls to any but Gentlemen. N.B. Unless he has none of his Acquaintance.

6. That Gentlemen crowding before the Ladies at the Ball, shew ill manners; and that none do so for the Future;—except such as respect nobody but Themselves.

7. That no Gentleman or Lady takes it ill that another Dances before them;—except such as have no Pretence to dance at all.

8. That the Elder Ladies and Children be content with a Second Bench at the Ball, as being past, or not come to Perfection.

9. That the Younger Ladies take notice how many Eyes observe them.—N.B. This does not extend to the Have-at-Alls.

10. That all Whisperers of Lies and Scandal be taken for their Authors.

11. That all Repeaters of such Lies and Scandal be shun'd by all Company;—except such as have been guilty of the same Crime. N.B. Several Men of no Character, Old Women and Young Ones of Questioned Reputation, are great Authors of Lies in this place, being of the Sect of Levellers.

Mr. Goldsmith, whilst approving of the matter of the Code, did not appreciate their literary style, and wrote, a little severely: 'These laws are written by Mr. Nash himself, and by the manner in which they are drawn up, he undoubtedly designed them for wit. The reader, however, it is feared, will think them dull. But Nash was not born a writer; for whatever honour he might have in conversation, he used to call his pen his torpedo: whenever he grasped it, it benumbed all his faculties.'

But there were unwritten, as well as written, Laws which must be kept by Beau Nash's subjects. The visitors to Bath must, for instance, dress in a suitable manner, as a mark of respect to the Beau himself, and to the rest of the company. The Beau took the strongest aversion to a white apron, and any lady who dared to appear at the Assembly dressed in such a manner was excluded, or, worse still, had the apron torn from her by the Beau. When, on one occasion, the Duchess of Queensberry dared to defy him in this respect, and appeared at one of the public balls in a white apron which was made of point lace, and cost five hundred guineas, Beau Nash tore it from her, and threw it into the back benches among the ladies' maids, with a strong reproof: 'None', he said, 'but Abigails appear in white aprons'. The Duchess of Queensberry, good-tempered and sweet-natured, instead of being angry, was amused, and begged the King of Bath's pardon, with great humility.

The offence of ladies wearing aprons paled, however, before that of gentlemen wearing boots. Such an indiscretion in costume was almost too much for the Beau, and the situation was made worse by the fact that insubordination about boots was more difficult to quell than outbreaks of aprons, because the fox-hunting squires of the district had got into the slovenly habit of appearing at the balls in their hunting costumes. 'The gentlemen's boots', said Goldsmith, 'made a very desperate stand against him.' So the Beau determined to make these ridiculous. Firstly, he wrote a song, denouncing both boots and aprons:

The Rules of Bath

Come, one and all, to Hoyden Hall,
For there's the Assembly this night,
None but prude fools,
Mind manners and rules;
We hoydens do decency slight.

Come, trollops and slatterns,
Cocked hats and white aprons,
This best our modesty suits;
For why should not we,
In dress be as free
As Hogs' Norton squires in boots?

Having written this awful indictment against the offending costumes, he next produced a puppet show, in which
Punch was shown in the dress of a country squire, with
boots and spurs, refusing to remove these before going to
bed. 'My boots', said Punch—'why, madam, you may as
well bid me pull off my legs. I never go without boots, I
never ride, I never dance, without them; and this piece of
politeness is quite the thing at Bath. We always dance at our
town in boots, and the ladies often move minuets in riding-
hoods.' In the end, as Punch continued in his refusal to
remove his boots, the lady on whom he had set his affections
kicked him off the stage.

After this reproof, few persons ran the risk of appearing
at the Assembly Rooms in hunting costume, boots, or spurs;
but if, by any chance, some unhappy gentleman, either
because he was in a hurry, or because he was forgetful, erred
in this manner, the Beau would approach him and ask, in a
very public manner, where he had hidden his horse. There
was, however, one notable person who defied him, and that
was Lord Peterborough, the great general, who, when he
visited the town on a certain occasion, lost his shoes, together with the rest of his luggage, and refused, absolutely

and finally, to buy any whilst he remained in Bath. He appeared, therefore, every day, whilst the visit lasted, in the offending boots, and Beau Nash was unable to do anything about the matter.

Having succeeded in enforcing his rules about these minor details—if we except the rebellion on the part of Lord Peterborough—Beau Nash now turned his attention to a most important reform, which was, indeed, to affect not only Bath, but the whole kingdom. Like all fashionable watering-places, Bath was a great gambling centre; there were quarrels at cards, and duels were fought very frequently. There were also minor causes of disturbances, such as the ill-behaviour of the chairmen, whose insolence and quarrelsomeness, led, very often, to gentlemen drawing their swords upon them. Beau Nash resolved, therefore, to put a stop to both duelling and street quarrels. This determination was largely the result of a very notorious duel between two professional gamblers, Taylor and Clark, who, according to Goldsmith, fought by torchlight in the Grove. 'Taylor was run through the body, but lived for seven years after, at which time, his wound breaking out afresh, it caused his death.' The unhappy and ruined gambler Clark, after the death of Taylor, made a pretence of joining the Quakers; but these looked at him askance, and avoided him; and he died, about eighteen years after, in great poverty and repentance for his past life. The death of Taylor was, then, the final cause of Beau Nash's determination to put a stop to outrages of the sort. He was resolved, he said, 'to hinder people from doing what they had no mind to'; and he published an edict which forbade, absolutely, both the fighting of duels, and the wearing of swords, at Bath. If any rumour of a challenge reached the Beau, he had the offenders arrested, immediately, before they could do each other any harm. He realised, however, that before he enforced this edict, he must show that he himself was not afraid of fighting, since he, of all the men in Bath, was the most likely to be challenged, and it must not be said that the law against duelling was passed in order to prevent this. Very characteristically, he chose to fight over an incident of a breach of good manners. A young gentleman having been too complimentary to a lady about her appearance in the Bath, and having expressed a wish that he were with her, Beau Nash set about gratifying that wish, and seizing the offender, threw him, fully dressed, into the water, to the great amusement of the onlookers. The young gentleman, furious, challenged the Beau to a duel, with the result that the Beau was wounded in the right arm. After this incident, the law against duelling and against the wearing of swords was made possible, as every one must now admit the courage of the lawgiver! The carrying out of this edict had, in the end, a civilising effect on the whole of the kingdom, for, as Lecky remarks in the *History of England* (Vol. II. chap. v. p. 198): 'Between 1720 and 1730 it was observed that young men of fashion in London had begun in their morning walks to lay aside their swords, which were hitherto looked upon as the indispensable sign of a gentleman. Beau Nash made a great step in the same direction by absolutely prohibiting swords within his dominions, and this was, perhaps, the beginning of a change of fashion, which appears to have been general in 1780, and which has a real historical importance as reflecting and sustaining the pacific habits that were growing in society.' Indeed, apart from this most important reform, the effect Beau Nash produced in civilising that society in minor matters can hardly be overrated. 'He was', said Goldsmith, 'the first who diffused a desire of society, and an easiness of address among a whole people, who were formerly censured by foreigners for a reservedness of behaviour and an awkward timidity in their first approaches. He first taught familiar intercourse between strangers at Bath and at Tonbridge, which still subsists among them.

The Rules of Bath

That easy and open access at first acquired there, our gentry brought back to the Metropolis, and thus the whole kingdom by degrees became more refined by lessons originally derived from him. . . . Regularly repressed pride, and that lessened, people of fortune became fit for society. Let the morose and grave censure an attention to forms and ceremonies, and rail at those whose only business is to regulate them; but, although ceremony is very different from politeness, no country was ever yet polite that was not first ceremonious.'

CHAPTER IV

The Ghosts of a Long Summer Day

THE AMUSEMENTS OF THE CITY OF BATH, AT THE time when Beau Nash ascended his throne, were not, as we have seen, of a very civilised kind. But with the accession of the Beau, his real talents came into play. It is true that not all the beauties of Bath sprang into being like those cities that were built by music. It was not, for instance, until 1720, that Killigrew enlarged the Assembly Rooms, and built Weymouth House—in the same year as that in which Thomas Greenway built the house in St. John's Court, whose splendour impressed Beau Nash so much that he bought it. Eight years later, in 1728, the elder John Wood built Wiltshire's Assembly Rooms, began the building of the North and South Parades, and laid the foundation-stone of Queen's Square; but many years had passed before the same great architect planned the superb Circus, with its fantastic and magnificent houses of the Ionic, Doric and Corinthian styles. (He did not live to see the completed work, but his son, John Wood, his successor, inherited his father's fame, not only by means of his genius in finishing his father's work, but also by his own erection of the magnificent Royal Crescent.)

Although, at the beginning of the Beau's reign, these glories had not been imagined, still less completed, yet roads were smoothed down, houses were cleaned and made more habitable, gardens were planted, musicians were brought from London, and the sound of flutes and stringed instruments mimicked the songs of the birds among the green arbours.

The Pump Room was rebuilt, and was put in charge of a special official, who could and would keep order. A theatre seemed to spring from the ground (though this, again, was later), the first Assembly Rooms were built by a man of the name of Harrison, and gardens were added to these Assembly Rooms, spreading far away into a tree-haunted silence. Year by year the city grew in size as it grew in fashion, and the elder Wood, and his son, built those squares in the town, those colonnaded terraces on the hills, which seem, always, to be haunted, sometimes by peaceful Roman ghosts, dark as the trees, sometimes by tittering ladies' maids in yellow chintz gowns and petticoats, sometimes by ladies in Isabella-colour kincock gowns flowered with green and gold, in yellow Atlas petticoats edged with silver—by ladies dressed in Shaggs and Tabbeys (for country lawns), mohairs (for satyr forests), grazets (for smooth lawns again), flowered damask (for moonlight); by ladies dressed in sarsnets, Italian mantuas, Spanish and English druggets, calamancoes (for those moon-coloured crescents); by other ghost-ladies in dresses of russets, shalloons, rateens, and salapeens, and those Indian stuffs that they wore on hot summer evenings when the moonlight sighed like a sea in the gardens; bafts and dark baguzzees, chelloes and chintz, mamoodies, guinea-stuffs, niccanees, quilts; pallampores, sovaguzzes, bulchauls and cuttanees, millaes and doorguzzies, gurracs and izzarees, humhums and allejars, atlasses, soosies, pelongs and paunches, succatums, doreas, bafraes and doodanies, gorgorans, sallampores, rehings and romalls, teapoys and china cherrys, humadees, tanjeebs and moorees, anjeringos and seerbeltees, sannoes, coffees, cherriderries, cuttances, cheaconines, jamdannies, chucklaes and mulmuls, culjees and luckhouries, tainsooks and brawls, seerbands and taffaties;—under the moonlit trees those floating glittering air-thin stuffs seem woven by the air-thin fingers of Alexander Pope's sylphs Zephyretta, Brillante, and Momentilla, in the lines which describe these hovering above the little almost unrippled waves:

'He summons straight his denizens of air;
The lucid squadrons round the sails repair:
Soft o'er the shrouds aerial whispers breathe,
That seemed but zephyrs to the train beneath.
Some to the sun their insect wings unfold,
Waft on the breeze, or sink in clouds of gold;
Transparent forms, too fine for mortal sight,
Their fluid bodies half dissolved in light.
Loose to the wind their airy garments flew,
Thin glitt'ring textures of the filmy dew,
Dipped in the richest tincture of the skies
Whose light disports in ever-mingling dyes;
While ev'ry beam new transient colours flings,
Colours that change whene'er they wave their wings.'

These were the early morning splendours, like those of the dew on the glittering strawberry-beds, and the moonlight splendours, that floated round the city of Bath; and on revisiting the city we find that these dreams and splendours haunt it still.

As for the beaux, the rakes, and the gamblers, we may still find dark shadows that have their shape, underneath the great sleeping trees of summer, or, at night-time, in the sleepy houses, when the shadows cast by the unsnuffed candles seem like ghosts in periwigs—in the Falbala periwig, or that named the Furbelow.

The beaux, the rakes, and the gamblers must have been, in many cases, haunted by a darkness more profound than that cast by the trees; but that shade deserted them in Bath; for at least the cold shade of the Debtors' prison was not there. In Bath, they might forget that cold darkness, for a while.

The Ghosts of a Long Summer Day

There was not a moment of dullness, or an unoccupied moment, in all the day.

Let us imagine that the clock has just chimed two hundred and twenty years ago—that we have sunk back, lazily and dreamily, into a mirage of the year 1711.

As soon as the arrival of fresh visitors is made known in the city—and even before they have recovered from the discomforts and dangers of the journey—the bells of the Abbey ring a peal to welcome them. A floating melody of bells, for this reason, hovers like a cloud over the city; but the invalids and the fashionable ladies and the beaux enjoy the sound, by means of which they may learn of every fresh arrival; and the ladies' maids and the footmen are sent running into the street, with every fresh cloud of bells, to enquire for whom the cloud has gathered.

The ringers of the bells are paid for their welcome before the visitors go to their lodgings, where they are serenaded by those bird-like sounds of flutes and stringed instruments, which, as a rule, float among the green arbours. The serenade having died away at last, in silence, Beau Nash appears, with great pomp and ceremony, to welcome the new arrivals. There are then various subscriptions to be made. We, together with the other visitors, must subscribe, for instance, if we wish to attend the balls and routs, two guineas to the entertainment fund; and if we are people of importance we must pay a guinea to be allowed to haunt the gardens of the Assembly Rooms. If we are not important, half a guinea is enough, for nobody will notice us. There is, as well, a small subscription to be given to the coffee-house, where the visitors write their letters, and where, for this small sum, the subscribers are allowed the use of paper, pen, and ink. Those who are readers, again, must subscribe half a guinea or five shillings to a library; and I, being a woman, shall subscribe, as well, to a house near to the Pump Room where I may read the papers, among which I shall find: *The London*

The Ghosts of a Long Summer Day

Post, The English Post, The New State of Europe, The Daily Courant, The Gazette de Londres, The British Apollo, The Tatler, the *Athenian News, British Mercury, The Guardian, The Lover*, and many others. I may also glance at the Almanacs, which bear such names as the following: 'Dove, Gadbury, Ladies' Diary, Moor, Partridge, Pond, Poor Robin, Salmon, Wing, Colepepper, Dade, Fly, Fowl, Perkins, Rose, Swallow, Trigge, and Woodhouse'. That strange work, which is called *Poor Robin*, is described as an Almanac of the Old and New Fashion; or an Ephemeris of the best and newest Edition. It contains this verse:

	Years since
'Geese without or Hose or Shoes went bare	5603
Maids did Plackets in their Coats first wear	4805
Plumbs were first put into Christmas Pies	1472
The Hangman did the riding knot devise	3999
Coffee came first to be us'd in London	0049
By Rebellion many a Man was undone	0050
Women did at Billingsgate first scold	0073
Summer was hot weather, Winter cold	5782'

On the first night of our arrival in Bath, neither we, nor the other new visitors, will leave our lodgings, because of the length and fatigue, and the discomforts of the journey we have undergone. Some of the roads approaching Bath might have been thrown up by a volcano; other roads resembled the Alps, whilst, as for the coaches, they threatened to fly to pieces at every jolt in the road; and, in addition, there was always the possibility of being held up by highwaymen. And, if we were not actually held up by highwaymen, we might, very possibly, have had our wigs stolen before we left London. For the *London Weekly Journal*, on 30th March, 1717, announced that 'the thieves have got such villainous ways now of robbing gentlemen, that they cut holes through the backs of hackney coaches, and take

63

away their wigs; or the fine headdresses of gentlewomen'. Even as late as 1743, Mrs. Montagu complained that 'A man set out with us from London, and kept us company for about seven miles. He often asked the footmen who we were, and whether we were going over Hounslow Heath; to the last he made no answer, but after being tired with his curiosity told him we were only lady's maids, after which he forsook us, either being too proud to accompany Abigails, or supposing we had not money enough to make it worth his while to go on to Hounslow Heath with us'.

Indeed, the journey was not one to be undertaken lightly; for not only was it dangerous and uncomfortable, but it seemed interminable, although the actual time taken by the coaches to reach Bath was reduced in the reign of Beau Nash. For whilst in 1667, the stage-coaches which set out every Monday, Wednesday, and Friday, at five o'clock in the morning from the Bell-Savage at Ludgate Hill, took three days in which to accomplish the whole journey, it is probable that in 1711, or thereabouts, when the first established coaches found they were faced with competition, the time taken by the journey was only from thirty to thirty-eight hours (and the charge for over-weight luggage was reduced to a penny, from having been three halfpence a pound).

Still, thirty-eight hours was quite long enough, and after such a journey the new arrivals were glad when the bells had stopped ringing, when the serenade was over, and Beau Nash had taken his leave, so that they might take their suppers and go to bed. But even when the ladies had fallen asleep, in the rooms beyond theirs, where the moonlight sounds like a tideless sea, the ladies' maids, running backwards and forwards like little winds, let fall drifts and soundless flakes of snow—their ladies' linen: white osnalrigs, dowlases, kentings, muslins, garlets, spotted lawns, sletias, white shorks, calicoes, damasks, huckabacks, and dimities.

64

The Ghosts of a Long Summer Day

Early next day, and every morning, we shall float in the baths, between the hours of six and nine—the gentlemen wearing drawers and jackets, the ladies wearing brown linen costumes and chip hats; whilst the attendants 'present you with a little floating Dish like a Basin, in which the Lady puts her Handkerchief, and a Nosegay, of late the Snuff Box is added, and some Patches; tho' the Bath occasioning a little perspiration, the patches do not stick as kindly as they should', so we are told by Defoe.

The ladies and the beaux walk about in the water, sometimes alone, sometimes accompanied by a guide, whilst there is a perpetual water-falling sound of music, compliments, and whispers. Here are the ghosts of some ladies, not separated by time—for what does it matter in two hundred years, if the clock has struck 1709 or 1739?

'There goes old Lady Hectick, a hundred years old if she is a day, and more like her shrivelled dust-coloured monkey than ever.' 'Oh, look! there is Miss Martha Blount, whom they say Mr. Pope is so fond of.' And, indeed, Mr. Pope wrote from Bath, in 1714, to tell Miss Teresa Blount how much he would enjoy seeing both the sisters in the water. 'Let me tell her' [Miss Patty] 'she will never look so finely, while she is upon earth, as she would here in the water. It is not here as in most instances; for those ladies, who would please extremely, must go out of their own element. She does not make half so good a figure on horseback as Christina, Queen of Sweden; but were she once in Bath, no man would part with her for the best mermaid in Christendom. You know, I have seen you often; I perfectly know how you look in black and white. I have experienced the utmost you can do in colours; but all your movements, all your graceful steps, deserve not half the glory you might here attain, of a moving and easy behaviour in buckram; something between swimming and walking free enough, and more modestly half-naked than you can appear anywhere

The Ghosts of a Long Summer Day

else: you have conquered enough already by land. Show your ambition, and vanquish, also, by water.' So here floats Miss Martha Blount, ' vanquishing by water'. Now she has gone again, and here comes Sarah, Duchess of Marlborough, with her face, slightly furred like a very large red strawberry, looking like all the Duke's battles combined in one. It is obvious that she is in a very bad humour. And after her floats Lady Mary Wortley Montagu, making a great splash, whose sound dies away as soon as it is made. She is the lady whose conversation ticks like a clock, telling always the hour, and speaking never of eternity—the lady whom all the Wits say must be a Beauty, and whom all the Beauties say must be a Wit. She has just given Miss Blount a very sharp look, for Miss Blount has kept her poet and has understood him—whilst never saying a cross word, in spite of all Lady Mary's attempts to wrest him from her. Here comes Catherine Hyde, Duchess of Queensberry, who, with her husband, treated poor John Gay as if he were their own child. Her delicate, sensitive features, her wide brow and almond-shaped, almond-sweet dark eyes are untouched by age, and her heart is warm, still, as the first spring days.

But now all the ghosts are flying from the bath, helter-skelter, in a great hurry. What can the matter be? The waters are rising and rising, and if the ghosts do not fly, they will be drowned. For Elizabeth, Duchess of Norfolk, that tall and gaunt woman, has entered the bath, and, heedless of the lives of the other ghosts, has ordered that the water shall flow in until it reaches her chin! And none of the other ghosts are of her stature. They fly, and only just in time, leaving the Duchess in sole possession of the bath.

Now that our bathing is over, we shall be carried back to our lodgings in the sedan-chairs in which we came. The 'old, ugly, or prudish', as a French writer said,[1] will keep their

[1]Chantreau, *Voyage dans les Trois Royaumes d'Angleterre, d'Ecosse, et d'Irlande.*

sedan-chairs hermetically closed. But the young, pretty, and gay, allow their little mouths like ripe strawberries, eyebrows like the wings of butterflies, to be seen glittering through the chinks of the sedan. So we are carried away, down the draughty, dark and narrow passages; but soon we shall meet again at the Pump Room, to drink the waters and gossip—and here, instead of the sound of running, and of falling waters, we have the bird-sharp sound of music.

After this, we shall have breakfast, either in one of the private or in one of the public parties, in Spring Gardens, or in the Assembly Rooms. (But I prefer Spring Gardens.) These breakfast parties are among the great ceremonies of the day.

Our sedan-chairs carry us, by means of the ferry-boat, across the grass-green Avon, to Spring Gardens, which, as Lydia Melford told Mrs. Willis in *Humphrey Clinker*, 'is a sweet retreat, laid out in walks and parks and parterres of flowers; and there is a long room for breakfasting and dancing'. Mondays and Thursdays are the days reserved for the public breakfasts, and we shall enjoy these, in the fruit-ripe open air, to the sound of the bird-noises of clarinets and French horns—and all for the sum of one shilling and sixpence.

But private breakfast parties are given every day, though without music, for the smaller sum of one shilling. These breakfasts are simple and countrified, but include 'Spring Garden Cakes and Rolls', which we may enjoy every morning from soon after nine o'clock, and the famous 'Sally Lunn'—dedicated to the memory of the cake-maker Sally Lunn, who lived in Liliput Alley.

It surprised and shocked John Gay, I may say at this time, that 'Lady Fitzwilliam . . . has so little resolution that she cannot resist buttered rolls at breakfast, though she knows they prejudice her health'. (Yet John Gay, himself, had a certain fondness for delicious food.) It seems, indeed, that the real, or the fictitious, good done by the waters, was destroyed, many times over, by those breakfasts in Spring Gardens.

Sometimes, when .breakfast was done, a minuet, or a cotillon, is danced on the smooth grass. The rose-full, rose-soft, hooped dresses are wet with dew that has been dead, now, for two hundred years; and the gentlemen's heels sound like satyr-hooves clattering.

When the dances are finished, and the music has died down, we will go to the daily service at the Abbey—not only, I am ashamed to say, for the sake of the service, but also because of the fashionable crowds that attend it.

This service, with its parade, is over by about twelve o'clock; and after this, the musicians may gather together for a concert, or the fashionable people may attend such darker, snuffier entertainments as a lecture on art or science. Sometimes the gentlemen and ladies, heavy from the effects of the Sally Lunn, tired with the country dances, go to read the papers in separate coffee-houses—the gentlemen, we are told, 'Make a Humming, like so many Hornets in a Country Chimney, not with their talking, but with their whispering over their Minuets and Bories'. And from these coffee-houses young girls will be excluded, because of the scandal —and not only because of the scandal, but also because of the weighty conversations on religion and philosophy— conversations unsuitable to that crowd of July roses. But the July roses will crowd together in the booksellers' shops, and will turn into girls—chattering and reading novels, plays, pamphlets, and newspapers (so Lydia Melford told Mrs. Willis), and all for the sum of a crown a quarter. And there they may hear all kinds of news which is scarcely suitable to young girls, and discuss them in whispers, whilst thanking their lovely and bright-shining stars that they are released from their imprisoning schoolrooms, where (according to Shadwell's *The Scourers*) a countrified young lady must learn such accomplishments as to feed Ducklings,

and cram Chickens, to see Cows milk'd, learn to Churn, and
make Cheese, to make Clouted Cream, and whip't Sillabubs,
to make a Carraway Cake, to make a Canary Cake, and raise
Pye Crust, and to learn the top of her skill in Syrrup, Sweetmeats, Aquæ Mirabilis, and Snayl water, or her great cunning in Cheese Cakes, several creams, and almond-butter;
and where, as well, she must learn 'The Needle, Dancing,
and the French tongue, a little music on the harpsichord or
spinet, and to read, write, and cast accounts in a small way'.

But now the young ladies are released from this bondage,
and may run over the water-green shaven grass that the
dew has spangled with great gold stars—from square to
square, from jewel-shop to toy-shop, and from there to the
shops where they sell silks.

'The shops are perfect gilded theatres, the variety of
wrought silks so many changes of fine scenes, and the
mercers are the performers in the operas . . . they are the
sweetest, fairest, nicest, most dished-out creatures; and by
their elegant and soft speeches, you would guess them to be
Italians.' As people glance within their doors, they salute
them with—'Garden silks, ladies, Italian silks, brocades,
tissues, cloth of silver, or cloth of gold, Geneva velvet,
English velvet, velvet embossed'. And to the meaner sort—
Fine thread satins both striped and plain, fine mohair silk,
satinets, burdets, Persianets, cintarines, silks for hoods and
scarves, hair camlets, druggets and sagathies, nightgowns
ready made, shalloons, durances, and right Scotch plaids'.

The young ladies 'flew into a shop which has three
partners; two of them were to flourish out their silks; and
after an obliging smile and a pretty mouth, made, Cicero-
like, to expatiate on their goodness; and the other's sole
business was to be gentleman usher of the shop, to stand
completely dressed at the door . . . and hand ladies in and
out'.

'This, Madam—my stars! how cool it looks. . . . Fan me,

ye winds, your ladyship rallies me! Should I part with it at such a price, the wearers should rise upon the very shop . . .'

These fellows are positively the greatest fops in the kingdom; they have their toilets and their fine nightgowns; their chocolate in the morning, and their green tea two hours after; Turkey polts for their dinner; and their perfumes, washes, and clean linen equip them for the Parade.

But by now the young ladies are tired of running from shop to shop, and will rest for a while at Mr. Gill's, the pastrycook's, pausing there for a jelly, a tart, or a small basin of vermicelli.

And now comes the time for some of the ladies and gentlemen to ride and walk—for dinner will be soon (at four o'clock). Whilst others, having dressed themselves in their full splendour, will sweep like great birds through Queen's Square and the Grand Parade, meeting their friends and their enemies, being hustled (so we are told by Smollett, later in the eighteenth century) by ' clerks and factors from the East Indies, loaded with the spoil of plundered provinces, planters, negro-drivers and hucksters, from the plantations, enriched they knew not how'. The ladies and gentlemen avoid these as much as possible, but when they meet their friends, they stop, and make arrangements for the moonlit summer evenings.

Here come the young ladies, once more, refreshed by the tarts and jellies from Mr. Gill's shop, and eager to see the celebrities and the fashionable people. They titter and whisper and nudge each other as the famous poets and wits and beauties pass them.

Look! Here comes Mr. Addison, that gentleman who was originally designed to have taken Orders, and who, according to Mr. Pope, who was not numbered among his admirers, was 'diverted from that design by being sent abroad in so encouraging a manner. It was from thence he began to think of public posts.' With him is Mr. Namby Pamby

The Ghosts of a Long Summer Day

Philips, the admired author of the *Pastorals*, in which he produced this confession:

> 'Ah silly I! more silly than my sheep,
> Which on the flowery plain I once did keep,'

and who is, as well, the author of this invocation:

> 'Teach me to grieve with bleating moan, my sheep'—

the moan in question echoing through all his verses in the most remarkable manner.

Mr. Philips is not only one of Mr. Addison's most admired poets, but he is, besides, a noted and prominent character at the famous London coffee-house, Button's. A loud and unceasing talker, he knows everybody, and is as vain of his red stockings and his appearance as he is of that poetry which is so much admired by the Whigs and by Mr. Addison. He thinks, indeed, that his appearance is the model on which every great man must necessarily be formed. One evening at Button's, when he was talking to a large company which included Dean Swift, he gave an amusing instance of this belief. The conversation had turned upon the personal appearance of Julius Caesar. 'I should take him', said Mr. Philips, 'to have been of a lean make, pale complexion, extremely neat in his dress, and five feet seven inches high' (for this was the appearance seen by Mr. Philips when he looked in the mirror, and it was inevitable, therefore, that a great man must look thus). Dean Swift was enchanted and interested, but could not agree. 'I', said the Dean, concealing his amusement and describing his own appearance, 'should have taken him to be a plump man, just five feet five inches high, not very neatly dressed in a black gown with pudding sleeves.'

Mr. Addison and Mr. Philips have passed, but here comes old Mr. Wycherley, hobbling along, for he is more gouty than ever; his overblown face, with that stupid, Jove-like,

The Ghosts of a Long Summer Day

bull-strong brow (one expects to see curls like those on the brow of a bull surrounding that forehead), is even redder than usual, and wears a queer, discomfited, rather angry look, for he has just seen young Mr. Alexander Pope, who was so pert to him a year or two ago, when Mr. Wycherley had paid him the compliment of asking for his help in reorganising a new edition of Mr. Wycherley's poems.

The reason for the compliment was this: Mr. Wycherley's memory had deserted him during an illness forty years ago, and refused to return, excepting at rare intervals when it was not wanted, but insisted on returning and in bringing with it all manner of erroneous impressions. On these occasions, the cold winds whistling through his empty head brought rags and tags of other people's poetry and wit and blew them round and round till he believed them to be his own; for the poor old man was in the habit of reading himself to sleep, nodding over the works of Montaigne, La Rochefoucauld, Seneca, or Gracian. Always an optimist, his ruined memory helped him in this respect, and by the time the morning came, those nocturnal readings had become works of genius issuing from his own brain. How, then, could Mr. Wycherley rely on that odd and wilful memory of his to come when it was wanted, and, when it did come, not to bring the works of other writers with it, now that he was faced with preparing a revised edition of his Miscellanies, which had been a failure, for the press? He thought it would be wiser to invoke the aid of somebody younger than himself, whose memory would not be likely to fly away at any moment and to keep odd company; so, having been much struck, in his bovine and staring way, by his young friend Mr. Pope's ability—Mr. Pope was, at that time, sixteen or seventeen years of age—he had asked him to 'look over that damned Miscellany of mine, to pick out, if possible, some that may be altered that they may appear in print'. Mr. Pope had, at first, contented himself with 'contracting some of the poems as we do sunbeams, to improve their energy and force! whilst with other verses, he pruned them away altogether, as we take branches from a tree to add to their fruit!' But the worst was still to come: for others, he said he had 'entirely new expressed and turned more into poetry'.

Mr. Wycherley did not like this; but he thanked his young friend, if rather sulkily. 'Let them undergo your purgatory'. Meanwhile, Mr. Pope's life was more than a little difficult; for Mr. Wycherley could never remember from one moment to another if they were friendly or if they had quarrelled; so 'sometimes they were out, sometimes in', as Pope told Spence. At last, after Mr. Pope had been 'plagued up and down for two years', the blow fell. For the intrepid youth actually suggested that with regard to a great many of those masterpieces, it would be well to destroy the whole design and fabric, and to print them as single thoughts in prose, in the manner of La Rochefoucauld's *Maximes*!

That was an end of Mr. Pope as far as Mr. Wycherley was concerned. But now they are brought face to face. Will Mr. Wycherley stop and speak to Mr. Pope, I wonder, or will Mr. Pope stop and speak to him? Mr. Pope slows down for a moment, as if he were going to try to speak to Mr. Wycherley; his face wears a half-kindly, half-mischievous smile. But old Mr. Wycherley, ignoring the furies in his feet, hobbles by at a very quick rate, with a muttered 'How de do, Sir?' For although he had forgotten many things in the last forty years, he had not forgotten Mr. Pope's behaviour.

Mr. Pope went on his way, accompanied by Dr. Arbuthnot, Colonel Disney (called Duke Disney, from his habit of using the word 'Duke' as an expletive) and Mr. Jervas, that kindly but conceited man, of whom Pope was very fond, who taught the poet to paint, and whose house was, for some time, Pope's headquarters when he was in London.

The Ghosts of a Long Summer Day

The conversation and behaviour of Mr. Jervas held many possibilities, the conversation of Duke Disney none. Mr. Jervas' conceit came, in part, from the fact that he had married a widow with a fortune of £20,000; but not from that fact alone, as we shall see. For when the Duchess of Bridgewater sat to him for her portrait, and asked, not unnaturally, in answer to Mr. Jervas' complaint that she had not a handsome ear, what *was* a handsome ear, he replied by showing her one of his own! On another occasion, having made a copy of a painting by Titian, he perceived immediately that he had outdone that master, and, looking from the copy to the original, exclaimed, 'Poor little Tit, how he would stare!' He had, however, some excuse, at that time, in believing his work to be above that of 'little Tit'—(as he set much store by money), for we find Swift writing, in his *Journal to Stella* (the 6th of March, 1713): 'I was to-day at an auction of pictures with Pratt, and laid out two pounds five shillings for a picture, and if it were a Titian, it would be worth as many pounds. If I am cheated, I'll part with it to Lord Masham; if it be a bargain I'll keep it to myself. That's my conscience.'

The conversation of Duke Disney, in contrast to that of Mr. Jervas, must have seemed monotonous; he must, in short, have been a good deal of a bore—although I admit that Swift did not think him one, for he said of him that he was 'a fellow of abundance of good humour, an old battered rake. It was he that said of Jenny Kingdom, the maid of honour, who is a little old, that since she could not get a husband, the Queen ought to give her a brevet to act as a married woman.'

The fourth member of the party, Doctor Arbuthnot, who walked a little ahead of the other three, was almost the greatest contrast to Duke Disney that could be found, for his wit in conversation, his learning and understanding were unbounded. Indeed, Duke Disney and Mr. Jervas were strange companions for Pope and Arbuthnot to have chosen. Doctor Arbuthnot was the remarkable Scotchman who had superseded the errant Doctor Radcliffe, that threatener of the peace of Bath, as Physician Extraordinary to Queen Anne in 1705. His art and kindliness were much appreciated by Swift, who believed that, as a wit, he exceeded all his friends, and by Pope. He was the author of *The History of John Bull, The Art of Political Lying*, and several other satires, but, far more important than this, he was one of the chief members of the Scriblerus Club, and was, with Pope and Parnell, one of the three authors of that strange work of genius, *The Origin of Sciences from the Monkeys of Aethiopia*, which is to be found among the supposed writings of Martin Scriblerus. He was as free of care as he was careless of fame—indeed, the latter meant so little to him that he was in the habit of allowing his children to make kites of his papers—and now, at Bath, he was determined to enjoy himself. The delays in starting the journey to Bath had been considerable, for, in the first place, Mr. Jervas had been unable to leave London, because the fashionable ladies whose portraits he was painting would not allow him to go; and then Doctor Arbuthnot, himself, had not been able to leave London because of his patients; and after that, there had been some obscure trouble about Mr. Pope's luggage. But, after all these delays, here they were at last, and Doctor Arbuthnot intended to make the most of his holiday.

In this he succeeded, as did Mr. Pope, who could and did enjoy any scene of real or pretended gaiety, and any opportunity of presenting himself in the character of a rake, a man of the world, a gallant, a sad dog, etc., as can be seen from this letter to Miss Teresa Blount, written during this visit:

'Madam, If I may be ever allowed to tell you the thoughts I have so often of you in your absence it is at this time, when I neglect the company of a great many ladies to write this letter. From the window where I am seated I command the prospect of twenty or thirty of the finest promenades in the world, every moment that I take my eye off from the paper. If variety of diversions and new objects be capable of driving our friends out of our minds, I have the best excuse imaginable for forgetting you; for I have slid, I can't tell how, into all the amusements of the place. My whole day is shared by the Pump assemblies, the walks, the chocolate houses, the raffleing-shops, medleys, etc. . . . . I endeavour, like all awkward fellows, to become agreeable by imitation: and, observing who are most in favour with the fair, I sometimes copy the civil air of Gascoin, sometimes the impudent one of Nash, and sometimes for vanity, the silly one of a neighbour of yours, who has lost [to] the gamesters here that money of which the ladies only deserve to rob a man of his age.'

The vanity in question caused him to add, in the hope of impressing the young ladies, and, perhaps, making them jealous: 'I am so much a rake as to be ashamed of being seen with Doctor Parnell. I ask people abroad who that parson is.'

But now the ghosts of Mr. Pope, and Doctor Arbuthnot, and Duke Disney have vanished into the darkness cast by the trees. The dream-like summer hours pass, and the clock strikes 1716.

Here comes the strawberry-faced old Duchess of Marlborough again, in a highly bad temper; for last night she lost at cards. But she was not so cross as she was destined to be, at a later time, when she brought her niece Lady Diana Spencer with her to Bath. For the redoubtable Duchess had hoped to win Frederick Prince of Wales as a husband for her niece, and she saw no prospect of that hope being fulfilled, since, whenever she made the attempt, it seemed as if she were, suddenly, plunged into a dark and silent forest.

Sarah, Duchess of Marlborough was walking, enveloped in rage, by the side of the Duchess of Shrewsbury, whose

mood equalled in amiability the crossness of her companion
—and this was an extra source of irritation to the Duchess
of Marlborough, who informed Lady Cowper: 'She plays
at Ombre upon the walks, that she may be sure to have
company enough, and is as well pleased in a great crowd of
strangers as the common people are with a bull-baiting or a
mountebank'. And the cross Duchess began to grumble: 'I
have been upon the Walks but twice', she complained, and
went on to say that the city smelt badly. Nothing, it seemed,
was right in the city of Bath, excepting the food. That, the
Duchess was obliged to admit, was excellent. She did, however, in spite of the disadvantages of Bath, make one new
friend, and that was Beau Nash, whom she liked, in spite of
the fact that he made her subscribe to charities, and whom
she consulted whenever such important matters were in
hand as the choosing of liveries for her footmen. But to-day,
the Duchess of Marlborough was in a very bad temper with
Beau Nash, in spite of his admirable advice on important
matters, because he had made her subscribe heavily, only
last night, when she had just lost a game of ombre, towards
supporting a starving clergyman and his family.

But the Duchess of Marlborough was not the only person
who was discontented and who found Bath insupportable.
The sound of grumbling arose from all the walks and gardens, floated down from all the windows, like the noise of a
little wind among the leaves, or like the chattering of a
thousand birds. This sound of grumbling was increased by
the rustling of a thousand letters; for those ladies and
gentlemen who have left the walks and gardens, are writing
to their favourite correspondents about the tortures of
ennui and of spleen from which they are suffering, in this
insupportable city of Bath.

Lady Orkney, for instance, had been extremely discontented (in September, 1711), and announced that since she
had been in Bath she had had nothing agreeable happen to

her, excepting a letter from the Countess of Oxford. She had found nothing to do in Bath, there was no conversation, no game was played excepting dice (and she vowed and declared that her head would not bear the noise of dice being thrown); there was a ball twice a week, and she had looked in at one, just as it began, and then she had been so bored that she went home again to rest. Indeed, she had only spent those few wasted moments at the ball, because it was supposed to be a crime not to appear in public. In future, however, Lady Orkney thought she would rather bear the censure than the inconvenience of the heat. But worse than all these troubles was her intense mortification at finding herself in a place made up of nobody but Lady Paulett. In short, Lady Orkney's visit to Bath was the first indication she had received that there *could* be a city in the world with not one reasonable creature in it.

Mrs. Bradshaw, too, was out of humour, and wrote to Mrs. Howard from Bath (30th August, 1721) that: 'Either I have no taste, or all the disagreeable people from all the four corners of the world are assembled together in this place, though my good lady Countess [of Bristol], who is never out of her way, can find amusement amongst them till twelve o'clock at night'.

A few days later (19th September) Lady Bristol had become even more trying, and Mrs. Bradshaw told Mrs. Howard:

'To me, it is all noise and nonsense; but the Countess finds her recreations; she cries every post-day for an hour because the Earl has not come; she dries up her tears about twelve, to play upon the walks, and an hour sooner, if anybody gives a breakfast (which happens about three times a week), we quarrel and are friends, and at it again after it is scolded out. I am only a humble spectator; for, as yet, I thank God, I have not been in any of them.'

Under these sad circumstances, it is a comfort to know

that Mrs. Bradshaw was a little deaf, which saved her from quarrelling as often or as much as she might have done; and to this deafness she added the virtue of silence. 'I came deaf', as she told Mrs. Howard in the same letter, 'and I believe I shall go home dumb; for I make very little use of my talking faculty, for fear of a quarrel. Nash says, if I go off without one, my statue shall be set up in the town.'

But though Mrs. Bradshaw found the ladies tiresome enough, she found the gentlemen still more so, and informed Mrs. Howard: 'There are a good many ladies that one knows, but the men (which you know is what interests me) are such unfinished animals, one would swear they were beholden to the hot spring for their creation, without any other assistance. Here is a Colonel Cotton, who is a good agreeable man; but the ladies are all so fond of him, that I believe he must take to his bed soon. If you see a footman in the street, his errand is to Colonel Cotton; he gives breakfasts, makes balls, plays, and does everything a lady can desire; but then he is but one man, and cannot turn himself to at least ten women that have fastened upon him, from which contests do often arise among us.'

As for Lady Anne Irwin, she discovered (on 24th September, 1729) that 'the company increases daily, but everybody complains they are people that nobody knows; for my part, I think it no great difference whether 'tis a crowd of quality or plebeians'.

The ladies were not the only people to be bored; for Lord John Hervey told Lady Mary Wortley Montagu (28th October, 1728) that he found 'so universal an affinity and resemblance among the individuals that a small paragraph will serve amply to illustrate what you have to depend upon. The Duchess of Marlborough, Congreve, and Lady Rich are the only people whose faces I know, the rest are a swarm of wretched beings, some with half their limbs, some with none, the ingredients of Pandora's box personified, who stalk about, half-living remnants of mortality, and by calling themselves human ridicule the species more than Swift's Yahoos.'

In short, everybody was bored, or discontented, or bent on quarrelling, or found nobody they knew, or else they had lost money at cards.

Mr. William Pulteney found the place an unlucky one (1735), for he had lost five or six hundred pounds at it; and he wished it was to be paid, like the Jew's of Venice, with flesh instead of money, for he thought he could spare some pounds of that without detriment. As for Lord Chesterfield, he complained to Lady Suffolk (1737): 'Were it not for the comfort of returning health, I believe I should hang myself; I am so weary of sauntering about, without knowing what to do, or of playing at low-play, which I hate, for the sake of avoiding high, which I love.'

But just before William Pulteney and Lord Chesterfield sat down to write their letters, many of the ghosts that remained among the shade of the flowering trees in the walks, moved away, fluttering their hands, raising their eyebrows, and looking shocked. For Lord Peterborough, that great general, but, from the fashionable ghosts' point of view, eccentric man, had appeared (the clock has struck 1731), carrying parcels of a nature which was scarcely suitable to his position, and wearing, horror of horrors, boots— which at that time were worn only when riding. Indeed, Beau Nash had taken the trouble to lay down the most stringent rule against the wearing of boots at Bath; but of this rule Lord Peterborough had taken not the slightest notice. He had, as well, lost all his luggage on the journey, and now refused categorically to buy any underlinen, preferring to go from friend to friend, and borrow theirs. 'Lord Peterborough has been here for some time', wrote Lady Hervey, 'though by his dress one would believe he had not designed to make any stay, for he wears boots all day, and, as I hear, must do so, having brought no shoes with him. . . . It is a comical sight to see him with his blue ribbon and star, and a cabbage under each arm, or a chicken in his hand, which after he himself has purchased at market, he carries home for dinner.'

These, then, are some of the famous men, some of the ghost-ladies of beauty, eminence, and wit, at whom the giggling young girls are staring with so much curiosity. These are the ghosts who have drifted out, from the shadow of the trees into the lovely summer day, whilst the afternoon casts down gold showers of motes, little lights like the feathers of bright exotic birds, upon their forgotten faces.

But now it is four o'clock, and dinner is ready. And after dinner, the gentlemen will nod a little, and the ladies will play with their parrot, bright as the afternoon light, bright as the grass and the feather-rippling river. Or they will play with their dust-coloured monkey, or their death-dark negro slave, and when this silent time is over, the whole company will gather together at the Pump Room, and then they will go to drink their tea at the Assembly Houses, and, after that, to pay calls, and flutter fans, and talk scandal.

Or, if it be a Tuesday or a Friday, they will go to a ball, and stay there until eleven o'clock, at which hour Beau Nash waves his hand, and the music stops.

CHAPTER V

The Balls at Bath

AT SIX O'CLOCK, ON TUESDAYS AND FRIDAYS, WHEN the evening lights trembled upon the ladies' dresses, the gentlemen's periwigs, when the silks shone like water, the balls began.

The same bird-like sounds that we had heard among the leafy arbours in the early morning, floated round the ball-room, but those shrill fruit-ripe sounds were hidden no longer by the green leaves. You would think all the birds in the world were singing—all through the voices of flute and hautbois, and the viol de gamba: not only such sweet-tongued birds as the nightingale and the blackbird, but, also, those bright-feathered or light birds with harsher voices, that were fashionable in that age—paroquets of Guinea, milk-white peacocks, white and dyed pheasants, bantams and furbelow fowls from the East Indies, and top-knot fowls, putting down their mincing feet with a little trilling movement, like the feet of the dancers, proudly and delicately.

Such was the sound of the music (sometimes chuckling, crowing or shrill, sometimes smooth as water or the green leaves among which those birds sang or uttered their cries) that floated round the ball-room.

How faded and ghostly that music would sound, if we could hear it now. And those dancers, after this long century, are nothing but little cold airs, wandering among the leaves that drift through the open windows, over the empty floors.

The Balls at Bath

Four years after the death of Beau Nash, a very strange and alien creature led the music in the Assembly Rooms, remaining there as conductor of the orchestra from 1766 till 1782. This young Hanoverian—he was aged twenty-eight when he arrived, with his sister, in Bath—was accustomed to the most threadbare poverty; he had received very little education in his own language, and none at all in ours, having no knowledge of it excepting for a few sentences which he had picked up during a short stay in Halifax. He had neither friends nor patrons in England, and his only education in music had been acquired in the military band of the Duke of Cumberland's army—in which he endured such misery that he deserted from his regiment. In Bath, where he and his sister had taken lodgings at No. 7 New King Street (moving, afterwards, in 1774, to Rivers Street, whence they returned in 1780, to 19 New King Street), the actual rigours of poverty were less than in the regiment, but the work was equally hard. Here William Herschel was not only conductor of the dance-band, but he was, as well, a teacher of music and an organist. His pupils, at moments, found their teacher's behaviour strange and unaccountable. Lessons were interrupted, for instance, in the oddest manner. The actor Bernard, who was one of Herschel's pupils, was much astonished, one January evening, to see his music master drop his violin and, with a shout of 'There it is at last', rush to a telescope and apostrophise a certain star, saying how glad he was to see it again. Mr. Bernard remarked, also, that 'His . . . lodgings . . . then resembled an astronomer's much more than a musician's, being heaped up with globes, maps, telescopes, reflectors, etc., under which his piano was hid, and the violoncello, like a discarded favourite, skulked away in one corner.'

This strange young man, whose goodness and simplicity had made him beloved by his pupils and the members of his orchestra, found time, in spite of lessons, of organ-playing, of conducting, to manufacture his own instruments on the pattern of a borrowed telescope. Having performed this feat, he then set about constructing telescopes more powerful than any which had hitherto been known; whilst his sister tells us that 'I was constantly obliged to feed him by putting the victuals by bits into his mouth'. This was once the case when, in order to finish a seven-foot mirror, he had not taken his hands from it for sixteen hours together. Then, just as 'a very busy winter was commencing, for my brother had engaged himself to conduct the oratorios conjointly with Ranzzini, and he had made himself answerable for the payment of the engaged performers, for his credit ever stood high in the opinion of everyone he had to deal with'—Herr Herschel (on 13th March, 1781) discovered that planet which was called, first *Georgium Sidus* (Herschel's name for it), then Herschel, and finally Uranus; and the ex-bandmaster received the gold medal of the Royal Society in honour of the discovery. He received, as well, the appointment of Director of the Royal Astronomical Observatory at Datchet, from the King, to whom he was presented. On this, Sir William Herschel's first presentation, the King looked at him thoughtfully for a moment, and then, drawing a paper from his pocket, handed it to the astronomer. It was a free pardon to the deserter for having left the Duke of Cumberland's army in such a hurried manner.

But these events, as we know, happened long after the reign of Beau Nash; and it was during that reign that the outward splendours of the balls were at their height.

The balls began punctually at six o'clock, with the dancing of a minuet, by one couple alone, whilst the rest of the company watched them in silence. The lady was the highest in rank amongst those who were at the ball.

The first minuet being over, the lady was escorted back to her chair, and the next in order of precedence was led forward by Beau Nash, to dance a minuet with the same part-

ner. Then a second couple occupied the attention of the
company, and then a third, until the minuet had been danced
for two hours—each couple taking their places according to
rank, and being watched by the whole company. The ladies'
hoops, sweeping across the floor in the dances of this age,
must have given the impression of a new Eden, or, at any
rate, a new garden, or a new ocean, or universe, springing
into being. For instance, on the occasion of a ball given in
honour of the Prince of Wales' birthday in 1739, we are told
that Selina, Countess of Huntingdon, that worldly-wise but
pious Methodist lady, wore 'a petticoat of black velvet embroidered with chenille, the pattern being a large stone vase
filled with ramping flowers that spread almost over a
breadth of the petticoat from the bottom to the top; between
each vase of flowers was a pattern of gold shells and foliage
embossed and most heavily rich. The gown was of white
satin embroidered with chenille mixed with gold, no vase on
the sleeve, but two or three on the tail; it was a most laboured piece of finery, the pattern much properer for a stucco
staircase than the apparel of a lady.'

But fine clothes were to be seen at all the balls and routs.
The Duchess of Bedford, for instance, according to Mrs.
Pendarves, wore at a certain ball in London a petticoat of
'green paduasoy, embroidered very richly with gold and silver and a few colours; the pattern was festoons of shells,
coral, corn, corn-flowers, and sea-weeds; everything in different works of gold and silver except the flowers and coral,
the body of the gown white satin, with a mosaic pattern of
gold facings, robings and train the same of the petticoat. . . .
Whilst at the same ball 'My Lord Baltimore was in light
brown and silver, his coat lined *quite throughout* with ermine'.

His lady, it appeared, was less successful in her appearance,
for, according to Mrs. Pendarves, she 'looked like a *frightened
owl*, her locks strutted out and most furiously greased, or
rather gummed and powdered'.

The Balls at Bath

On another occasion, the Duchess of Queensberry, who was remarkable for her beauty, but not, as a rule, for her smartness, wore 'a dress of white satin embroidered, the bottom of the petticoat *brown hills* covered with all sorts of weeds, and every breadth had an old stump of a tree that ran up almost to the top of the petticoat, broken and ragged and worked with brown chenille, round which twined nastersians, ivy, honeysuckles, periwinkles, convolvules, and all sorts of twining flowers which spread and covered the petticoat, vines with the leaves variegated as you have seen them by the sun, all rather smaller than nature, which made them look very light: the robings and facings were little green banks with all sorts of weeds, and the sleeves and the rest of the gown twining branches of the same sort as those on the petticoat: many of the leaves were finished with gold, and part of the stumps of the trees looked like the gilding of the sun'.

These splendours appeared as much in the Assembly Rooms at Bath as in the ball-rooms of London.

It was in honour of such strange gardens as these, that the bird-noises of the music chuckled and floated down from the galleries.

In the presence of such splendours, beneath the watchfulness of such a multitude, the ordeal of a very young girl, making her appearance for the first time at these balls, was a terrifying one. Lady Bristol (the same lady who, according to Mrs. Bradshaw, screamed and cried every post-day because her husband had not arrived), writing to that gentleman on May the 29th, 1723, told him that 'The most extraordinary thing of all was Betty [her daughter] to make the greatest compliments she cou'd to the day, danced four minuets; the first time she trembled and was so out of countenance I thought she would not have been able to go thro' with it; but the second time she performed very well. . . .' *The New Prose Guide* remarks, 'How many fine women do we see totter with Fear, when they are taken out to dance? And is it not possible that such who cannot walk firmly should be able to dance gracefully? . . .' And certainly the minuet can not, as a rule, have been graceful, for Mrs. Elizabeth Montagu, that enchanting blue-stocking (to whom I suspect that the dreary rattle who bore her surname—Lady Mary Wortley Montagu—owed her reputation for wit), announced that 'Grace of person is more important to a woman than a man; but the capacity of dancing a minuet is more serviceable to a man, for, by so doing, he obliges many young ladies, while the minuet miss seldom pleases any girl but herself. Unless a girl is very well-shaped, and very genteel, she gives little pleasure to the spectators of her minuet; and, indeed, so impolite are the setters-by in all assemblies that they express a most ungrateful joy when the minuets are over. For my part, tho' I feel as great ennui as my neighbours on these occasions, I never allow myself to appear so; for I look upon a minuet to be generally an act of filial piety, which gives real pleasure to fathers, mothers, and aunts. . . . In France minuets are clapped; but I believe no nation arrived at such a degree of civilisation as to encore them.'

However this may be, the ordeal of the young ladies, as Beau Nash grew older, became even more alarming, for the Beau contracted the habit of reproving them publicly when they showed any disinclination to dance. The following letter ascribed to Quin the actor is, however, like several letters which Quin is supposed to have written about his old friend, apocryphal. 'A young lady', according to this, 'was asked to dance a minuet. She begged the gentleman would be pleased to exquise her, as she did not chuse to dance; upon this old Nash call'd out so as to be heard by all the company in the room: "G—d d—m you, Madam, what business have you here, if you do not dance?" Upon which the lady was so affrighted she rose and danced. The ress't of the company was so much offended that not one lady more would dance a minuet that night'. It is impossible to believe this story, but it is, at the same time, certain that the Beau was severe—though not in this odious manner—upon any breach of his rules.

After the Minuets, came the Country Dances, but these were of a very stately order, and not of the kind that alternately pleased and shocked Mr. Budgell (one of the victims of Pope's *Dunciad*)—when he accompanied his daughter to a dancing-class—to such an extent that he found it necessary to write about them in the *Spectator*.

'They began', he tells us, 'a Diversion which they call Country Dancing, and wherein there were also some things not disagreeable, and divers Emblematical Figures, compos'd, as I guess, by wise Men for the Instruction of Youth.

'Amongst the rest, I observed one, which I think they call "Hunt the Squirrel", in which while the Woman flies, the Man pursues her; but as soon as she turns, he runs away, and she is obliged to follow.

'The Moral of this Dance does, I think, very aptly recommend Modesty and Discretion to the Fair Sex.'

But then comes a darker note.

'But as the best Institutions are liable to Corruption, so, Sir', Mr. Budgell continues sadly, 'I must acquaint you, that very great abuses are crept into the Entertainment. I was amazed to see my girl handed by, and handing young Fellows with so much Familiarity; and I could not have thought it had been in the Child. They very often made use of a most impudent and lascivious Step called Setting, which I know not how to describe to you, but by telling you that it is the very reverse of Back to Back. At last an impudent young Dog bid the Fiddlers play a Dance called Mol Patley, and after having made two or three Capers ran to his Partner, locked his Arms in hers, and whisked her round Cleverly above ground in such a manner, that I, who sat upon one of the lowest Benches, saw further above her Shoe than I can think fit to acquaint you with. I could no longer endure these Enormities, therefore, just as my girl was going to be made a Whirligig, I ran in, seized on the Child, and carried her home.'

I wonder what was Miss Budgell's fate when she reached that haven of refuge; and, indeed, what would have been Mr. Budgell's feelings if he had been brought face to face with such impudent and lascivious Steps as the Two Step, and other Enormities of this present civilisation.

These, then, were among the dances of the times, but I do not think that either 'Hunt the Squirrel' or Mol Patley would have been endured by the Beau, who stood among the dancers, ready to reprove any lack of proper behaviour, and dressed with the utmost splendour. Indeed, he appeared at a ball given in honour of the King's birthday in 1734, in gold-laced clothes of such magnificence that Chesterfield remarked 'He looked so fine that, standing by chance in the middle of the dancers, he was taken by many at a distance for a gilt garland'.

Beau Nash was, indeed, a peculiarly suitable arbiter of the behaviour and decorum of the dances and the dancers, since he was himself, according to the Dedication of *Characters at the Hot Well, . . . and at Bath*, an exceedingly accomplished dancer. Among the other eulogies contained in this dedication, we find this passage: 'I don't mention your great dexterity in French dances, because you don't affect dancing them, in which, I think, you show your judgment: though, no doubt, you might as well excel in a minuet or riggadoon, as in "Bartholemy Fair", or "Thomas I cannot".'

What, therefore, with the decorum enforced by Beau Nash, and the stateliness enforced by the excessively advanced age and stiff joints of some of the gentlemen, we may take it that Hunt the Squirrel and Mol Patley were not admitted.

Indeed, the advanced age of some of the gentlemen taking

part in the minuets and country dances was most remarkable. But it seems to have been no sort of hindrance to their enjoyment.

'Since my coming to Bath', John Earl of Orrery wrote to Councillor Kempe on November the 20th, 1731, 'I am perfectly convinced that the ancient patriots were a thoughtless race of people who loved country dances and breakfasted on hot rolls and butter. They lived to an immense length of days merely by leading the same kind of life that is prevalent at this place, where the Methusalems and the Abrahams dance with as much vigour at the Balls as if they had not flourished in a Courrant at Charles the Second's restoration. To be more particular: Here is a Brocas (now in his 97th *currente anno*) who avers that he was never sick in his life, nor ever paid a groat for a pennyworth of physick, which athletic constitution he attributes to an utter inattention either to the cares of the public or the various fortunes of his private friends. He thanks Heaven, he always had a clean pair of gloves and a neat pair of pumps at command, and therefore it was of little consequence to him who was King of England, or which of his relations was married or hanged. But the less he regards public affairs, the more he attends public places. He is at Bath in May, at Tonbridge in July, at Bath again in September, and every day during Parliament time amongst the rarities of the Court of Requests. The pale-faced girls are all fond of him, and they are sure to be well-tangled when he leads up the Kissing Dance. Do not imagine from hence that he is a dangerous or a poisonous animal. No, he is perfectly harmless; Mothers trust him with their daughters alone in the dark. The virgin plays with him, and the married woman takes his advice in laces and tippets. Some curious people call him a dangler, and maliciously whisper in his ear that

"a Dangler is of neither sex
a creature born to tease and vex."

The Balls at Bath

But his patience surmounts and baffles all brutalities by a grave grin that at once denotes inward satisfaction and outward philosophy. *Nec deficit alter*. We have an Ingram "who whistles as he goes for want of thought". He is an old Brobdignaggian, or rather a Stahlberg of the first magnitude. Yet the ladies, notwithstanding his dreadful aspect, are grown familiar with often seeing him, and all venture to romp with him as if he were no bigger than a monkey.'

But not all these aged gentlemen were so agile as to be dancers. Lord Orrery continues: 'Here are antedeluvians of lesser note and fewer years. A Brigadier Warren who is forced to make use of a cane in his 79th year. Here is also one Dockry, a moneylender, and one Laydeman of the same trade: but these are looked upon as really immortal, being true sons of Mammon in human shapes. Here is Mr. Pitt with a swinging nose, and two eyes looking each a different way.'

There seems, indeed, to have been a plague of dotards in the city of Bath; and although the pale-faced girls, according to Lord Orrery, appreciated the attentions of the ancient Brocas, certain ladies with a taste for nimbleness of wits (as well as for nimbleness of legs) did not. Both at balls and at games of cards, they found the attentions of these ancient and chilly gallants disheartening.

'Lord Berkshire', that witty and delicate-featured bluestocking Elizabeth Montagu tells us, in 1740, 'was wheeled into the room on Thursday night, where he saluted me with much snuff and civility, in consequence of which I sneezed and curtseyed abundantly; as a further demonstration of his loving kindness, he made me play at commerce with him. You may easily guess at the charms of a place where the height of happiness is a pair royal at commerce and a peer of fourscore. Last night I took to dancing, and am nothing but a fan (which my partner tore) the worse for it; our beaux here may make a rent in a woman's fan, but they will never make

91

a hole in her heart. For my part, Lord Noel Somerset [afterwards fourth Duke of Beaufort] has made me a convert from toupets and pumps to tye-wigs and a gouty shoe. Ever since my Lord Duke reprimanded me for admiring Lord Crawford's nimble legs, I have resolved to prefer the merit of the head to the agility of the heels; and I have made so good a progress in my resolution as to like the good sense which limps, better than the lively folly which dances.'

But, as we have seen, it was not lively folly alone which danced. Self-satisfied piety, and unrelieved learning, these also cast a shadow over the splendour of the balls. I cannot believe, to mention one instance of the first quality, that the presence of Selina, Countess of Huntingdon added much gaiety to those assemblies, for she was a lady who was determined to save other people's souls, publicly, at the most inopportune moments, and in the most inopportune manner— as we shall see in another chapter. On one occasion, having lured Lady Suffolk, the mistress of George the Second, into attending her chapel, the darts and arrows which flew, with their usual recklessness, about that building, were aimed so obviously at this visitor (or so she supposed) that, after a public pitched battle between the ladies, all communication between Lady Suffolk and Lady Huntingdon ceased.

Of Lady Huntingdon's war on behalf of truth and goodness, I shall speak in another chapter, but her attitude towards other fighters in the great cause, when they were tactless and attracted undue attention, was both firm-minded and instructive. Piety and worldly wisdom were present in equal proportions. 'One day', says Barbeau (in his *Life and Letters at Bath in the Eighteenth Century*), 'when Lady Huntingdon was present in the Pump Room, a Quakeress suddenly saw fit to lift up her voice against the follies and vanities of this world, the assembled company gave noisy expression to their impatience, whereupon Lady Huntingdon, rising from her seat, went to the preacher, praised aloud her courage and zeal (although she differed widely from her in her own religious opinions), then, taking her by the hand, *accompanied her to the door, and quietly returned to her seat.*' (The italics are mine.)

But dark as was the shadow cast by piety of this particular kind, that cast by unrelieved learning was darker still, since it contained no possibilities of amusement for the onlooker. In the case of the illustrious Porson, it was cast when the century was almost exhausted, and long after the reign of Beau Nash, who, I feel, would not have put up with that gentleman for a moment.

'Once', said Warren in his *Literary Recollections*[1], 'I had the pleasure of conversing with the illustrious Porson; and, strange to say, it was at a Ball in the Lower Rooms, on an unusually crowded night. A very ingenious friend of mine, Dr. Davis of Bath, who was this same learned Theban's chaperon on the occasion, did me the favour of introducing me to him. The Professor appeared to be quite at sea, and neither to understand nor to relish the scene before him. On separating from him, Mr. King, the Master of the Ceremonies, addressed me: "Pray, Mr. W., who is the *man* you have been speaking to? I can't say I much like his appearance." And to own the truth, Porson, with lank, uncombed locks, a loose neckcloth, and wrinkled stockings, exhibited a striking contrast to the gay and gorgeous crowd around. "Who is that gentleman, Mr. King?" replied I, "the greatest man that has visited your rooms since their first creation. It is the celebrated Porson, the most profound scholar in Europe, who has more Greek under that mop of hair than can be found in all the heads in the room; ay, if we even include those of the orchestra."

' "Indeed!" said the Monarch—and ordered a new dance.'

In spite, however, of Mr. Warren's awed admiration, and

[1]Vol. II., Chapter XIII., p. 5.

his dignified reproof to the Master of the Ceremonies, I feel that had Beau Nash been reigning at the time, he would, in all probability, have emulated Lady Huntingdon in her tactful behaviour towards the Quakeress, and that he, whilst praising aloud the courage of the illustrious Porson, would have 'taken him by the hand, accompanied him to the door, and quietly returned to his seat'.

It is not remarkable, therefore, that the *New Prose Guide*, in a fit of dudgeon, informs us that 'It is always remarked by Foreigners that the English Nation, of both sexes, look as grave when they are dancing, as if they were attending the Solemnity of a Funeral'.

But the evening is wearing on; the little lovely feathers of the light have turned duskier and duskier, and the darkness seems rustling like water in the gardens beyond the Assembly Rooms; though inside those rooms a thousand exotic suns are still shining over a wide horizon. It is nine o'clock, and time for a pause in the dancing, and for the gentlemen to hand tea to the ladies. Sometimes, on occasions of great ceremony, tea was not sufficient, and there was a supper. Mrs. Montagu tells us of one of these occasions, when there was 'a table of sweetmeats, jellies, wine, biscuits, cold ham and turkey set behind the screens, which at nine o'clock were taken away, and the table discovered . . . above stairs there was a hot supper for all that would take the trouble to go up'.

As soon as this interlude was over, the dancing would begin again, and last until eleven o'clock, when Beau Nash, careful for the health of the real and the imaginary invalids, would hold out his hand. The bird-noises of the music stopped . . . one by one the enormous gold summer suns, whose rays seemed like rustling wheat-sheaves, withered, until only one was left; and, after the airs from the open windows had cooled the dancers, the company dispersed, and the last sun of all was extinguished.

The Balls at Bath

There were, however, moments when the younger and even the older dancers became restive under Beau Nash's orders that the music must stop at eleven o'clock, although, until Princess Amelia, the daughter of George the Second, arrived at Bath in 1728, nobody had dared to tell him so. The Princess, however, was a firm-minded woman, and one who was not accustomed to being contradicted.

Vastly unpopular, it was she who, as Ranger of Richmond Park, kept that Park closed, to all but her royal relations and her friends; and no amount of respectfully-worded representations that other and humbler people had as much right to walk through the Park as had these, produced the slightest effect upon her. At last some of the people of Richmond had the temerity to go to law on this point, and, worse still, to win their lawsuit, whereupon the Princess ordered the most unsafe and rickety ladders that could be found, to be placed against the walls, and intimated that anyone who wished to enter the Park could do it by those means, or not at all.

This firm action on the part of the Princess did not add to her popularity; and, in the end, the inhabitants gained their point, and she was forced to open one of the gates, although she continued to grumble, complaining that she 'thought the world must be coming to an end when the Vulgar dared thus to keep standing on their rights in defiance of a Princess'. Eventually, she was so disgusted with the Vulgar, that she resigned her position as Ranger, and announced that 'the downfall of England commenced with the opening of Richmond Park'.

Horace Walpole, in a letter to 'Our Legate in Tuscany', in 1752, shows much astonishment at the lady's behaviour. 'Princess Emily', he writes, 'who succeeded my brother in the rangership of Richmond Park, has imitated her brother William's unpopularity, and disobliged the whole country, by refusal of tickets and liberties that had always been allowed. They are at law with her, and have printed in the

Evening Post a strong memorial, which she had refused to receive. The High Sheriff of Surrey, to whom she had denied a ticket, but on better thought had sent one, refused it, and said he had taken his part. Lord Brooke, who had applied for one, was told he couldn't have one: and to add to the affront, it was signified that the Princess had refused one to my Lord Chancellor. Your old nobility don't understand such comparisons. But the most remarkable event happened to her about three weeks ago. One Mr. Bird, a rich gentleman, near the Palace, was applied to by the late Queen for a piece of ground that lay convenient for a walk she was making. He replied that it was not proper for him to pretend to make a Queen a present, but if she would do what she pleased with the ground, he would be content with the acknowledgment of a key and two bucks a year. The bucks were denied, and he himself once shut out, on the pretence that it was fence-month (the breeding-time, when tickets used to be excluded, keys never). The Princess was soon after going through his grounds to town. She found a padlock on his gate. She ordered it to be broken open. Mr Shaw, her deputy, begged a respite, till he could go for the key. He found Mr. Bird at home. "Lord, sir, here is a strange mistake. The Princess is at the gate and it is padlocked." "Mistake! no mistake at all. I made the road; the ground is my own property. Her Royal Highness has thought fit to break the agreement which her royal mother made with me; nobody goes through my grounds but those I choose should".'

It was this redoubtable, but not invariably victorious lady who, disliking the idea of the Ball being closed at eleven o'clock, told Beau Nash that she wished for another country dance. 'One more dance', said the Princess. The Beau looked at her with visible amazement. 'Remember', the Princess warned him, 'I am a Princess'. 'Yes, Madam', replied the Beau, 'but *I* reign here, and *my* laws must be kept'. It was now the Princess's turn to be amazed, but, after renewed and futile attempts to have her own way she smiled, and not only forgave the Beau, but actually became good friends with him, and was often to be seen accompanied by him on her visits to the gambling tables.

So, even on this occasion, the ball closed at eleven o'clock, and, as soon as the ladies were cooled by the airs from the windows, their sedan-chairs bore them home through the dark squares and crescents. The feet of the chairmen falling on the pavements, dry with the summer heat, sounded like satyr hooves splashing through deep water.

Next morning, one or another of the ladies might be awakened by such a terrifying experience as that which befell Mr. Addison, who tells us about it in the *Tatler* (No. 88).

'I was awakened this morning by a sudden shake of the house, and as soon as I had got a little out of my consternation I felt another, which was followed by two or three repetitions of the same convulsion. I got up as fast as possible, girt on my rapier, and snatched up my hat, when my landlady came up to me and told me "that the gentlewoman of the next house begged me to step thither, for that a lodger she had taken in was mad, and she desired my advice", as indeed everybody in the whole lane does upon important occasions. I am not like some artists, saucy, because I can be beneficial, but went immediately. Our neighbour told us "she had the day before let her second floor to a very genteel youngish man, who told her he kept extraordinarily good hours, and was generally home most part of the morning and evening at study; but this morning he had for an hour together made this extravagant noise which we then heard". I went upstairs with my hand upon the hilt of my rapier, and approached the new lodger's door.

'I looked in at the keyhole, and there I saw a well-made man look with great attention on a book, and on a sudden jump into the air so high, that his head almost touched the

ceiling. He came down safe on his right foot, and again flew
up, alighting on his left; then looked again out his book, and
holding out his right leg, put it into such a quivering motion,
that I thought he would have shaked it off. He then used the
left after the same manner, when, on a sudden, to my great
surprise, he stooped himself incredibly low, and turned
gently on his toes. After this circular motion, he continued
bent in that humble posture for some time, looking on his
book. After this, he recovered himself with a sudden spring,
and flew round the room in all the violence and disorder
imaginable, until he made a full pause for want of breath.

'In this interim, my women asked "what I thought". I
whispered "that I thought this learned person an enthusiast,
who possibly had his first education in the Peripatetic way,
which was a sect of Philosophers, who always studied when
walking". But observing him much out of breath, I thought
it the best time to master him if he were disordered, and
knocked at his door. I was surprised to find him open it, and
say with great civility and good mien "that he hoped he had
not disturbed us". I believed him in a lucid interval, and
desired "he would please to let me see book". He did so,
smiling. I could not make anything of it, and therefore asked
"in what language it was writ". He said "it was one he
studied with great application; that it was his profession to
teach it, and he could not communicate his knowledge without a consideration". I answered "that I hoped he would
hereafter keep his thoughts to himself, for his meditations
this morning had cost me three coffee dishes, and a clean
pipe".

'He seemed concerned at that, and told me "he was a
dancing master, and had been reading a dance or two before
he went out, which had been written by one who had been
taught at an Academy in France". He observed me at a stand,
and went on to inform me "that now articulate Motions as
well as Sounds were expressed by Proper Characters, and

that there is nothing so common as to communicate a Dance by a letter". I besought him hereafter to meditate in a ground room.'

Mr. John Ashton explains this to us in his *Social Life in the reign of Queen Anne* (Vol. I.). Such dances as the Louvre and the French Brittagne were, apparently, so elaborate, that a fresh literature was devoted to their cult. 'This seems to have been started by one Thoinet Arbeau, in a book published by him in 1588, and he may be called the originator of the ballet. Both Beauchamp and Feuillet wrote on this subject in French. Feuillet's book was translated and improved upon by Siris, in 1706. John Weaver wrote on this subject (in his *Orchesography*) about 1708, and John Essex (in the *Treatise of Choreography*) in 1710. The object was to teach the different steps and dances, by means of diagrams. Thus coupées, bourrées, fleurets, bounds or tacs, contretemps, chassés, sissones, pirouettes, capers, entrechats, etc., all had their distinguishing marks.'

It was, therefore, to Messieurs Arbeau, Feuillet and Siris, to Messrs. Beauchamp, Weaver and Essex, that Mr. Addison, and, in all probability, many of the ladies who attended the balls in Bath, owed their early awakenings.

CHAPTER VI

The Games of Hazard

DURING THE EIGHTEENTH CENTURY, THE UNI-
versal and perpetual sound of the shuffling of cards
produced the effect of a storm of sultry summer rain,
each drop falling heavy and distinct, though the interval
between the drops could scarcely be heard by the ear.
Gentlemen in periwigs as thick as the heavy, snuffy
green trees of summer, ladies in hooped petticoats that
seemed like the plumage of some bright, great bird, these
played cards, on the walks of Bath, like the Duchess of
Shrewsbury—'that she may be sure to have company
enough'—or in the Assembly Rooms; whilst below stairs in
the lodging-houses, the tittering ladies' maids, the negro
pages, and the impertinent footmen—these, too, had their
gambling parties. This universal bond of card-playing could
even make people forget their political differences. . . .
'Whist has spread an opium over the whole nation', Walpole
wrote to Mann in 1742; 'it makes the courtiers and patriots
sit down to the same pack of cards'. And 'at Bath', according to Lecky, in the *History of England*[1], 'which was then the
centre of fashion, it (gambling) reigned supreme; and the
physicians even recommended it to their patients as a form
of distraction'. Yet, whilst the physicians recommended it
and everybody, from the Duchess of Shrewsbury and Lord
Chesterfield down to the Duchess's Abigail and Lord
Chesterfield's negro, played cards, nobody, so far as we can

[1]Vol. II., Chap. V., p. 156.

make out, ever recorded his or her winnings; each recorded only the fact of the losses they incurred; and every post-day the coach from Bath was snowed under by letters full of complaints about money lost, and hopes destroyed.

One of the favourite games of the time was Ombre, which was played by Pope's Belinda, in Canto III. of *The Rape of the Lock.*

The name Ombre was derived from the Spanish, and does not mean, as might be thought, 'Shadow', but 'I am the Man'—because the gambler who undertook to stand the game must exclaim, 'Io l'Hombre'; this game took the place of its rather primitive ancestor Primero, which was a variation, or rather foreshadowing, of Ombre. To this day we can find it masquerading in Spain under the name of Tresillo, and in Spanish South America under the name of Rocamber.

But far more dangerous and exciting for a professional gambler than any game of Ombre, Tresillo, or Rocamber, was the game called Basset, and this bore a certain resemblance to Faro. Another favourite game of that time, Picquet, is still played by ancient ladies—or was, when I was a child. I remember my grandmother, Lady Londesborough, that link with the eighteenth century (she used to tell us stories told her by her great-grandmother about *that* lady's great-grandmother, Arabella Churchill, and, too, she had often drunk tea, as a small child, with two very old ladies, the Misses Berry, the friends of Horace Walpole's old age), playing picquet in a small room looking out on to a lawn as smooth as green baize. There were many other games besides these: Cribbage, All Fours, Ruff and Honours, French Ruff, Marlborough's Battles, Rolly Polly, Costly Colours, Pharaoh, Bon Ace, Putt, Plain Dealing, Queen Nazareen, Pennech, Post and Pair, Banhafalat, and Beast, Whisk or Whist, Brag, Lanterloo, or Lancre Loo (in which Pam or the Knave of Clubs was the highest card), and, more important than all, there was the Eo, which was to prove, in part, the downfall of poor Beau Nash.

The cards with which these games were played were as various as the games themselves. They were so small and thin that they seemed like the first young leaves on the trees, but they were many-dyed, and glittering like the fish in a lake, and were not confined to bearing representations of hearts, diamonds, clubs, and spades, and the Kings, Queens and Knaves of these; for there were also geographical and astronomical cards, Orange cards (representing the reign of the late King James, and the expedition of the Prince of Orange), cards representing the Plots of the Papists, the Bishops in the Tower and their Trial, the Consecrated Mock Prince of Wales, the Popish Midwife, the Fight at Reading, the Pope's Nuncio, Captain Tom (whoever he may have been), the Murder of Essex, Burning Mass Houses, and the Army going over to the Prince of Orange—as well as Sacheverell cards, cards from Vigo (after the great victory of 1702), and Proverb Cards.

These, then, were the games that were played, these were the cards that were shuffled, by the amiable Duchess of Shrewsbury on the flowered walks in Bath, and in the Assembly Rooms by that cross old Duchess who had said: 'Books! Prithee, don't talk to me about books! The only books I know are men and cards'. These were the games that were played by Lord Chesterfield, who preferred gambling with sharpers to playing with gentlemen, because, if he played with sharpers and won, he was sure to be paid; but if he won from gentlemen, they frequently behaved so genteelly, that he got words and polite apologies instead of his money.

So here was Lord Chesterfield (according to a letter written on 29th March, 1755, by Horace Walpole, who could not be numbered among his admirers), 'while England and France are at war, and Mr. Fox and Mr. Pitt going to war, coolly amusing himself at picquet at Bath with a Moravian Baron who would be in prison if his creditors did not occasionally release him to play and cheat my Lord Chesterfield, as the only chance they have for recovering their money'.

The ladies were as inveterate gamblers as the men; and Steele, in the *Guardian* (No. 174, 30th September, 1713), remarks ironically: 'I must own that I receive great pleasure in seeing my pretty countrywomen engaged in an amusement which puts them upon producing so many virtues. Hereby they acquire such a boldness as raises them near the lordly creature man. Here they are taught such contempt of wealth as may dilate their minds, and prevent many curtain lectures. Their natural tenderness is a weakness here easily unlearned, and I find my soul exalted when I see a lady sacrifice the fortune of her children with as little concern as a Spartan or a Roman dame. . . . But I am satisfied that the gamester ladies have surmounted the little vanities of shaming their beauty, which they so far neglect as to throw their features into violent distortions, and wear away their lilies and roses in tedious watching and restless lucubrations. . . . It is to me an undoubted argument of their ease of conscience that they go directly from church to the gaming table; and so highly reverence play as to make it a great part of their exercise on Sundays.'

As for the professional gamblers, Ward, in the *London Spy*, gives a gloomy picture of them: 'Pray, said I, what do you take those knots of gentlemen to be, who are so merry with one another? They, replyed my Friend, are gamesters, waiting to pick up some young Bubble or other as he comes from his Chamber; they are Men whose Conditions are subject to more Revolutions than a weather Cock, or the Uncertain Mind of a Fantastical woman. They are seldom two Days in one and the same Stations, they are one day very richly drest, and perhaps out of Elbows the next; they have often a great deal of Money, and are as often without a Penny in their Pockets; they are as much Fortune's Bubbles, as young Gentlemen are theirs; for whatever benefits she bestows upon 'em with one Hand, she snatches away with t'other; their whole Lives are a Lottery, they read no books but cards, and all their Mathematicks is to truly understand the odds of a Bet; they very often fall out, but very seldom Fight, and the way to make 'em your friends is to quarrel with them. . . . They generally begin every Year with the same Riches; for the Issue of their Annual Labours is chiefly to enrich the Pawnbrokers. They are seldom in debt, because no Body will Trust 'em; and they never care to Lend Money, because they know not where to Borrow it. A pair of false dice, a pack of mark'd cards sets 'em up; and an hour's unfortunate play commonly breaks 'em.'

In spite of this unhappy state of the lower ranks of professional gamblers, the higher ranks earned for themselves as much fame as did experts in any other profession, and they came, also, from every class of society. Among the famous gamblers in the reign of Queen Anne—men whose names have come down to us—were St. Evremond, that strange old gentleman who (according to Alexander Pope) 'would talk for ever, was a great epicure, and as great a sloven. He lived, you know, to a great old age, and in the latter part of his life used to be always feeding his ducks; or the fowls that he kept in his chamber. He had a great variety of them, and other sorts of animals, all over his house. He used always to say, "that when we grow old, and our own spirits decay, it reanimates one to have a number of living creatures about one, and to be much with them". Indeed, the higher ranks of gamblers considered their profession in that time much as a soldier regarded his; it was a dangerous calling, but not one of which one need be ashamed. "They cry fie upon men engaged in play", said

The Games of Hazard

Barry Lyndon, but I should like to know how much more honourable *their* modes of livelihood are than ours. The broker of the Exchange who bulls and bears, and buys and sells, and dabbles with lying loans, and trades on State secrets, what is he but a gamester? The merchant who deals in teas and tallow, is he any better? His bales of dirty indigo are his dice, his cards come up every year.'

The dangers attached to the profession were, however, only too real, for, apart from the risk of duels, the risk of murderous attacks, if the gambler was detected in cheating, was great. One gambler who was caught in the act of cheating was, for instance, thrown out of a first floor window by the gentlemen whom he had fleeced. This incident afterwards gave Foote an opportunity for exercising his wit; for when 'The Baron', the cheat in question, met Foote some time after, and, complaining loudly of this usage, asked what he should do? 'Do?' says the wit: 'why, it is a plain case. Never play so high again as long as you live.' Another unhappy creature, one Newman, had his hand pinned to the table by a fork. 'Sir', said his adversary, 'if you have not a card hidden under that hand, I apologise.' (Newman committed suicide at Bath in 1789.) Suicide or death by duelling was the common fate of many gamblers; and although duels were forbidden by Beau Nash, who, at any rumour of a challenge, had both parties arrested, his vigilance was at moments evaded, and there were such tragic events as the duel 'that has been fought lately [Lord Orrery to Lady Kaye] between one Jones, a gamester, and one Mr. Price (a gentleman's son, but of the same profession), and has put us in great confusion. Price is kill'd and Jones has made his escape'. After Beau Nash's death, when the gamblers had no longer to fear his authority, there were more frequent duels—and the *Bath Chronicle*, of 26th November, 1778, states that 'a later encounter that made a great sensation was that in which a French adventurer, the Vicomte de Barré, was killed in 1788 by his accomplice Rice, who had challenged him for some reason never explained'.

In this world of pleasure, dawdling, high play, duels, despair and suicide, Beau Nash, himself a professional gambler, spared no pains to save the young, the inexperienced and the unwise, from the consequences of their own folly. His benevolence towards these unhappy creatures was untiring. For, said Goldsmith, 'a thousand instances might be given of his integrity, even in this infamous profession (that of gamester), where his generosity often impelled him to act in contradiction to his interest; wherever he found a novice in the hands of a sharper, he generally forewarned him of the danger; whenever he found any inclined to play, yet ignorant of the game, he would offer his services, and play for them'. And Goldsmith produces many evidences of this kindness and integrity. A typical example of these was his treatment of a certain giddy-headed young man who had just resigned his Fellowship at Oxford, in order to gamble at Bath. On his visit to that city he was foolish enough to bring his whole fortune with him, and, though it amounted to very little, to risk the whole at the tables. At first his luck was greater than he had dared hope, for, though he had neither experience nor skill, he won a sum which might have pleased any man of moderate hopes. Indeed, in a short time, he had added four thousand pounds to his former capital. Just about this time it happened one night that Beau Nash, after losing heavily to this foolish youth, invited him to supper, and took the opportunity of warning him, in the strongest terms, against continuing in his present ways. 'Sir', cried this honest though inveterate gamester, 'perhaps you may imagine I have invited you, in order to have my revenge at home; but I scorn so inhospitable an action. I desired the favour of your company to give you some advice, which you will pardon me, Sir, you seem in need of. You are now high in spirits, and drawn away by a torrent of success: but there will come a time, when you will repent having left the calm of a college life for the turbulent profession of a gamester. Ill runs will come, as sure as day and night succeed one another. Be therefore advised, remain content with your present gains; for be persuaded, that had you the Bank of England, with your present ignorance of gaming, it would vanish like a fairy dream. You are a stranger to me; but to convince you of the part I take in your welfare, I'll give you fifty guineas, to forfeit twenty, every time you lose two hundred at one sitting.' Unhappily, the advice was in vain, for the young man refused the Beau's offer, and was, after a short time, ruined.

Another instance of Beau Nash's attempts to save young men from ruin is shown by his behaviour to the third Duke of Bolton, whose second wife was Lavinia Fenton, the actress, who became celebrated in the character of Polly in *The Beggars' Opera*. The Duke, much distressed at having lost a large sum in gambling, begged Nash to prevent him, in some way, from playing deep in the future. The Beau, therefore, gave him a hundred guineas on condition that he would forfeit ten thousand, whenever he lost that amount in gambling, at one sitting. The Duke, whose passion for gambling was very great, lost eight thousand guineas, soon after this compact, at hazard; and he was about to throw for three thousand more, when Nash, catching hold of the dice box, reminded him what penalty he must pay if he lost. The Duke desisted for the time, but in the end his passion became too strong for him, and, having lost an immense sum at Newmarket, he paid the penalty without murmuring.

There was, too, the case of the Earl of T——, quoted by Goldsmith. This very young man, who had a passion for cards, was never so pleased as when the Beau was his antagonist. The Beau, who understood only too well the danger in which the young man found himself, determined to cure him of this passion, however painful the remedy might be. Experienced and skilful as a gambler, whilst the young man had neither experience nor skill, the Beau engaged him in single play for a very large sum. Very naturally, the young man lost each game, and, each time that he lost the game, he lost his temper too. But the more he lost, the more he seemed determined on ruin, for, till the last, he hoped that his luck might change. At last, the Beau had won from him his whole estate—then his entire fortune, and finally even his carriage, which was the last possession he had to stake. Then Beau Nash, that good-hearted, generous, and honourable gambler, seeing that the young fool was punished sufficiently, returned to him his property, his fortune, and his carriage—in short, everything that he had won from Lord T——, stipulating only that he should be paid £5,000 if ever he were in need. He never asked for the fulfilment of this promise in the young man's lifetime, but, after his death, when Beau Nash found himself in great poverty, he reminded Lord T——'s heirs of the promise, which they, very honourably, paid without any hesitation.

This, then, was the man who saved many from destruction, and who, in his old age, when his company had become tedious, could find but few to pity and relieve his misery.

But these were early days, the shadow of poverty had not fallen upon the Beau as, swashbuckling and splendid, he swaggered about Bath, and travelled to Tunbridge in a post chariot with six greys, with outriders, footmen, French horns, and every other sign and appendage of his royalty. 'He always wore a white hat', said Goldsmith, 'and, to apologise for this singularity, said he did it purely to secure it from being stolen: his dress was tawdry, though not perfectly genteel; he might be considered as a beau of several generations, and in his appearance he, in some measure, mixed the fashions of the last age with those of the present. He perfectly understood elegant expense, and generally passed his time in the very best company, if, Goldsmith continues, with some

The Games of Hazard

degree of gloom, persons of the first distinction deserve that title.'

Alas, that elegant expense was largely dependent upon gambling, and, in 1739, an Act was passed which in the end, after many long years, played a large part in the Beau's lawsuit, effecting ruin, though at first the decline in his fortunes was so gradual, so slight, as to be almost imperceptible. The state he kept was undiminished until within seven years of his death; but the Gaming Act, even at the time it was made law, cast a faint shadow of decay over Bath and over the uncrowned king.

Until the Gaming Act of 1739, there had been no genuine effort on the part of the authorities to prevent public gambling, although in 1633 an Act had been passed releasing any person who had lost more than £100 at one sitting, in any form of gambling, from paying the same; whilst in 1710 the law was made that bonds and securities lost in gambling were not recoverable, and that anyone losing more than £10 might sue the person who won that sum for its recovery; but it was hardly likely, however, that any gambler would dare take advantage of the Acts, for he would, in all probability, be challenged to a duel and killed; and if he were not killed, he would be ostracised by common agreement for the rest of his life. The Act of 1739, however, was a very different matter, for not only were all private lotteries, and the games of Basset, Hazard, Faro, and the Ace of Hearts, made illegal, but the law demanded as well that 'all and every person or persons who shall set up, maintain, or keep the same games shall forfeit and lose the sum of £20'.

This law, very naturally, affected the city of Bath, which depended largely on gambling for its resources, and Beau Nash, who was in the same condition, deeply. So the gamblers determined to invent new games, which would be safe, since they had not been pounced upon by the authorities. They invented, therefore, Passage, Roly-Poly, Bragg (which was a form of poker), and, most important of all, the Eo; and it was the Eo, in the end, which was to bring about Nash's impoverishment.

The Eo, which, according to the *New English Dictionary*, was 'a game of chance, in which the appropriation of the stakes is determined by the falling of a ball into one of several niches marked E. and O. respectively', appears to have been invented by a man of the name of Cook, and to have been played, in the first place, at Tunbridge Assembly Rooms, where the inventor, Cook, and the proprietor of the Rooms, A——e, ruled over the tables. This state of affairs went on for some time, during which both gentlemen earned for themselves the distinction of being called reptiles by Mr. Goldsmith, in his *Life of Nash*. At last, however, A——e, acting up to Mr. Goldsmith's name for him, realised the immense amount of money which was being made, and turned the inventor out of the Rooms. But that outraged gentleman, who did not see why he was to make A——e a present of his invention, hired the town-crier to denounce the game. Faced with the exposure of any frauds that may have been perpetrated, A——e at once bethought himself of Beau Nash, who was already on the verge of poverty; and, seeking him out, he promised that if the Beau would have the proceedings stopped, he should retain a fourth share of the bank. I am sorry to say that Beau Nash, under the shadow and threat of the direst want, honourable and upright as he was, sank to this meanness; which, as Goldsmith rightly says, was the greatest blot in his life; and thus, it is hoped, will find pardon.

Meanwhile Cook, as soon as he found that Beau Nash had entered into league with A——e, tried to induce the Beau to throw that gentleman over, and to set up another table in partnership with Cook. The Beau declined, and Cook chose, instead, a certain Joye as his partner. Eventually, however, Nash induced A——e and Cook to become partners again, and to divide the gains into three shares; one for A——e, one for Cook, and one for himself.

At last, being much struck with the game of Eo, Beau Nash decided that it should be introduced to the world of fashion at Bath; and, having consulted various lawyers as to whether it could be found illegal under the new gaming law, and being assured that it could not, he suggested to the proprietors of the Assembly Rooms that a table for the Eo should be set up in each house; Beau Nash's share of the profits amounted to one-fifth of the total. No sooner were the tables set up than flocks of birds of prey arrived from all the corners of England and from all the gambling places on the Continent, scenting ruin from afar, and ready to gorge themselves on their fellows' misfortunes. The two Assembly Rooms grew richer and richer. But Beau Nash did not. For his employés, the keepers of the Assembly Houses, acting according to their natural instincts, cheated him. Year by year they paid him less and less, until he found that he had lost not less than £20,000—£2,000 of which seems to have been lost through the cheating of A——e and Joye at Tunbridge. 'Taking them to be honest', he said in his Memorial, 'I never enquired what was won or lost, and thought they paid me honestly, till it was discovered they had defrauded me of two thousand guineas. I arrested A——e, who told me I must go to Chancery, and that I should begin with the people of Bath, who had cheated me of ten times as much; and told my attorney that Joye had cheated me of five hundred. . . . Upon my arresting A——e, I received a letter not to prosecute Joye, for he would be a very good witness. I writ a discharge to Joye, for £125 in full, though he never paid me a farthing. Every article of this I can prove from A——e's own mouth, as a reason he allowed the bank keepers but 10 per cent. because I want twenty, and his suborning . . . to alter his information.'

Beau Nash went to law against A——e of Tunbridge and

Walter Wiltshire of Bath, and sued them for the money owing to him; but the only result was that he was told that, under the Gaming Act, the money could not be recovered, and that the public realised that he was a partner in the gaming-houses. This gave his enemies an opportunity to blacken his character, and they were not slow to take it. From that time onwards, although the Beau continued in authority till the end of his days, although nobody dared contradict him as to what should and what should not be done, at the Balls, at the Assemblies, and in all public places, —although he was still the arbiter of fashion and of good manners, yet he was, as a result of this mistake, 'every day calumniated with some new slander'. He tried to obviate the effect of these slanders by a series of printed papers, which he handed about among his acquaintance, and which were distributed, in general, among the visitors to Bath; but these apologies were, as a rule, so badly written, confused, obscure, and wandering, that it was difficult for any reader, however much interested, to conceive what the Beau was aiming at. The only facts that transpired with any clearness were that he had been cheated by the proprietors of the Assembly Rooms, and that they had made large fortunes, while he, their benefactor, and his nephew, for whom he had secured one of the Rooms at first, were left in an equal distress.

One can only deplore the moment in which Beau Nash's poverty and weakness landed him in such an undertaking; and the only consolation to be found is that, as a result of the Beau's unwise lawsuit, the detestable Wiltshire was sued by the Vestry of St. Peter and St. Paul, under the new gaming law, and forced to pay £500 as a fine.

The life of a professional gambler in the eighteenth century was, indeed, no happier than it is now; it may even have been more unhappy, and more unfriended. We may guess at this from a lengthy letter found among Beau Nash's papers after his death. No amount of bad writing could obscure the tragedy that lay behind that letter. For here was a man telling the heart-rending truth about his own suffering—the sad experience of nearly ninety years of life.

DISSUASIVE AGAINST GAMING, IN A LETTER FROM MR. —— IN TUNBRIDGE TO LORD —— IN LONDON

'My Lord:—What I foresaw has arrived, poor Jenners, after losing all his fortune, has shot himself through the head. His losses to Bland were considerable, and his playing soon after with Spedding contributed to hasten his ruin. No man was ever more enamoured of play, or understood it less. At whatever game he ventured his money, he was most usually the dupe, and still foolishly attributed to his bad luck those misfortunes that entirely proceeded from his want of judgment.

'After finding that he had brought on himself irreparable indigence and contempt, his temper, formerly so sprightly, began to grow gloomy and unequal: he grew more fond of solitude, and more liable to take offence at supposed injuries; in short, for a week before he shot himself, his friends were of opinion that he meditated some such horrid design. He was found in his chamber fallen on the floor, the bullet having glanced on the bone, and lodged behind his right eye.

'You remember, my lord, what a charming fellow this deluded man was once. How benevolent, just, temperate, and every way virtuous; the only faults of his mind arose from motives of humanity: he was too easy, credulous, and good-natured, and unable to resist temptation, when recommended by the voice of friendship. These foibles the vicious and the needy soon perceived, and what was at first a weakness they soon perverted into guilt; he became a gamester, and continued the infamous profession till he could support the miseries it brought with it no longer.

The Games of Hazard

'I have often been not a little concerned to see the first introduction of a young man of fortune to the gaming-table. With what eagerness his company is courted by the whole fraternity of sharpers; how they find out his most latent wishes, in order to make way to his affections by gratifying them, and continue to hang upon him with the meanest degree of condescension. The youthful dupe no way suspecting, imagines himself surrounded by friends and gentlemen, and incapable of even suspecting that men of such seeming good sense and so genteel an appearance, should deviate from the laws of honour, walks into the snare, nor is he undeceived till schooled by the severity of experience.

'As I suppose no man would be a gamester unless he hoped to win, so I fancy it would be easy to reclaim him, if he was once effectually convinced, that by continuing to play he must certainly lose. Permit me, my lord, to attempt this task, and to shew, that no young gentleman by a year's run of play, and in a mixed company, can possibly be a gainer.

'Let me suppose, in the first place, that the chances on both sides are equal, that there are no marked cards, no pinching, shuffling, nor hiding; let me suppose that the players also have no advantage of each other in point of judgment, and still further let me grant, that the party is only formed at home, without going to the usual expensive places of resort frequented by gamesters. Even with all these circumstances in the young gamester's favour, it is evident he cannot be a gainer. With equal players, after a year's continuance of any particular game it will be found that, whatever has been played for, the winnings on either side are very inconsiderable, and most commonly nothing at all. Here then is a year's anxiety, pain, jarring, and suspense, and nothing gained; were the parties to sit down and professedly play for nothing, they would contemn the proposal; they would call it trifling away time, and one of the most insipid amusements in nature; yet, in fact, how do equal players differ? It is allowed that little or nothing can be gained; but much is lost; our youth, our time, those moments that may be laid out in pleasure or improvement, are foolishly squandered away in tossing cards, fretting at ill-luck, or, even with a run of luck in our favour, fretting that our winnings are so small.

'I have now stated gaming in that point of view in which it is alone defensible, as a commerce carried on with equal advantage and loss to either party, and it appears, that the loss is great, and the advantage but small. But let me suppose the players not to be equal, but the superiority of judgment in our own favour. A person who plays under this conviction, however, must give up all pretensions to the approbation of his own mind, and is guilty of as much injustice as the thief who robbed a blind man because he knew he could not swear to his person.

'But, in fact, when I allowed the superiority of skill on the young beginner's side, I only granted an impossibility. Skill in gaming, like skill in making a watch, can only be acquired by long and painful industry. The most sagacious youth alive was never taught at once all the arts and all the niceties of gaming. Every passion must be schooled by long habit into caution and phlegm; the very countenance must be taught proper discipline; and he who would practise this art with success, must practise on his own constitution all the severities of a martyr, without any expectation of the reward. It is evident, therefore, every beginner must be a dupe, and can only be expected to learn his trade by losses, disappointments, and dishonour.

'If a young gentleman, therefore, begins to game, the commencements are sure to be to his disadvantage; and all that he can promise himself is, that the company he keeps, though superior in skill, are above taking advantage of his ignorance, and unacquainted with any sinister arts to correct fortune. But this, however, is but a poor hope at best, and, what is worse, most frequently a false one. In general, I might almost have said always, those who live by gaming are not beholden to chance alone for their support, but take every advantage which they can practise without danger of detection. I know many are apt to say, and I have once said so myself, that after I have shuffled the cards, it is not in the power of a sharper to pack them; but at present I can confidently assure your lordship that such reasoners are deceived. I have seen men both in Paris, the Hague, and London, who, after three deals, could give whatever hands they pleased to all the company. However, the usual way with sharpers is to correct fortune thus but once in a night, and to play in other respects without blunder or mistake, and a perseverance in this practice always balances the year in their favour.

'It is impossible to enumerate all the tricks and arts practised upon cards; few but have seen those bungling poor fellows who go about at coffee-houses perform their clumsy feats, and yet, indifferently as they are versed in the trade, they often deceive us; when such as these are possessed of so much art, what must not those be, who have been bred up to gaming from their infancy, whose hands are not like those mentioned above, rendered callous by labour, who have continual practice in the trade of deceiving, and where the eye of the spectator is less upon its guard.

'Let the young beginner only reflect by what a variety of methods it is possible to cheat him, and perhaps it will check his confidence. His antagonists may act by signs and confederacy, and this he can never detect; they may cut to a particular card after three or four hands have gone about, either by having that card pinched, or broader than the rest, or by having an exceeding fine wire thrust between the folds of the paper, and just peeping out at the edge. Or the cards may be chalked with particular marks, which none but the sharper can understand, or a new pack may be slipped in at a proper opportunity. I have known myself, in Paris, a fellow thus detected with a tin case, containing two packs of cards, concealed within his shirt sleeve, and which, by means of a spring, threw the cards ready packed into his hands. These and an hundred other arts may be practised with impunity and escape detection.

'The great error lies in imagining every fellow with a laced coat to be a gentleman. The address and transient behaviour of a man of breeding are easily acquired, and none are better qualified than gamesters in this respect. At first, their complaisance, civility, and apparent honour is pleasing, but upon examination, few of them will be found to have their minds sufficiently stored with any of the more refined accomplishments which truly characterise the man of breeding. This will commonly serve as a criterion to distinguish them, though there are other marks which every young gentleman of fortune should be apprized of. A sharper, when he plays, generally handles and deals the cards awkwardly like a bungler; he advances his bets by degrees, and keeps his antagonist in spirits by small advantages and alternate success at the beginning; to show all his force at once, would but fright the bird he intends to decoy; he talks of honour and virtue, and his being a gentleman, and that he knows great men, and mentions his coal-mines, and his estate in the country; he is totally divested of that masculine confidence which is the attendant of real fortune; he turns, yields, assents, smiles, as he hopes will be most pleasing to his destined prey; he is afraid of meeting a shabby acquaintance, particularly if in better company; as he grows richer he wears finer clothes; and if ever he is seen in an undress, it is most probable he is without money; so that seeing a gamester growing finer each day, it is a certain symptom of his success.

'The young gentleman, who plays with such men for considerable sums, is sure to be undone, and yet we seldom see even the rook himself make a fortune. A life of gaming must necessarily be a life of extravagance, parties of this kind are formed in houses where the whole profits are consumed, and while those who play mutually ruin each other, they only who keep the house or the table acquire fortunes. Thus gaming may readily ruin a fortune, but has seldom been found to retrieve it. The wealth which has been acquired with industry and hazard, and preserved for ages by prudence and foresight, is swept away on a sudden; and when a besieging sharper sits down before an estate, the property is often transferred in less time than the writings can be drawn to secure the possession. The neglect of business, and the extravagance of a mind which has been taught to covet precarious possession, brings on premature destruction; though poverty may fetch a compass and go somewhat about, yet will it reach the gamester at last; and though his ruin be slow, yet it is certain.

'A thousand instances could be given of the fatal tendency of this passion, which first impoverishes the mind, and then perverts the understanding. Permit me to mention one, not caught from report, or dressed up by fancy, but such as has actually fallen under my own observation, and of the truth of which I beg your lordship may rest satisfied.

'At Tunbridge, in the year 1715, Mr. J. Hedges made a very brilliant appearance. He had been married about two years to a young lady of great beauty and large fortune; they had one child, a boy, on whom they bestowed all that affection which they could spare from each other. He knew nothing of gaming, nor seemed to have the least passion for play; but he was unacquainted with his own heart; he began by degrees to bet at the tables for trifling sums, and his soul took fire at the prospect of immediate gain: he was soon surrounded with sharpers, who with calmness lay in ambush for his fortune, and coolly took advantage of the precipitancy of his passion.

The Games of Hazard

'His lady perceived the ruin of her family approaching, but at first without being able to form any scheme to prevent it. She advised with his brother, who at that time was possessed of a small fellowship in Cambridge. It was easily seen, that whatever took the lead in her husband's mind, seemed to be there fixed unalterably; it was determined, therefore, to let him pursue fortune, but previously take measures to prevent the pursuits being fatal.

'Accordingly, every night this gentleman was a constant attender at the hazard tables; he understood neither the arts of sharpers nor even the allowed strokes of a connoisseur, yet still he played. The consequence is obvious; he lost his estate, his equipage, his wife's jewels, and every other moveable that could be parted with, except a repeating watch. His agony on this occasion was inexpressible; he was even mean enough to ask a gentleman, who sate near, to lend him a few pieces, in order to turn his fortune; but this prudent gamester, who plainly saw there were no expectations of being repaid, refused to lend a farthing, alleging a former resolution against lending. Hedges was at last furious with the continuance of ill-success, and pulling out his watch, asked if any person in company would set him sixty guineas upon it: the company was silent; he then demanded fifty; still no answer; he sunk to forty, thirty, twenty; finding the company still without answering, he swore that it should never go for less, and dashed it against the floor, at the same time, attempting to dash out his brains against the marble chimney-piece.

'This last act of desperation immediately excited the attention of the whole company; they instantly gathered round, and prevented the effects of his passion; and, after he again became cool, he was permitted to return home, with sullen discontent, to his wife. Upon his entering her apartment, she received him with her usual tenderness and satisfaction; while he answered her caresses with contempt and severity;

his disposition being quite altered with his misfortunes. "But, my dear Jemmy," says his wife, "perhaps you don't know the news I have to tell; my mamma's old uncle is dead; the messenger is now in the house, and you know his estate is settled upon you." This account seemed only to increase his agony, and looking angrily at her, he cried, "there you lie, my dear, his estate is not settled upon me."—"I beg your pardon," says she, "I really thought it was, at least you have always told me so."—"No," returned he, "as sure as you and I are to be miserable here, and our children beggars hereafter, I have sold the reversion of it this day, and have lost every farthing I got for it at the hazard table."—"What, all!" replied the lady.—"Yes, every farthing," returned he, "and I owe a thousand pounds more than I have to pay." Thus speaking, he took a few frantic steps across the room. When the lady had a little enjoyed his perplexity: "No, my dear," cried she, "you have lost but a trifle, and you owe nothing; our brother and I have taken care to prevent the effects of your rashness, and are actually the persons who have won your fortune: we employed proper persons for this purpose, who brought their winnings to me; your money, your equipage, are in my possession, and here I return them to you, from whom they were unjustly taken; I only ask permission to keep my jewels, and to keep you, my greatest jewel, from such dangers for the future." Her prudence had the proper effect, he ever after retained a sense of his former follies, and never played for the smallest sums, even for amusement.

'Not less than three persons in one day fell a sacrifice at Bath to this destructive passion. Two gentlemen fought a duel, in which one was killed, and the other desperately wounded; and a youth of great expectation and excellent disposition, at the same time ended his own life by a pistol. If there be any state that deserves pity, it must be that of a gamester; but the state of a dying gamester is of all situations the most deplorable.

The Games of Hazard

'There is another argument which your lordship, I fancy, will not entirely despise: beauty, my lord, I own is at best but a trifle, but such as it is, I fancy few would willingly part with what little they have. A man with a healthful complexion, how great a philosopher soever he be, would not willingly exchange it for a sallow hectic phyz, pale eyes, and a sharp wrinkled visage. I entreat you only to examine the faces of all the noted gamblers round one of our public tables; have you ever seen anything more haggard, pinched, and miserable? And it is but natural that it should be so. The succession of passions flush the cheek with red, and all such flushings are ever succeeded by consequent paleness; so that a gamester contracts the sickly hue of a student, while he is only acquiring the stupidity of a fool.

'Your good sense, my lord, I have often had an occasion of knowing, yet how miserable it is to be in a set of company where the most sensible is ever the least skilful; your footman, with a little instruction, would, I dare venture to affirm, make a better and more successful gamester than you; want of passions, and low cunning, are the two great arts; and it is peculiar to this science alone, that they who have the greatest passion for it, are of all others the most unfit to practise it.

'Of all the men I ever knew, Spedding was the greatest blockhead, and yet the best gamester; he saw almost intuitively the advantage on either side, and ever took it; he could calculate the odds in a moment, and decide upon the merits of a cock or a horse, better than any man in England; in short he was such an adept in gaming, that he brought it up to a pitch of sublimity it had never attained before; yet, with all this, Spedding could not write his own name. What he died worth I cannot tell, but of this I am certain, he might have possessed a ministerial estate, and that won from men famed for their sense, literature and patriotism.

'If, after this description, your lordship is yet resolved to hazard your fortune at gaming, I beg you would advert to the situation of an old and luckless gamester. Perhaps there is not in nature a more deplorable being: his character is too well marked, he is too well known to be trusted. A man that has been often a bankrupt, and renewed trade upon low compositions, may as well expect extensive credit as such a man. His reputation is blasted: his constitution worn, by the extravagance and ill hours of his profession; he is now incapable of alluring his dupes, and like a superannuated savage of the forest, he is starved for want of vigour to hunt after prey.

'Thus gaming is the source of poverty, and still worse, the parent of infamy and vice. It is an inlet to debauchery, for the money thus acquired is but little valued. Every gamester is a rake, and his morals worse than his mystery. It is his interest to be exemplary in every scene of debauchery, his prey is to be courted with every guilty pleasure; but these are to be changed, repeated, and embellished, in order to employ his imagination, while his reason is kept asleep; a young mind is apt to shrink at the prospect of ruin; care must be taken to harden his courage, and make him keep his rank; he must be either found a libertine, or he must be made one. And when a man has parted with his money like a fool, he generally sends his conscience after it like a villain, and the nearer he is to the brink of destruction, the fonder does he grow of ruin.

'Your friend and mine, my lord, had been thus driven to the last reserve, for he found it impossible to disentangle his affairs, and look the world in the face; impatience at length threw him into the abyss he feared, and life became a burthen, because he feared to die. But I own that play is not always attended with such tragical circumstances: some have had courage to survive their losses, and go on content with beggary; and sure those misfortunes which are of our own production, are of all others most pungent. To see such a poor disbanded being an unwelcome guest at every table, and often flapped off like a fly, is affecting; in this case the closest alliance is forgotten, and contempt is too strong for the ties of blood to unbind.

'But however fatal this passion may be in its consequence, none allures so much in the beginning; the person once listed as a gamester, if not soon reclaimed, pursues it through his whole life; no loss can retard, no danger awaken him to common sense; nothing can terminate his career but want of money to play, or of honour to be trusted.

'Among the number of my acquaintance, I knew but of two who succeeded by gaming; the one a phlegmatic heavy man, who would have made a fortune in whatever way of life he happened to be placed; the other who had lost a fine estate in his youth by play, and retrieved a greater at the age of sixty-five, when he might be justly said to be past the power of enjoying it. One or two successful gamesters are thus set up in an age to allure the young beginner; we all regard such as the highest prize in a lottery, unmindful of the numerous losses that go to the accumulation of such in frequent success.

'Yet I would not be so morose as to refuse your youth all kinds of play; the innocent amusements of a family must often be indulged, and cards allowed to supply the intervals of more real pleasure; but the sum played for in such cases should always be a trifle; something to call up attention, but not engage the passions. The usual excuse for laying large sums is, to make the players attend to their game; but, in fact, he that plays only for shillings, will mind his cards equally well with him that bets guineas; for the mind habituated to stake large sums, will consider them as trifles at last; and if one shilling could not exclude indifference at first, neither will an hundred in the end.

'I have often asked myself, how it is possible that he who is possessed of competence, can ever be induced to make it precarious by beginning play with the odds against him; for wherever he goes to sport his money, he will find himself overmatched and cheated. Either at White's, Newmarket, the Tennis Court, the Cock Pit, or the Billiard Table, he will find numbers who have no other resource but their acquisitions there; and if such men live like gentlemen, he may readily conclude it must be on the spoils of his fortune, or the fortunes of ill-judging men like himself. Was he to attend but a moment to their manner of betting at those places, he would readily find the gamester seldom proposing bets but with the advantage in his own favour. A man of honour continues to lay on the side on which he first won; but gamesters shift, change, lie upon the lurch, and take every advantage, either of our ignorance or neglect.

'In short, my lord, if a man designs to lay out his fortune in quest of pleasure, the gaming-table is, of all other places, that where he can have least for his money. The company are superficial, extravagant, and unentertaining; the conversation flat, debauched, and absurd; the hours unnatural and fatiguing; the anxiety of losing is greater than the pleasure of winning; friendship must be banished from that society the members of which are intent only on ruining each other; every other improvement, either in knowledge or virtue, can scarce find room in that breast which is possessed by the spirit of play; the spirits become vapid, the constitution is enfeebled, the complexion grows pale, till, in the end, the mind, body, friends, fortune, and even the hopes of futurity sink together! Happy, if nature terminates the scene, and neither justice nor suicide are called in to accelerate her tardy approach. I am, my lord, &c.'

CHAPTER VII

The Religious Revival in Bath

THE GAMBLERS, AND THE DANCERS, AND THE light bright ladies, were not, however, in spite of what we have seen in the previous chapters, to have everything their own way. For a Methodist Revival, with Whitfield, and the redoubtable Lady Huntingdon, descended upon these butterflies like a shower of rain, and damped them considerably.

The state of the Established Church, in the first half of the eighteenth century, was such an exact mirror of the life of the countryside, that it might have been a mimicry of this. A drowsy sermonising and hymn-singing, like the innocent baa-ing of a woolly flock, leaders who had no more intellect than their followers—a complete lack of either hope or aspirations, a humdrum round of small and meaningless duties—this constituted the religious life of the time. Those Bishops who had any pretensions to intellect—such as Pope's friend, Bishop Atterbury—were statesmen rather than churchmen, were more of this world than of the next; whilst those who were churchmen refused to take any interest in this world at all, and could scarcely, therefore, have been of much use to its inhabitants.

But whilst the religious life in the country was drowsy, that in London, and in Bath, was a travesty of smart assemblies. The religious life in London, as far as church-going went, was nothing but an excuse for parading dresses, and for fashionable people meeting fashionable people, whilst the sermon was drowned by a sea of whispering, and by the sounds made by the hooped petticoats as their wearers turned in their seats, and by the fans as they were furled and unfurled—a sound like all the birds in the world preening their plumage, and all the leaves in the world welcoming the summer air.

Sylvanus Urban, Gent., of the *Gentleman's Magazine*, was informed by some correspondent, in May, 1753, of 'a dozen designs, elegantly executed, which at a late celebration of the Communion in a certain church of this metropolis were actually displayed by way of screens to so many pretty faces, disposed in a semi-circular arrangement about the Holy Table. 1. Darby and Joan with their attributes. 2. Harlequin, Pierrot, and Columbine. 3. The Prodigal Son, copied from the Rake's Progress. 4. A Rural Dance, with a band of music consisting of a fiddle, a bagpipe, and a Welsh Harp. 5. The Taking of Porto Bello. 6. The solemnities of filiation. 7. Joseph and his Mistress. 8. The Humours of Change Alley. 9. Silenus with his proper symbols and supporters. 10. The first interview of Isaac and Rebecca. 11. The Judgment of Paris. 12. Vauxhall Gardens with the decorations and company.'—In this way, and by these means, were the rigours of the sermon softened, the musty, snuffy, dry-as-dust atmosphere made glittering by the light and dancing motes of life.

In the countryside, where even the amusement of staring in church must have palled after a while, since there was never an unknown person to stare at, we find Sir Roger de Coverley, that typical squire of his time, marshalling his tenants and marching them to church (if the words 'marshalling' or 'marching' could be applied to such unenergetic and sleepy movements). Sir Roger performed this duty under the spell, probably, of some wool-gathering idea that church-going was a meaningless affair of good manners and inherited instincts, rather like drinking toasts in honour of some king who had never lived within his dominions, and who had never been seen, or would, or could, be seen by his subjects. Also, absence from church led, in his belief, to every form of criminality. For, as the *Spectator* remarks: 'In the printed confessions of persons that are hanged, Sabbath-breaking is the crime the poor wretches always begin with. If they kill'd father or mother, they would not mention that article, till after having profess'd how often they had broke the Sabbath.'

Sir Roger de Coverley, therefore, remembering these awful warnings, and wishing to save his tenants from such an untimely end, thought it better that these should go to church, whether they liked it or not, every Sunday. 'My friend, Sir Roger, being a good churchman, has beautified the inside of his church with several texts of his own chusing: he has likewise given a handsome pulpit cloth, and railed in the Communion Table at his own expense.' Sir Roger's tenants, however, remained unmoved, even by such attractions as these; so even stronger measures became necessary. 'He has often told me, that at his coming to his Estate he found his parishioners very irregular; and that in order to make them kneel and join in the responses, he gave every one of them a hassock and a common prayer book: and at the same time employed an itinerant singing master, who goes about the country for that purpose, to instruct them rightly in the tunes of the psalms; upon which they do now very much value themselves, and indeed out-do most of the country churches that I have ever heard.

'As Sir Roger is landlord to the whole congregation, he keeps them in very good order, and will suffer nobody to sleep in it besides himself; for if by chance he has been surprised into a small nap at sermon, upon recovering out of it he stands up and looks about him, and if he sees anybody else nodding, either wakes them himself or sends his servant to them. As soon as the sermon is finished, nobody presumes to stir till Sir Roger is gone out of church. The knight walks down from his seat in the chancel between a double row of his tenants, that stand bowing to him, on each side; and every now and then enquires how such and such an one's wife or mother, or son, or father, do, whom he does not see at church; which is understood as a secret reprimand to the person that is absent.'

But whilst the flock of the Church of England fell asleep immediately on entering the penn, it could be awakened and roused to fury by any person who refused to fall asleep there, and preferred to remain awake in some other sacred building. The choice of sects by whom it could be roused was very large, and according to Mr. John Ashton, in his learned, and enchanting, history of *Social Life in the Reign of Queen Anne*, included Antinomians, Hederingtonians, Theaurian Joanites, Seekers, Waiters, Reevists, Brownists, Baronists, Wilkinsonians, Familists, Ranters, Muggletonians, etc., etc. And, after giving this peculiarly depressing list of names, he quotes Missan as saying (with a certain degree of gloom): 'All these, and nothing at all, are just one and the same thing: Christianity is overwhelm'd with sects enough already, without our studying them chimerically. . . .'

The most unpopular form of all forms of Christianity, however, was Roman Catholicism—largely because fears were entertained about the political actions of the Roman Catholics, who were subjected to the most disgraceful persecutions. Next in disfavour came the Quakers, and the dislike of these seems to have been aroused, partly, by the fact that the men refused to wear wigs, and that the women insisted on wearing steeple-crowned hats.

It was, therefore, in a world which grew drowsy over the form of religion known to it, and turbulent over the forms of religion to which it was unused, that John Wesley brought his ardour, his fine intellect, and his clear beliefs.

The fashionable world at Bath was curious to see him, but none too pleased when it had seen him, on the occasion of

his preaching at that city in 1739, the year after his first appearance as a Methodist preacher in London. The thought
of him, however, did not disturb that world's card-playing,
and when subscriptions for a new card-room and for the
expenses of church services were opened at the same time, it
could not be denied that the card-room won.

> 'The books were opened t'other day,
> And all the shops, for church and play.
> The church got six, Hoyle sixty-seven.
> How great the odds of Hell to Heaven.'

I cannot help feeling, however, that the conversations of
the Countess of Huntingdon, whom we have met already in
the chapter on Balls, and who was Wesley's principal sup-
porter in Bath, must have painted Heaven in such tones that
we cannot be surprised at sinners flying from any danger of
conversion.

No matter where Lady Huntingdon found herself, no
matter what her company, she would insist on the conversation being turned upon religion, the terrible sins of those
present, the hopelessness of their future state as compared
with hers, her own former sinfulness and present righteous-
ness, her virtue in contrast to her companions' lack of virtue,
and other matters of the same kind. 'There was a publicity in
her religion', we are told by her biographer in *Life and Times
of Selina Countess of Huntingdon, by a member of the Houses of
Shirley and Hastings*, 'that no one else, Dissenter, Puritan, or
Anglican, had admitted, at least since the Reformation. . . .
Wherever she went, she produced an extraordinary degree of
attention to religious subjects. . . . Wherever she was, and in
whatever company, her conversation was on religion, in
which there was this peculiarity, that she spoke of the sins
and errors of her former life, her conversion to God, the
alteration of her heart and conduct, and she plainly said to all
that it was absolutely necessary that the same change should

take place in them, if they would have any life in death.' In short, 'the sternest Calvinism', as Barbeau exclaims in an ecstasy of admiration, 'breathed from all her utterances'.

We can see her still, in an engraving after a portrait by Russell, with her long and rather flabby face framed by un-powdered hair, which seems to be of the colour of pepper and salt, and a white headdress which is carried under her chin. Her eyes, which are sunken and lightless, seem fixed (if so strong a word can be used) with some reflectiveness, but without any great interest, on a distant sky. Her lips are thin and shapeless, and her whole face, though it wears a sunken look of piety, makes one think of a colourless evening after a rainy day! Everything is a little too flat and soft and taste-less, like a fillet of boiled plaice.

Lady Huntingdon, however, in spite of her feeble ap-pearance, found nobody's business too heavy to be borne upon her frail shoulders. Certain of her social position in this world as in the next, she would use the former in order to enhance the latter. Nobody was safe from her. We have seen, in the chapter on Balls, how she dealt with the Quaker lady who had the effrontery to forget that effacement which would have graced her humble position in life. Lady Huntingdon was always particularly admirable with sinners. Lady Suffolk, whose rank in this world, but not in the next, equalled her own, was routed for good, though not, I am afraid, until Lady Suffolk had made a public scene. When Lady Hunting-don's relative, Earl Ferrers, was indicted and condemned for murder, that great woman, 'whose company', as Lord Fer-rers said, 'was better than no company', insinuated herself into his prison, and, according to one of her most fervent admirers, managed to induce the gaoler to cut off Lord Fer-rers' wine allowance, and to take away his playing cards, so that he might spend the last remaining days of his life, with-out wine, and without distractions, in uninterrupted con-templation of his impending fate.

The Religious Revival in Bath

The admirer who claimed that Lady Huntingdon had performed this feat may, however, have been carried away by enthusiasm, for Horace Walpole gives quite another version of the affair to Sir Horace Mann: 'Lord Cornwallis, governor of the Tower, shortened his [Lord Ferrers'] allowance of wine after his conviction, agreeably to the late strict acts on murder. This he much disliked, and at last pressed his brother the clergyman to intercede that at least he might have some more porter; for, said he, what I have is not a draught. His brother represented against it, but at last consenting (and he did obtain it), then said the Earl, "Now is as good a time as any to take leave of you—Adieu!"

Mr. Walpole's view of this affair was probably the right one, as he cannot be accused of being prejudiced in favour of the Methodists. Indeed, he told the Rev. William Cole, in a highly libellous letter dated the 16th of April, 1768, that 'that arch-rogue' Whitfield was in the habit of encouraging the people to forge, murder, etc., in order to have the benefit of converting them on the gallows!

Whether Horace Walpole was right or wrong, it must be said for Lady Huntingdon that she prevented Lord Ferrers' three illegitimate children from being present at the gallows when their father was executed, and that she did take them to the prison to bid him farewell—though nobody will ever know if this gave the slightest satisfaction to either father or offspring.

Lord Ferrers was by no means the only sinner whose business she took upon her shoulders. The actor, Shuter, for instance, with whom Lady Huntingdon was unacquainted, was accosted by that great lady, simply because she saw him walking in the street at Bath; he was invited to her house, and, when there, was urged to give up his calling as an actor. History does not relate, however, if Lady Huntingdon offered to make the sinner even the smallest allowance, if he consented to throw away his livelihood in order to follow her tenets. It may be, of course, that she thought that the spiritual rewards would be sufficient.

Lady Huntingdon was no respecter of persons. Hearing that the Archbishop of Canterbury and his wife were in the habit of giving parties (on Sundays, too!), Lady Huntingdon, who was unacquainted with them, induced a mutual friend to take her to Lambeth Palace, and, when there, reproved her host and hostess, with a good deal of severity, for their behaviour. It is sad to think that the Archbishop paid no attention to the rebuke of his new acquaintance, and that the only reason why the Archbishop's wife paid it such marked attention, was in order that she might give a lifelike imitation of Lady Huntingdon at the parties in question. In the end, Lady Huntingdon, realising that her rebuke had been administered in vain, made a personal complaint to the King and Queen about the scandal at Lambeth, with the result that the King wrote a letter of the greatest severity to the Archbishop, and that Lambeth became, on all the subsequent Sundays of that reign, the haunt of gloom, and the habitation of owls.

As I have said, Lady Huntingdon was particularly admirable with sinners, and home truths flew about her chapel during the services to such an extent that the Duchess of Buckingham, who was the natural daughter of King James II., saw no reason why, if Lady Huntingdon could indulge in these, she should not indulge in them also. She therefore called that great lady to order in a strong-minded and delightful letter. The Methodist doctrines, the Duchess considered, were 'most repulsive, and strongly tinctured with impertinence and disrespect towards their superiors, in perpetually endeavouring to level all ranks and do away with old distinctions. It is monstrous to be told that you have a heart as simple as the common wretches that crawl the earth. This is highly offensive and insulting, and I cannot but wonder that your Ladyship should relish any sentiments so much at variance with high rank and good breeding.' The Duchess then, having delivered this rebuke, accepted an invitation to Lady Huntingdon's chapel, which, at that moment, occupied much the same position in the social world as the Opera at Covent Garden occupies to-day. Indeed, Horace Walpole, in a letter to Horace Mann (23rd March, 1749) wrote: 'Methodism is more fashionable than anything but brag; the women play devilish deep at both—as deep, it is much suspected, as the matrons of Rome did at the mysteries of the Bona Dea.'

But then Walpole could scarcely be counted as an admirer of Methodism, for in another letter to the same correspondent (3rd May, 1749) he informed him: 'If you ever think of returning to England, as I hope it will be long first, you must prepare yourself with Methodism. I really believe that by that time it will be necessary: this sect increases as fast as almost ever any religious nonsense did. Lady Fanny Shirley has chosen this way of bestowing the dregs of her beauty upon Jesus Christ; and Mr. Lyttleton is very near making the same sacrifice of the dregs of all those various characters that he has worn. The Methodists love your big sinners, as proper subjects to work upon—and indeed they have a plentiful harvest—I think what you call flagrancy was never more in fashion.'

As for the preachers, they also were at variance with high rank and good breeding, and, according to Graves, 'inveighed with great severity against luxury in dress, cards, dancing, and all the fashionable diversions of the place, and even against frequenting the rooms with the most innocent intentions of recreation and amusement'. Certain of the sect believed that 'no recreation, considered as such, could be innocent', whilst dancing was regarded as particularly sinful. Yet Lady Huntingdon, as we have seen, went to a Ball in honour of the Prince of Wales' birthday, and went dressed in such a manner, moreover, that she was much remarked.

The Religious Revival in Bath

But perhaps she did not regard dancing as 'a recreation, considered as such'.

John Wesley's first sermon at Bath was preached in 1739, and, drawn by a powerful curiosity, four thousand hearers were present. When he preached for the second time, there was an audience of one thousand, which included several fashionable people. Of these, Wesley wrote in his Journal, 22nd May, 1739: 'There were several fine gay things among them, to whom specially I called "Awake, thou that sleepest, and arise from the dead, and Christ shall put thee right".'

A fortnight after this time, we find Wesley writing in his Journal, after he had announced that he would preach the third time, 'There was great expectation at Bath of what a noted man' [Beau Nash] 'was to do with me there: and I was much intreated not to preach, because no one knew what might happen. By this report I also gained a much larger audience, among whom were many of the rich and great. I told them plainly "the Scripture had included them all under sin, high and low, rich and poor, one with another". Many of them seemed to be not a little surprised, and were sinking apace into seriousness, when the champion appeared, and coming close to me asked "By what authority I did these things?" I replied, "By the authority of Jesus Christ, conveyed to me by the (now) Archbishop of Canterbury, when he laid his hands upon me, and said: 'Take thou authority to preach the Gospel'." He said, "This is contrary to Act of Parliament. This is a Conventicle". I answered: "Sir, the Conventicles mentioned in the Act (as the Preamble shows) are seditious meetings. But this is not such. Here is no shadow of sedition. Therefore it is not contrary to the Act." He replied, "I say it is. But besides, your preaching frightens people out of their wits." "Sir, did you ever hear me preach?" "No." "How then can you judge of what you have never heard?" "Sir, by common report." "Common report

134

is not enough. Give me leave, Sir, to ask, is not your name Nash?" "My name is Nash." "Sir, I dare not judge of you by common report. I believe it is not enough to judge by." Here he paused a while, and having recovered himself, asked: "I desire to know what these people come here for?" On which one replied: "Sir, leave him to me. Let an old woman answer him. You, Mr. Nash, take care of your body. We take care of our souls, and for the food of our souls we come here".'

The Beau, having decidedly got the worst of this battle, walked away, leaving the audience in some confusion; and the news of the encounter spread rapidly round the city, with the result that, to quote once more from Wesley's Journal: 'As I returned, the street was full of people hurrying to and fro and speaking great words. But when any of them asked "Which is he?" and I replied "I am he", they were immediately silent. Several ladies followed me into Mr. Marchant's house, the servant told me: "There were some wanted to speak to me." I went to them and said: "I believe, ladies, the maid mistook; you only wanted to look at me." I added, "I do not expect that the rich and great should want either to speak with me or hear me, for I speak the plain truth: a thing you little hear of and do not desire to hear".'

After this ill-tempered and ill-mannered remark, a few more words passed between Wesley and his visitors, and he then returned to his host.

Meanwhile, Beau Nash, who disapproved strongly of the Methodists because they were, according to his lights, a disturbing influence, and because they preached against those pleasures over which he ruled, returned to the charge. He was happy enough to find an adversary who was less quick-witted than Wesley, and gained an immediate victory over this gentleman, who had been unwise enough to boast that, whilst the Church of England was either too sleepy or too unsure or too stupid to preach extempore, the Methodist clergy invariably did so. Nash, who approved of the clergy of the Church of England because they did not interfere with him, replied, tartly, that 'It was no difficult matter for the Methodist to preach extempore, since they had a certain string of words and expressions that they consistently used on every subject'. The Methodist promptly lost his temper and muttered: 'It is such a string as must draw you to Heaven, if ever you intend to go there'. Whereupon 'I thank you', replied the Beau, 'but I don't choose to go to Heaven on a string'.

Not content with this small victory, Beau Nash, according to Graves' *Spiritual Quixote*, carried on a silly and bad-mannered guerilla warfare of annoyance and noise against the Methodists. . . . 'Mr. Nash, though he himself had greatly reformed and regulated the manners and behaviour of his subjects in the public room, yet, being orthodox in his tenets and very well content with the present state of religion amongst them, he did not desire any reformation in that article. Having notice, therefore, of this intended preachment, he got ready his band of music, with the addition of two or three French horns and kettledrums, and as soon as the Orator had exhibited his person on the Parade, stretched forth his hand, and, like Paul in the cartoon, was about to speak, Nash gave the signal for the grand chorus of "God Save the King"; the music struck up; and playing so loyal a piece of music no one had the hardiness to interrupt them. Nay, a majority of the company were probably pleased with Nash's humour; and it being now breakfast time, the mob was easily dispersed.'

Beau Nash found himself, however, in a rather awkward position when he realised that Lady Huntingdon and her great social influence were behind the Methodists. The position was a delicate one; he realised, too, that in spite of Lady Huntingdon's rather embarrassing conversation, her influence was likely to prevent any public outbreaks of eccentricity on the part of her sect. He thought it better and wiser, therefore, to discuss the beliefs of the Methodists with Lady Huntingdon, and at last he even went so far as to hear Whitfield preach in her house. But this led to unfortunate results; for his friends and associates having, in some way, got to hear of this odd behaviour on the part of the Beau, overwhelmed him with congratulations on his supposed conversion, whilst verses on the subject were posted up in the Pump Room and in the Assembly Rooms, and printed broadsheets announcing the Beau's conversion from his former lamentable way of life, and his resignation from the post of Master of the Ceremonies, and the date of his first sermon, were showered on the visitors.

Beau Nash was so infuriated by this, that he never visited Lady Huntingdon again—although she could scarcely be blamed in the matter.

But though Beau Nash would never visit Lady Huntingdon again, there were others who would, and did. Lord Bolingbroke, for instance, whose decline of life was, according to Goldsmith's *Life* of him, 'less brilliant, because more amiable', not only heard Whitfield preach at her house, but actually wrote to Lady Huntingdon: 'You may command my pen when you will: it shall be drawn in your service. For, admitting the Bible to be true, I shall have little apprehension of maintaining the doctrines of predestination and grace against all your revilers.' Lord Chesterfield, 'notwithstanding his own private feeling and sentiments', offered her twenty pounds toward the building of a new tabernacle—although he would not, could not, be converted to Methodism by her. Whitfield could, and did, convert Lady Chesterfield, through the medium of Lady Huntingdon, whilst Lady Gertrude Hotham and the Countess Delitz, Chesterfield's sister and sister-in-law, were deeply involved in the movement; but Lady Huntingdon waited in vain, as far as Lord Chesterfield himself was concerned.

The Religious Revival in Bath

Those who were not frightened away by the shafts and arrows aimed at them, were, occasionally, more than a little irritated by the services. Horace Walpole, for instance, found both the service and Mr. Wesley very hard to bear.

'My health', he informed John Chute, in a letter dated the 10th of October, 1766, 'advances faster than my amusement. However, I have been at one opera, Mr. Wesley's. They have boys and girls with charming voices, that sing hymns, in parts, to Scotch ballad tunes; but indeed so long that one would think they were already in eternity, and knew how much time they had before them. The Chapel is very neat, with true Gothic windows (yet I am not converted); but I was very glad to see that luxury was creeping in upon them before persecution; they have very neat mahogany for branches, and brackets of the same in taste. At the upper end is a broad *haut pas* of four steps, advancing in the middle: at each end of the broadest part are two of *my* eagles', (can these have been a present from the hypocritical Mr. Walpole?) 'with red cushions for the parson and clerk. Behind them rise three more steps, in the midst of which is a third eagle for pulpit. Scarlet armchairs to all three. On either hand, a balcony for elect ladies. The rest of the congregation sit on forms. Behind the pulpit in a dark niche, is a plain table without rails; so you see the throne is for the apostle. Wesley is a lean, elderly man, fresh-coloured, his hair smoothly combed, but with a soupçon of curls at the end. Wondrous clean, but as evidently an actor as Garrick. He spoke his sermon, but so fast and with so little accent that I am sure he has often uttered it, for it was like a lesson. There were parts of eloquence in it; but towards the end he altered his voice, and acted very ugly enthusiasm; decried learning, and told stories, like Latimer, of the fool of his college who said, "I *thanks* God for everything". Except a few from curiosity and some *honourable women*, the congregation was mean. There was a Scotch Countess of Buchan, who is carrying a pure rosy vulgar face to heaven, and who asked Miss Rich if that was *the author of the poets*. I believe she meant me and the Noble Authors.'

Lady Huntingdon was probably aware of Horace Walpole's real feelings, but she was by now so accustomed to ruling everybody she met (with those two very remarkable, and strongly contrasted, exceptions, the Duchess of Buckingham and John Wesley), that it would have been difficult for her to realise the possibility of ridicule attaching to anything, mortal or immortal, to which she had given her patronage. By now, she had become 'a mother in Israel'; she was the fourth member of a directing Council—with John and Charles Wesley, and Whitfield, as her companions, she had founded a seminary at Trevecca in Wales, which she proceeded to rule as though she were a bishop; finally, she tried to rule John Wesley himself, and found that, strangely enough, he had the temerity to refuse to be ruled. For some time, he had found her exceedingly trying—remarking that she always spoke of '*my* college, *my* masters, *my* students;— "I" mixes with everything', whilst Lady Huntingdon, who had always regretted the strange vein of obstinacy in Wesley which made it impossible for her to like him as she would have done, had he been more amenable to reason, found that not only was he obstinate, but that his doctrines were all wrong. They savoured of Arminianism. She broke with him with some vehemence, and, after this, busied herself with sending pastoral letters, in which she taught everybody their duty to God and to herself, to 'My well-beloved friends of the Congregation of my Chapel, Bath'.

Southey, who could not be numbered among her admirers, announced tersely, in his *Life of John Wesley*, that there was insanity in her family—a charge which was rebutted with some indignation by her biographer and relation.

She must, I imagine, have been a remarkable woman, inasmuch as she had zeal and energy (she had, as well, great physical courage, and, although she feared the disease, nursed a friend through an attack of smallpox), but we find our sympathies wandering to Wesley, as we contemplate those long years in which her guidance and spiritual help were placed, with such generosity, at his disposal.

CHAPTER VIII

Splendours and Miseries

IN THE YEAR 1738 THAT STRANGE AND GALLANT gambler-adventurer and man of honour, Richard Nash, was at the height of his fortune, controlling the fashions, and the manners of the fashionable, and ruling his kingdom like an autocrat. He was the benevolent tyrant over the aristocracy, and the friend of royalty. Ten years ago Princess Amelia had forgiven him his obstinacy in refusing her request for a dance after the hour of eleven, and, during the rest of her visit, she invariably chose him as escort when she played at the tables. In 1734, the good but unattractive Prince of Orange, who was visiting Bath for the sake of the waters, might often have been seen in the Beau's company—Nash's swagger and large figure making a strange contrast to the Prince's appearance, of which the odious Lord Hervey had written: 'If you looked at him behind, you would say he had no head, and if you looked at him in front, you would say he had no legs.' And now, in the autumn of 1738, the Prince and Princess of Wales paid Bath a visit, and overwhelmed the Beau with their attentions. Indeed, the Prince, before leaving the city, did the uncrowned King the signal honour of presenting him with a large gold-enamelled snuff-box.

Delighted with such a signal mark of the royal favour as the gold snuff-box, Beau Nash was seized with the idea of erecting an obelisk, which was designed by John Wood, and paid for by the Beau. The obelisk was erected, and filled not only Beau Nash, but Mr. Oliver Goldsmith, with an awed admiration. Unfortunately, the obelisk did not inspire the same feelings in Mr. Alexander Pope, who was chosen by the Beau to write the inscription upon this Memorial.

I think I cannot do better than to quote Goldsmith in order to do justice both to the Memorial, and to the very unworthy backslidings of genius which were connected with it. 'This handsome memorial in honour of the good-natured Prince is erected', said Goldsmith in his *Life of Richard Nash*, 'in Queen Square. It is enclosed with a stone balustrade, and in the middle of every side there are large iron gates. In the centre is the obelisk, seventy feet high, and terminating in a point. The expenses of this were eighty pounds, and Mr. Nash was determined that the inscription should answer the magnificence of the pile. With this view, he wrote to Mr. Pope at London, requesting an inscription.' The poet, to Mr. Nash's (and Mr. Goldsmith's) surprise and indignation, wriggled violently, and tried to escape. He owned himself unequal to the task, 'even granting it possible to express an inexpressible idea', and he actually ended the letter by suggesting, firmly enough, that the Beau should write the inscription himself! But Mr. Nash was nothing if not tenacious; he pinned the poet down, and the end of that affair was that Pope wrote an inscription that rendered Goldsmith almost, but not quite, speechless with disappointment.

The inscription ran thus:

IN MEMORY OF HONOURS BESTOW'D
AND IN GRATITUDE FOR BENEFITS CONFERR'D
ON THIS CITY
BY HIS ROYAL HIGHNESS
FREDERICK PRINCE OF WALES
AND HIS ROYAL CONSORT
IN THE YEAR 1738,
THIS OBELISK IS ERECTED BY
RICHARD NASH ESQRE.

Splendours and Miseries

'Naught can be more frigid', as Goldsmith very rightly observes, 'though the subject was worthy of the utmost exertions of genius.'

Beau Nash's victory, on this occasion, was a doubtful one; in fact, the honours were nearly, though not quite, equal.

But the Beau's battles, when they were fought in the cause of charity, as was nearly always the case, ended, invariably, in triumph. He fought and vanquished, among other rebels, his old friend, the redoubtable and parsimonious Sarah, Duchess of Marlborough, in one of these campaigns—this time on behalf of the Mineral Water Hospital, for the building of which he was raising funds. The Beau was walking from table to table, in one of the gaming rooms, collecting money from the players, by means of holding out his famous white hat towards them, when the Duchess, after a vain attempt to escape, said, 'You must put down a trifle for me, Nash, for I have no money in my pocket'. 'Yes, Madam', says he, 'that I will with pleasure if your Grace will tell me when to stop'; then taking a handful of guineas out of his pocket, he began to tell them into his white hat—'One, two, three, four, five——' 'Hold, hold', exclaimed the Duchess, 'consider what you are about.' 'Consider your rank and fortune, Madam', replied the Beau, and drawing another handful of guineas from his pocket, passed these, also, into his hat, 'six, seven, eight, nine, ten.' Here the Duchess became more than a little angry, but to no avail, for Nash, after begging her to compose herself, and not to interrupt the work of charity, continued counting out his guineas. When the fifteenth guinea dropped into the hat, the Duchess tried to catch hold of the Beau's hand, but his only response was to promise her she should have her name in letters of gold on the front of the hospital. 'Sixteen, seventeen, eighteen, nineteen', counted the Beau. When, however, he had reached the twentieth guinea, the Duchess raged at him, and swore that she would not pay a farthing more.

'Charity hides a multitude of sins', remarked Nash. 'Twenty-two, twenty-three, twenty-four, twenty-five.'

'Nash', said the Duchess, 'I protest you frighten me out of my wits. Lord, I shall die.' 'Madam', was the reply, 'you will never die with doing good; and if you do it will be the better for you'—and he plunged his hand into his pocket once more, but, then, seeing the Duchess was in a serious passion, 'a parley ensued, when he, after much altercation, agreed to stop his hand and compound with her Grace for thirty guineas'. The Duchess's bad temper lasted until nearly the end of the evening, and whenever the Beau approached the table at which she was playing, she told him to 'Stand further, an ugly devil, for she hated the sight of him'. In the end, however, the Duchess won at cards, and this caused her to forgive the Beau, although she still thought him, and called him, a fool; 'but', she continued, 'to show you I am not angry there is ten guineas more for your charity. But this I insist on, that neither my name nor the sum shall be mentioned.'

In the end, although the Duchess insisted that her name should not be mentioned, the names of the King and the Prince and Princess of Wales *were* mentioned, in the list of the second subscription for the hospital (1742): 'The King, per Mr. Nash, £200. The Prince of Wales, do. The Princess of Wales, £50.' Whilst Mr. Nash himself was put down for £100.

Since the year 1716, the scheme for the hospital had been in the thoughts of Beau Nash and Dr. Oliver (the famous Bath physician who invented the biscuit which bears his name). Ralph Allen, who offered to give the stone from the quarries in which he was interested, and the great John Wood, had the scheme equally at heart. £10,000 was collected during the first few years, but this sum was not enough, nor could a suitable site be found until 1737, when, owing to the closing of the first theatre in Bath, the com-

mittee were enabled to buy the site of this. Meanwhile, John
Wood, who had promised to design the hospital without a
fee, had made 'several new designs, attended with great in-
cidental expenses, . . . to answer various situations and
various purposes of the Trustees'.

The first stone of the hospital was laid on 6th July, 1738,
and, four years later, to the delight of Wood, Nash, Allen
and Dr. Oliver, the hospital was opened to such patients as
were 'in such a situation in life that the expenses attendant
upon a long residence in Bath would be more than could be
afforded'. The splendours of the hospital were great, as far
as the list of Governors were concerned. Lord Chesterfield,
for instance, was one of the first of these.

Goldsmith remarks, gloomily, that 'the disorders of the
poor who could expect to find relief at Bath, were mostly
chronical' . . . and, after beating about the bush for the space
of a page and a half, adds: 'the hospital . . . is at present
fitted up for the reception of one hundred and ten patients,
the cases mostly paralytic or leprous'.

I have, indeed, seen a print, portraying the good Dr.
Oliver interviewing some of his patients, one of whom,
according to the letterpress, suffered from rheumatism, the
second from paralysis, and the third, who appeared to me to
be hustling the paralytic a little impatiently, from leprosy.

But the subject is gloomy, and we shall be happier if we
return to Beau Nash and his charities. He was, as Captain
Thicknesse was obliged to admit, never tired of working in
the cause of private or public charity. There was, for instance,
the case of the unhappy clergyman who had come to Bath in
the hope of obtaining a cure for his wife, and whose ragged-
ness was such, that the Beau, with the coarseness which was
his worst trait, nicknamed him Dr. Cullender, because of the
holes in his coat.

No sooner, however, had the Beau invented this name,
than he found that the man upon whom he had bestowed it

was, with his wife and six children, starving upon the sum of thirty pounds a year. Nash, at once, started a subscription, headed by his own donation, and, going from table to table at a tea-drinking at Harrison's, raised two hundred pounds within the space of two hours. This unexpected mercy had a better effect upon the wife's health than could be effected by the waters; and Nash's efforts did not cease with the raising of the subscription; for he induced a nobleman of his acquaintance to present the clergyman with a living of £160 a year, which, according to Goldsmith, who tells the story, 'made that happiness he had before produced, in some measure permanent'.

In the severe winter of 1739 Nash made a practice of seeking out cases of want, going unexpectedly into the houses of those who were too proud to beg, and relieving their wretchedness out of his own pocket.

The state of the colliers was particularly terrible, and Nash raised a subscription for these, heading the list with a gift of ten guineas; he also gave a dinner to the weavers, who came begging to Bath, in a body, and, when they left, gave to each a week's subsistence.

Nor was Nash's charity a matter of money alone. His kindness and chivalry when he saw young women in danger of ruining themselves, or contracting foolish marriages, was untiring.

There was, for instance, the happy and romantic story of the mysterious Miss L—— whom Beau Nash saved from a runaway marriage when that marriage would have meant her ruin, and whose happiness, when that marriage would no longer be an imprudence, he brought about.

Miss L. was a young lady who was heiress to her father's large fortune. Her father wished her to marry a certain nobleman, but she had set her heart upon young Colonel M., who was as thoughtless as Lord X. was thoughtful—and who was gay, charming, and as extravagant as he was poor.

Indeed, his extravagance landed him in such trouble that he was obliged to sell the annuity arising from his commission in order to maintain his usual splendid appearance. Miss L. and Colonel M. (they are Miss L. and Colonel M. to us still, after nearly two hundred years—those dark and shining ghosts whose faces we cannot see, whose names we shall never know, but who meet, still, and live over again those hours of wonder and of deep and abiding love, under the heavy trees of summer)—these young lovers met by stealth under the deep trees when the moonlight lay like snow on the wooded paths that glistened with frost till they shone like the strawberry paths of early summer. They planned, at last, to make a runaway marriage, but Beau Nash heard of their intention, and knowing that it would bring about their ruin, warned Miss L.'s father. The old gentleman removed his daughter from Bath, and offered Beau Nash a large sum of money as a reward for his kindness, a present which Beau Nash refused with dignity.

Meanwhile, Colonel M., who suspected Beau Nash of warning the girl's father, asked the Beau if he had done so, and was told the truth. The young man challenged the Beau to a duel, but Nash, who was conscious that he had acted only according to a sense of duty, and who, as well, had forbidden duelling at Bath, refused to fight. Soon after this, the attentions of Colonel M.'s creditors became so unremitting that he was obliged to leave Bath, and was forced by his extreme poverty to sign on as a common soldier in the Dutch army in Flanders. There, in addition to having no pay, he was starved, overworked, clothed in rags, and suffered every misery of body and mind, whilst, in England, his friends invented and circulated the story that he had been killed in battle. It is possible that Miss L. believed this story, but Beau Nash, as certainly, did not, and spared no efforts to find out what had become of the young man, for old Mr. L. had died, and left his daughter in possession of £1,500 a year, and there was no longer any reason why the lovers should not marry. Beau Nash, at last, discovered that Colonel M. had returned to England (under an assumed name, in order to avoid his creditors), and that he was sunk in such poverty that he was reduced to the misery and humiliation of a strolling player's life, with all its hopelessness, hunger, and uncertainty. He was, indeed, acting at Peterborough at that very moment. Beau Nash at once invited the young lady to a theatre party at Peterborough, and they set out together in the Beau's famous coach, with the postillions, the outriders, the footmen, and the French horns, driving through the country lanes with, for their only spectators, the nodding wild flowers, the bunched hen-coloured wild columbines. The young lady found herself in the first row, next to the stage, with the impatient Beau beside her. It was some little time before Colonel M., who, miserable as were all the players, played the most humble part of all, appeared upon the stage. But the next moment, the girl fainted away in the arms of Beau Nash, and the young man, scarcely knowing what he was doing, rushed from the stage and caught her in his arms.

'Colonel', said Nash, when they had left the theatre, 'you once thought me your enemy, because I endeavoured to prevent you both from ruining each other; you were then wrong, and you have long had my forgiveness. If you love well enough now for matrimony, you fairly have my consent, and confusion to him that attempts to part you.' 'Their nuptials', said Mr. Goldsmith, primly, 'were solemnized soon after, and affluence added a zest to all their future enjoyments. Nash had the thanks of each; and he afterwards spent several agreeable days in that society which he had contributed to make happy.'

But Nash could not save the wretched Fanny Braddock, the daughter of General Braddock, who was young, and beautiful; but who, unfortunately for her, inherited a large

fortune from her father, and who, equally unfortunately, fell
in love with a man whose fickleness and extravagance were
known to all. At last, his debts grew to such an extent that he
was arrested and put in prison. Miss Braddock was then
seized with what Goldsmith calls the 'fatal resolution' of
paying his debts and freeing him from prison.

On hearing of this resolution, Beau Nash, who was then in
London, implored her to listen to reason, representing to
her that the only result of her action would be that men
would despise her, and that women would think her reputation lessened. He added that if she rescued Mr. S. from prison
it would only be a temporary relief, and that 'a mind so
generous as his would become bankrupt under the load of
gratitude; and instead of improving in friendship or affection, he would only study to avoid a creditor he could never
repay; that though small favours produce good will, great
ones destroy friendship'. But all his advice was in vain, and
the poor girl, whose fortune had vanished by these means,
found that her friends and her former admirers had vanished
too. All, that is, excepting Richard Nash, who promised her
that if she returned to Bath, he would introduce her to the
best society to be found there; and, accordingly, on her
return, she found that she was treated with great kindness
and civility. But, although she still went from party to party,
from ball to ball, she seemed like a ghost floating through
those well-known places, unheeding and uncaring; and in
spite of all Nash's efforts to protect her, it was not long
before this 'poor, thoughtless, deserted girl' had fallen into
the clutches of Dame Lindsay, and was being used by that
harpy in her gambling exploits—but never for Miss Braddock's profit, only for the profit of others.

It was then that Beau Nash induced his friend Wood, the
architect, to take this friendless and unfortunate creature
into his house, as governess to his children. The Wood
family felt an affection for her which she returned, but

nothing could restore the happiness she had lost; and after a while, when she had neither fashionable clothes, nor money, and when the outside world she had known had deserted her, she sank into a settled melancholy. At last, on a night when Mr. Wood was in London, and she was alone in the house with the children and an old servant, she spent the remaining hours before bedtime, nursing two of Mr. Wood's children on her knee. Then, before she went to her own room, she went into the nursery to say good-bye to a little child who was sleeping in his cradle.

She must, it is thought, have walked about her room for hours, as was her custom when she wanted sleep, before, dressed in a gown that was pinned over her bosom, as the swaddling clothes of a child are pinned, she ended her misery. The rope she used to hang herself with was a pink silk girdle, mixed with a stronger girdle of silver thread.

It was not till two o'clock on the next afternoon that the old and wool-gathering but devoted maid, and some workmen, broke into her room, and found her dead body still hanging from the cord.

I wonder if, many years after, when Beau Nash lay dying, he remembered this girl whom he had tried to save, and other girls whom he had succeeded in saving, and ragged Doctor Cullender with his hollow face; or if his thoughts were with the great and fashionable crowd, with the tall and immaculate Lord Chesterfield, the splendours of whose entertaining had been used to enhance the splendours of the Beau—Lord Chesterfield who joked with, and patronised him, and helped him with the scheme of the hospital. Or if his thoughts were with his friend, the cross Duchess of Marlborough, or the Prince of Wales and that gilded snuff-box.

CHAPTER IX

The Old Age of Beau Nash

ON A CERTAIN LOVELY MORNING IN JUNE, 1760, a sedan-chair which had once been very gaudy, but by now was rather battered and dimmed, might be seen making its way through the shadows, that were so kind to the age of the figure within the chair. Beau Nash was by now more than eighty-five years old. He wore a very carefully brushed waistcoat, and, when he was not in his sedan-chair, a tall white hat set at a jaunty angle over a heavy purplish face, adorned by particularly meaningless and watery eyes, and several chins. Even when he was young and everybody wanted to see him, and to know him, Beau Nash had never been handsome. Goldsmith had said of him, that his person was too large and awkward, that his features were harsh, strong, and particularly irregular, though one of his admirers, or rather, one of the admirers of his power and prestige, had, in a dedicatory preface, described, in a burst of enthusiasm, 'the very agreeable oddness of your appearance, your black wig, scarlet countenance, and brown beaver hat'.

Alas, old age had not improved that very agreeable oddness, nor that scarlet countenance, nor had it made those watery eyes more intelligent—those eyes which had searched, so unceasingly, for cases of poverty that might be relieved from the Beau's now empty pockets. Those watery and unintelligent eyes had often, as Goldsmith tells us, been seen to shed tears when the Beau was unable to relieve distress, for 'the sums he gave away were immense, and in old age, when at last he grew too poor to give relief, he gave, as the poet has it, a tear. . . . Poverty now denied him the indulgence, not only of his favourite follies, but of his favourite virtues. The poor solicited him in vain; for he was himself a more pitiable object than they.'

On such a lovely morning as this, Beau Nash felt younger than ever, in spite of his eighty-five years. The air was like floods of white wine; the little bee-winged lights of summer buzzed happily, with a far-off sound, among the lime-trees of the arbours, those trees that were older, even, than Beau Nash; and, as he was carried from his sedan-chair to the coffee-house, great golden stars of dew splashed upon the Beau's coat, and the green dust of the lime-bloom, poignant as the memories of youth, brushed the old man's face, and fell upon that imposing white hat.

The distance from the Beau's house to the coffee-house, though not great, had seemed considerable. The sedan-chair jolted the ancient bones of the man who, in his prime, had driven in a coach drawn by six dapple-grey horses, with an escort, footmen, outriders, and French horns. Though just as young as ever, he felt very tired. But it would never do for him to be absent from the coffee-house—for had he not been the uncrowned King of Bath? He must attend all the balls, all the routs, as well as the coffee-houses, although many years before this, Lord Orrery had written to Lady Kaye: 'In my mind, he seems to labour under the unconquerable distemper of old age, and though he attends the balls as usual, his dancing days are over.' But though his dancing days were over, he could still keep order. Mrs. Delany told, in a letter, the story of how 'Mr. Sloper, who is here with Madame Cibber and a daughter by her (a young woman), had been much offended that his daughter was not taken out to dance; she was the first night, but a sensible clever woman whose daughter was taken out after her refused to let her dance; this put a stop to Miss Cibber's being asked again; and on a Sunday night, in the midst of the room, Mr. Sloper collared poor Collett, abusing him at the same time, and asking if he had been the occasion of the affront put upon his daughter; he said it was "by Mr. Nash's direction"—the poor wretch is now wheeled into the room; Mr. Sloper had some discourse with him, and so the matter ended.'

And now Beau Nash was making his way to the coffee-house; for if he did not appear there, people would miss him. They would miss that tall white hat of which Lady Luxborough had written to Shenstone, in a letter dated 15th February, 1752: 'His white hat commands more respect than the crown of some kings, though now worn on a head that is in the eightieth year of its age. To promote society, good manners, and a coalition of parties and ranks, to suppress scandal and late hours are his views; and he succeeds better than his fellow monarchs usually do.' No matter how tired the Beau felt, he must visit the coffee-house, for if he did not, the young men would say he was getting old—he who, when he was young, had been so dashing that, for a wager, he rode through a village, on the back of a cow, and stark naked; he whose friends had, for fun (according to his story), invited him on board a man-of-war, and made him drunk, so that he was carried far out to sea, and was forced to take part in a naval battle, amidst the very inelegant and pigtailed mariners. And how proud he was of the resultant wound in his leg—though if that wound had ever been inflicted, nobody could tell (owing to a painful habit of perfectly harmless lying on the part of the Beau), whilst, on the other hand, nobody could know for certain that it had *not* been inflicted, as the Beau had an unanswerable way of putting a stop to indiscreet enquiries. He would, for instance, invite incredulous ladies of quality, such as Sarah, Duchess of Marlborough, at the slightest sign of unbelief on their parts, to 'receive further information and feel the ball in my leg', an invitation which they, not being of an adventurous character, never accepted. The Beau, however, whilst expecting a credulous and respectful, though wondering, audience, when he was the narrator, was not always so ready to believe other people's stories, even if they happened to be true, and when he doubted the truth of a story, he had no hesitation in saying so—or at any rate in showing incredulity by a smile. On one occasion, a naval captain was telling the company in one of the Assembly Rooms of some strange sight he had seen from his ship, when, happening to look round, he saw the Beau smiling to himself, and enquired if his story was not believed. 'Why, Sir, did you see it?' enquired Beau Nash, in a very incredulous tone. 'Yes, I did', the Captain replied with some asperity. 'Well, if you saw it, I will believe it', said the Beau, 'but I would not if I had seen it myself.' The Captain was silent for the moment, but, soon after, was able to repay the Beau in his own coin; for when the latter had embarked upon one of his interminable, and apocryphal stories, the captain, after listening intently, gave a grunt of disbelief. 'And so, Captain, you won't believe this?' enquired the Beau, in a hurt tone. 'Why yes, I will, Nash, to oblige you', retorted the Captain, 'but I would not believe such another damned lie for any other man upon the face of the earth.'

The sedan-chair swung from side to side in the great squares, in the moon-coloured crescents, until the Beau's reveries about wounds, real or imagined, about adventures of the same dubious reality, and about rides on cows, were cut short by his arrival at the coffee-house. As he was wheeled through the smart and fluttering crowd, a curious silence fell upon it—a sign, so the Beau thought, of these smart young men's respect for the uncrowned King of Bath. But another strange phenomena had, for some time, obtruded itself upon the notice of the Beau, and had caused him a certain bewilderment, for he observed that immediately on his arrival, the young, and even the middle-aged persons who

were nearest the table to which his chair was wheeled, remembered inevitably some important engagement, and left
the coffee-house without delay, unless they were so hemmed
in that they were unable to do so. The Beau was very pleased
to see his young friends, and, realising that they took a profound interest in his departed grandeur, indeed, in everything pertaining to the uncrowned King of Bath, began to
enliven those listeners who remained (because they were
unable to make their escape) with one of the stories of his
former physical prowess. 'Here I stand, gentlemen, that
could once leap forty-two feet upon level ground, at three
standing jumps, backward or forward. One, two, three,
dart like an arrow out of a bow. But I am old now. I remember once I leaped for a hundred guineas with Count Klop-
stock, the great leaper, leaping-master to the Prince of
Nassau; you must all have heard of him. First he began with
the running jump, and a most damnable bounce it was, that's
certain: everybody concluded that he had the match hollow;
when only taking off my hat, stripping off neither coat, shoes,
nor stockings, mind me, I fetches a run, and went beyond
him one foot, three inches, and three quarters, measured,
upon my soul, by Captain Pately's own standard.'

Alas, on this occasion, as always when the Beau was telling
a story, several young men who had been able to disengage
themselves from behind his chair, gave 'a running jump, a
most damnable bounce', and, muttering something about a
most important engagement which they must on no account
miss, left the coffee-house. The Beau looked after them with
a smile of commiseration, for they were about to miss one of
his best stories, then began the narration in question: 'I'll tell
you something to that purpose . . .'(the young men, according to Goldsmith, were, at that moment, discussing either
Elizabeth Gunning or a German war—but the Beau swept
any subject which did not suit him aside), 'I'll tell you something to that purpose that I fancy will make you laugh. A

certain old person, as rich as the devil, scraped a fresh acquaintance with me several years ago at Bath. I knew him when he and I were students at Oxford, where we both studied damnationally hard; but that's neither here nor there. Well, very well. I entertained him in my house in John's Court—no, my house in John's Court was not built then; but I entertained him with all the city could afford; the rooms, the music, and everything in the world. Upon his leaving Bath, he pressed me very hard to return the visit, and desired me to let him have the pleasure of seeing me at his house in Devonshire. About six months after, I happened to be in that neighbourhood, and was resolved to see my old friend, from whom I expected a very warm reception. Well: I knocks at his door, when an old queer creature of a maid came to the door, and denied him. I suspected, however, that he was at home; and going into the parlour, what should I see but the person's legs up the chimney, where he had thrust himself to avoid entertaining me. This was very well. "My dear", says I to the maid, "it is very cold, extreme cold, indeed, and I am afraid I have got a touch of the ague: light me the fire if you please." "La, Sir", says the maid, who was a modest creature to be sure, "the chimney smokes monstrously; you could not bear the room for three minutes together." By the greatest good luck there was a bundle of straw in the hearth, and I called for a candle; the candle came. "Well! good woman", says I, "since you won't light me a fire, I'll light one myself", and in a moment the straw was all in a blaze. This quickly unkennelled the old fox; there he stood in an old rusty nightgown, blessing himself, and looking like a . . . hem . . . egad.'

Then, just as the Beau was beginning, to the terror of those of the company whom he had succeeded in hemming in, and who were, therefore, unable to escape, another of those well-known and interminable stories, in crept an even more miserable spectre than Beau Nash, a creature so famine-stricken that his very humanity seemed destroyed, and only his gaze full of despair remained to show that those bones still retained their life. This mimicry of death held by his hand a little boy, as hopeless as himself. When the Beau saw these, he stopped in his story and felt in his pocket, with a grand and a flourishing gesture. Alas, no happy jingle answered the movement; the poor old man's face fell, his old hanging lip drooped still further, and a kind of hunted shame appeared in his eyes. He withdrew his hand from his pocket with the only coin that pocket held tightly clasped in it, and placed this in the beggar's hand, avoiding his eyes; 'Good day to ye', he said.

But the surrounding company were spared the rest of that long and well-known story, and after about ten minutes of complete silence on the part of Beau Nash, the poor harmless old man left the coffee-house, planting his white hat at even a jauntier angle than before (alas, he must take off that insignia of his royalty as he entered the sedan-chair!), and was carried home to his small, and by now almost empty, house in Saw-Close. The chairmen went away without their fares, for they must wait to be paid until the first Monday of next month, when the Beau would receive £10 from the Corporation, the monthly pension they had seen fit to give him in return for his past services.

During the last few years, even the last and happiest luxury which remains to us, that of helping others, had been denied to the Beau, for he had fallen on evil times, and had grown poorer and poorer since the Gaming Act of 1745, suppressing gambling-houses and making card-debts not recoverable by law, had been passed. For, although the law was not applied very rigidly, the authorities were liable to fits and starts of energy, and nobody knew when the gambling-houses might be raided; so the players showed increasing signs of nervousness about visiting the card-houses; and the company dwindled away until few but soldiers of fortune and professional gamblers were left, for those who had more to lose in the way of reputation, preferred to play in the security of their own or their friends' houses. It is true that this state of affairs came about but gradually, each year bringing a noticeable change, but, though the change was gradual, the city of Bath, which depended largely on gambling for its resources, and especially the poor uncrowned King of Bath, suffered badly. Matters had been made much worse, as we have seen in another chapter, by the Beau's unwise lawsuit against his former partners, and by the fact that cruel and perfectly unjust accusations of fraudulent dealings had been brought against him by various pamphleteers and writers in the press, who, aware of the falsity of their charges, did not even dare to sign their names, but preferred to remain anonymous. In 1748, Richard Nash, who had impoverished and nearly ruined himself by subscriptions to such charities as the Bath Hospital, was accused of having misappropriated the funds raised by him to benefit some charity. For once, Beau Nash was roused to protest; and, for the only time in that long life (as Mr. Melville remarks), he was forced to a reference to his generosity. He protested against the cruelty and injustice of such a charge, in the Bath Journal, and called on God and man to witness that it was a lie: for 'it has cost me more annually in the public account, than any ten that ever came to Bath, and if it was not for the sake of Bath and company, I would leave 'em to the confusion I found 'em in'.

The accusations against Nash, I am glad to say, caused some indignation, and certain inhabitants of Bath, together with some of Nash's friends, subscribed, in August, 1752, towards buying a white marble statue of the Beau, which they placed in the Pump Room, as a mark of their gratitude and esteem. And grateful, indeed, they should have been, for the Beau, by his own efforts alone, had changed Bath from its former state, which was that of a small and unfashionable (and exceedingly uncomfortable and dirty) city, into being the most celebrated watering-place in England.

But a white marble statue in his honour, though it flattered the Beau's vanity, did not help him financially; and, although he had raised Bath to its present state, Bath now, in his time of need, would help him but little—until the moment came for his funeral. This ceremony, naturally, gave the civic authorities every chance to show their munificence (and, incidentally, to attract new visitors to the city), and, being men of business, they were not prepared to let such an opportunity pass. But Beau Nash, when alive, over eighty years old, peevish, and a bore, was a very different matter. It is true that when in 1754, his friends, distressed at his poverty, raised a public subscription—to save the old man's pride, this was supposed to be in order that *The History of Bath and Tonbridge for these last fifty years, by Richard Nash, Esq., with an Apology for the Author's life*, might be written— the Corporation headed the list by subscribing for twenty-five copies of Mr. Nash's book; but it was not until February the 17th, 1760, exactly a year before he died, that they had the decency to allow the old man, who was, by now, eighty-five years old, who had practically created the wealth and popularity of their city, and who had spent a large part of his fortune in benefiting it, even such a wretched pittance as that of £10 on the first Monday of every month. In such a fashion were his services rewarded when he, who had done so much to help the city, was, himself, in need of aid. As for the public subscription, Beau Nash lived on this till it was exhausted. Goldsmith believes that the poor old man had really intended to write the book for which the subscription was, ostensibly, raised. But he was, by now, far too old and too weak to make such an effort, and no draft of the work was found among his papers after his death. It is sad to think that even this small attempt to help the Beau in his desperate state, was resented by some. Most surprisingly, the usually charming Sarah

Scott, in a singularly odious letter to Mrs. Montagu, dated the 17th November, 1754, wrote: 'Some have subscribed ten guineas, some five, and a great many hundred pounds are already subscribed. It is to be kept open for life, and people give to him, who will not part with a guinea to relieve the greatest real and unmerited distress imaginable. The pretence is that he has little more than £200 a year, which is not supposed true, but if it was, surely it is full equal to his merits, whether one considers them as moral or entertaining. To such ladies as have secret histories belonging to them he hints that he knows everyone's private life and shall publish it.'

The last sentence in this detestable letter is a deliberate lie, for Beau Nash's invariably chivalrous conduct towards women was well known. The rest of the letter is a disgrace to the woman who wrote it; she was a general gossip, but it is strange to find that her heart was so shrivelled that she could grudge a poor old man, whose unbounded generosity and kindness to others had helped to bring about his ruin, freedom from actual want during the last few wretched years of that most harmless and most charitable life. 'In this variety of uneasiness', says Goldsmith, 'his health began to fail.' However, when the money from the subscriptions was spent, and when that magnificent collection of snuff-boxes of which the Beau had been so proud, had all, with the exception of those which were the gifts from Frederick, Prince of Wales, Princess Amelia, and a few other royalties, been sold, that he might have food and a fire, the ungenerous pension he received from the Corporation of Bath saved him from actual starvation, although, as Goldsmith points out, it was 'far too trifling to enable him to support the character of a gentleman. Habit, and not nature, makes almost all our wants; and he who has been accustomed in the early parts of life to affluence and prodigality, when reduced to a hundred and twenty-six pounds a year must pine in actual indigence.'

Indeed, such was his poverty that not only the collection of snuff-boxes, but the magnificent house in St. John's Court, had to be sold, that Beau Nash might eke out the last threadbare years of that long life, and the Beau moved to a small house in Saw-Close, next door to the scene of his former magnificence.

It was to this small house that the Beau was carried, after his morning in the coffee-house. Once in the shelter of his, by now, almost empty house, the uncrowned King of Bath sat down on a chair which had once been gaudy, but which now, like its owner, was dimmed and shabby with age, and, calling for Mrs. Juliana Papjoy, his aged voice floating, with a strange hollow ghostly sound, through the narrow house, ordered a cup of coffee. For he had a slight sinking feeling, due, no doubt, to that episode with the beggar. At first, there was no answer to that eerie, hollow call. Then Mrs. Juliana Papjoy, or Lady Betty Besom, who had once been a dressmaker, crept up the stairs, like a ghost, noiselessly. Her queer face with its straight black locks of hair, its pointed chin, its bird-black eyes that seemed shadowed by the boughs of trees, peered at the Beau through the half-open door of his empty, dusty room. She was the one being who now, in his old age, remained to him, tended him, treated him with kindness, though all the luxuries he had lavished on her had gone— gone was the dapple-grey horse on which she had ridden through the streets of Bath, carrying a many-thonged whip, in those far-off days of Beau Nash's splendour.

The tall white hat had been put away with care by Mrs. Juliana Papjoy, so had his smart clothes, and now the Beau, dressed in a very ancient nightgown of red and white broad stript thread satin, lined with a green and white Persian, proceeded to read his letters.

There were no invitations among these; indeed, the letters which reached him now were, in nearly every case, from clergymen, urging him to repentance, reproaching him for the (purely imaginary) sins they attributed to him, reminding him that he must die, threatening him with fire and brimstone. Yet as Goldsmith very rightly remarks: 'In the name of piety, what was there criminal in his conduct? He had long been taught to consider his trifling profession as a very serious and important business. He went through his office with great gravity, solemnity, and care. Why then denounce peculiar torments against a poor harmless creature, who did a thousand good things, and whose greatest vice was vanity. He deserved ridicule, indeed, and he found it; but scarce a single action of his life, except one, deserved the asperity of reproach.'

By the time the Beau had finished his letters, he was trembling a little, perhaps because he was so very old. Day by day letters such as these poured in, for the clergymen of all denominations in Bath, whether resident or visiting, were in a state of fermenting hysteria, owing, very largely, to the religious revival brought about by that irritating woman Lady Huntingdon. The Beau continued to read the letters, for, having begun them, he was hypnotised by fear and a sense of his own isolation, into finishing such exhortations as the following:

'This admonition comes from your friend, and one that has your interest deeply at heart. It comes on a design altogether important, and of no less consequence than your everlasting happiness, so that it may justly challenge your careful regard. It is not to upbraid or reproach, much less to triumph or insult over your misconduct or misery; no, 'tis pure benevolence, it is disinterested goodwill, prompts me to write. I hope, therefore, I shall not raise your resentment. Yet be the consequence what it will, I cannot bear to see you walk in the paths that lead to death without warning you of the danger—without sounding in your ear the awful admonition, "Return and live! Why do you such things? I hear of your evil dealings by all this people".

The Old Age of Beau Nash

'I have long observed and pitied you, and must tell you plainly, Sir, that your present behaviour is not the way to reconcile yourself to God. You are so far from making atonement to offended justice that each moment you are aggravating the future account, and heaping up an increase of His anger. As long as you roll on in a continued circle of sensual delights and vain entertainments, you are dead to all the purposes of pity and virtue. You are as odious to God as a corrupt carcase that lies putrefying in the churchyard. You are as far from doing your duty, or endeavouring after salvation, or restoring yourself to the Divine favour, as a heap of dry bones nailed up in a coffin is from vigour and activity . . .

'Think, Sir, I conjure you, think upon this, if you have any inclination to escape the fire that will never be quenched. Would you be rescued from the fury and fierce anger of God? Would you be delivered from weeping and wailing, and incessant gnashing of teeth? Sure you would! But be certain that this will never be done by amusements, which at best are trifling and impertinent, and for that, if for no other reason, foolish and sinful. 'Tis by seriousness, 'tis by retirement and mourning, you must accomplish this great and desirable deliverance. You must not appear at the head of every silly diversion, you must enter into your closet and shut the door—commune with your own heart and search out its defects. The pride of life and all its superfluity of follies must be put away. You must make haste, and delay not, to keep every injunction of heaven. You must always remember that mighty sinners must be mightily penitent, or else mightily tormented.

'Your example and your projects have been extremely *prejudiced*—I wish I could not say *fatal* and *destructive*—to many. For this there is no amends but an alteration of your conduct, as signal and remarkable as your *person* and *name*. If you do not by this method remedy in some degree the evils that you have sent abroad, and prevent the mischievous consequences that may ensue . . . wretched will you be, wretched above all men to eternity. The blood of souls will be laid to your charge. God's jealousy, like a consuming flame, will smoke against you; as you yourself will see in that day, when the mountains shall quake and the hills melt, and the earth be burnt up at His presence.

'Once more then I exhort you as a friend; I beseech you as a brother; I charge you as a messenger from God in His own most solemn words, "Cast away from you your transgressions, make you a new heart, and a new spirit; so iniquity shall not be your ruin".

'Perhaps you may be disposed to contemn this, and its serious purport, or to recommend it to your companions as a subject for raillery. . . . Yet let me tell you beforehand, that for this, as well as for other things, God will bring you to judgement. He sees me now I write. He will observe you while you read. He notes down my words; He will also note down your consequent procedure. Not then upon me—not upon me, but upon your own soul will the neglecting or the despising my sayings turn. "If thou be wise, thou shalt be wise for thyself; if thou scornest, thou alone shall bear it".'

Having read this, the Beau put down his letters, beside the empty coffee-cup. He must, he thought, try to conquer this foolish, and uncontrollable, shaking of his head, for this habit made him look older than he was, and nearer to death, and it was, perhaps, owing to this that he received so many letters warning him of his fate after death. He knew quite well that all the people who had flattered him and had sought his conversation when he was young and rich, and before his stories had become so lengthened and so weakened by age— these people were waiting for him to die. He knew perfectly well that, in 1752, when he was only seventy-seven years old (and now he was nearly eighty-six), Lady Jane Coke had written from Tunbridge Wells that he 'had had a fit'—which was quite untrue—but that he did not seem to mind having had the fit, 'though he looks just a-going'. He knew perfectly well that in the same year, Lady Luxborough had written—in the very same letter which expressed admiration of the white hat and the respect that was paid to it—exhorting Shenstone, if he wished to look upon Mr. Nash, to 'hasten then your steps, for he may soon be carried off the stage of life, as the greatest must fall to the worms' repast'. He was quite aware, too, that, cruellest of all, this entry appeared in White's Betting Book of 1755: 'Lord Mountford bets Sir John Bland twenty guineas that Nash outlives Cibber.' Cibber was at this time eighty-four years of age, and Nash eighty-one, yet they outlived Lord Mountford and Sir John Bland, the makers of this heartless wager, for both the parties to the wager committed suicide before either of the old men had sunk into his grave.

Beau Nash was quite aware of the watchful eyes that were waiting to see him fall, he was aware of the letters and the bet, because certain people who found amusement in cruelty had been only too willing to tell him of these.

And a fresh bitterness lay in wait for him, only a few months away (in October, 1760). For the poor Beau was about to know, or to think that he knew, that James Quin, the actor, his own familiar friend, a man whom he himself had persuaded to live in Bath, was trying to supplant him as Master of the Ceremonies. These were the letters he was to receive, four months after this June day, and after his death they were found among his papers.

'London, Oct. 8, 1760.

'Dear Nash, Two posts ago I received a letter from Quin, the old player, covering one to my lord, which he left open for my perusal, which after reading, he decided I might seal up and deliver. The request he makes is so extraordinary, that it has induced me to send you the copy of his letter to my lord, which is as follows:

The Old Age of Beau Nash

' "My der Lord, Old Beaux Knash has mead himself so dissagreeable to all the company that comes here to Bath that the Corperation of this city have it now under their consideration to remove him from being master of the ceremonies, should he be continuead the inhabitants of this city will be rueind as the best companey declines to come to Bath on his acc^t. Give me leave to show to your Lordship how he beheaved at the first ball he had here thiss season, which was Tus'day last. A younge Ladye was asked to dance a minueat she begg the gent^m would be pleased to exquise here as she did not chuse to dance; Upon thiss old Nash called out so as to be head by all the companey in the room, G—— dam yo, Madam, what business have yo here if yo do not dance, upon which the Lady was so afrighted, she rose and danced, the res'et of the company was so much offended at the rudeness of Nash that not one Lady more would dance a minueat that night. In country houses no person of note danced except two boys, Lord S—— and T——, the res't of the companey that danced waire only the families of all the haber'dashers Machinnkes and innkeepers in the three kingdoms brushed up and colexted togither. I have known upon such an occaison as thiss seventeen Dutchess' and Contiss' to be at the opening of the ball at Bath now not one. This man by his pride and extravagancis has outlived his reasein, it would be happy for thiss city that he was ded; and it is now only fitt to reed Shirlock upon death by which he may seave his soul and gaine more than all the profitts he can make, by his white hatt, suppose it was to be died red: The fav^r I have now to reques't, by which I now have wrote yo, is that your Lordship will speke to Mr. Pitt, for to recommend me to the corporeation of this city to succede this old sinner as master of the ceremonies, and yo will much oblige, my Lord.

' "Yord Lord^s ob^t Servt "

The Old Age of Beau Nash

'N B. There were some other private matters and offers in Quin's letter to my lord, which do not relate to you.'

It was quite impossible that anything in Quin's character could lay him open to a charge of committing, or trying to commit, such a cruel act of treachery towards his old friend and benefactor. Nor was this the only reason why we may believe this charge to be baseless. Quin was sixty-seven years old at the time this obviously forged letter was written, and he had come to Bath for peace and seclusion. Why, then, should he wish to undertake all the tiring duties of Master of the Ceremonies? It is obvious that this letter, with its cruel implications, was forged in order to inflict an extra wound upon the heart of Beau Nash. And that heart had sustained many, from the desertion of friends and of those whom he had benefited.

But, on the lovely June afternoon in which we now find ourselves, Beau Nash had not, as yet, received this supposed letter from James Quin. He returned to the letter from the officious clergyman, and read part of this again, then put it aside. The Beau did not like being reminded that he must die: he did not like these 'admonitions of the grave, who aggravated his follies and vices'. It was better not to think about these subjects. So, refreshed and strengthened by his cup of coffee, he, 'whose greatest vice was vanity', drew some old, tattered, and ear-marked papers from a case, and began to read them. They were mostly dedications, made to Beau Nash in the days of his prosperity, when everybody wanted to know him and to hear him talk.

One very odd dedication was from Mr. Poulter, *alias* Baxter, a highwayman who had been apprehended for trying to rob and murder a certain eminent Doctor, as well as for more successful attempts, and who escaped the judicial reward for his industry by denouncing his associates, and assuring to them the reward in question.

The dedication runs thus:

The Old Age of Beau Nash

'To the Honble Richard Nash, Esqr.

'May it please your Honour,—with humblest submission I make bold to present the following sheets to your Honour's consideration and well-known humanity. As I am industrously careful, in respect to His Majesty and good subjects, to put an end to the unfortunate misconduct of all I know, by bringing them to the gallows. To be sure, some may censure, as if from self-preservation I make this ample discovery; but I communicate this to your Honour and gentry, whether the life of one person being taken away, would answer the end, as to let escape such a number of villains, who has been the ruining of many a poor family, for whom my soul is now much concerned. If my inclinations were ever so roguish inclined, what is it to so great a number of villains, when they consult together. As your Honour's wisdom, humanity, and interest are the friend of the virtuous, I make bold to lay at your Honour's feet the following lines, which will put every honest man upon his defence against the snares of the mischievous; and am, with greatest gratitude, honoured Sir, your Honour's most truly devoted and obedient servant,

'John Poulter, *alias* Baxter.
Taunton Jail. June 2nd.'

It is difficult to know which to admire most: Mr. Poulter's (*alias* Baxter's) virtuous indignation against 'unfortunate misconducts', his pleasure that virtue should be rewarded, in his own case, by being spared a hanging, his anxiety that vice should be punished, or his grammar.

At the time when this dedication was made, Beau Nash was too modest to allow it to be printed; but he had kept it by him, and now it afforded him considerable pleasure.

The Beau turned next to a less astounding proof of the admiration he had, invariably, inspired in the days of his unchallenged power. This was a dedication from a Professor of Cookery, prefixed to a work which was named

The Old Age of Beau Nash

The Complete Preserver; or a new method of preserving fruits,
flowers, and other vegetables, either with or without sugar, vinegar,
or spirits, etc.

The dedication ran thus:

'To the very Honourable Richard Nash, Esqr.

'Honoured Sir, As much as the oak exceeds the bramble,
so much do you exceed the rest of mankind in benevolence,
charity, and every other virtue that adorns, ennobles, and
refines the human species. I have therefore made bold to
prefix your name, though without permission, to the following work, which stands in need of such a patron, to
excuse its errors with a candour only known to such a heart
as your own, etc., etc.'

This dedication was still pleasing to the patron, though it
could not be said that the work to which it was prefixed was
so useful to him now as in former days. For to be frank,
there were not now, in the Beau's house, many of either
'fruits or other vegetables, to be preserved with, or without,
sugar, vinegar, etc.'.

The Beau finished reading and re-reading these flattering
tributes, and then grew tired from watching the little golden
feathers of the light, flying so lightly and happily outside his
room, in the nectarine-ripe afternoon. His head began to
nod, for he was drowsy from old age and the lovely summer
weather.

When he awoke, the shadows had invaded his room in
their silent companies; they seemed small and shaggy like
the 'sort of little Satyrs from Aethiopia who were hairy one
half of their body, and who accompanied Osiris for the
civilisation of mankind'. Beau Nash's former acquaintances,
Mr. Alexander Pope and Doctor Arbuthnot, had written of
these, among the *Works of Martin Scriblerus (the Treatise on*
the Origin of Sciences). And, by now, those shadows, like the
later satyrs, had seemed to enter 'a great and memorable
æra in which they began to be silent.' In the reign of Con-

stantine, one of these philosophers of the race of old Silenus was 'taken in a net and brought to Alexandria, round whom the people flocked to hear his wisdom; but as Ammanius Marcellinus reporteth he proved a dumb philosopher, and only instructed by his action'.

Such were the shadows, and they grew darker still, until they were like those ape-philosophers' 'unparalled monarchs in India', of whom the one was 'Perimal the Magnificent, a prince most learned, . . . the other, Hanimaut the Marvellous, his relation and successor, whose knowledge was so great, as made his followers doubt, if even that wise species could arrive at such perfection; and therefore they rather imagined him and his race a sort of gods formed into apes'. To what were those shadows pointing, and what speech lay buried in their silence? Those small and shaggy satyrs, in the 'great and memorable æra in which they began to be silent', crept nearer and nearer to the Beau, until at last, Juliana Papjoy, or Lady Betty Besom, flitted into the room, in her pink gown bunched like a rose, carrying a small taper which seemed darting like a fire-fly, so quick and so soundless were her movements.

From that time, Beau Nash seemed more sunk than ever under the weight of his eighty-five years; he suffered, too, from gout, but refused to see a doctor until Juliana Papjoy invited one to the house without the Beau's knowledge. For he had always disliked doctors, and now, he not only disliked them, but dreaded them as well, because they reminded him of the death which he could not escape, which heeded not past splendours, nor could be kept at bay by the ghosts of those vanished crowds of fawning fashionable beaux and belles, who, when Beau Nash was young, had thrust that black shade so far into the distance.

The shade dogging his aged footsteps grew nearer and nearer, and Richard Nash was, by now, too tired even to attempt to escape it. He died at his house in the Saw-Close, on the night of February the 12th, 1761, or in the early morning on the following day, having passed eighty-six years and four months in this life.

Two days after his death, the Corporation of Bath, to which he owed so little in these last sad years, met together and voted that 'the funeral of Mr. Nash be defrayed at a sum not exceeding fifty guineas, under the direction of Mr. Mayor and Mr. Chamberlain'. But even so, there was one member of the Corporation who objected to so large a sum being spent in burying the old man who had created the splendours of their city.

Beau Nash lay in state for four days, after which time he was carried, with great pomp, to the Abbey Church. The procession left the Beau's house at about five o'clock. First came the charity-girls walking two and two, and followed by the boys of the charity-school, singing, from time to time, a hymn. After these marched the city musicians, and the dead Beau's own orchestra, playing a dirge. The coffin, which was adorned with thick smoky black plumes, and whose pall was supported by the six senior aldermen of Bath, was preceded by three clergymen. The chief mourners—and this was but natural and right—were Mr. Wiltshire and Mr. Simpson, the Masters of the Assembly Rooms, and these were followed by several members of the Corporation, and the beadles of the hospital to which Beau Nash had subscribed so largely, in the days of his power and plenty, marching in solemn formation. Then, last of all, came those who had the deepest cause of all to grieve that the Beau had gone—the unhappy patients from the hospital, whose pain had moved him to so much pity, to so many strenuous efforts on their behalf. These, 'the lame, the emaciated, and the feeble, followed their old benefactor to his grave, and lamenting themselves in him'.

The crowds filled the streets, and people came from far away to see the Beau carried to his grave. 'Even the tops of the houses were covered with spectators', we are told by one news-sheet. 'Each thought the occasion affected themselves most; as when a real king dies, they asked each other, where shall we find such another? Sorrow sate upon every face, and even children lisped that their sovereign was no more. The awfulness of the solemnity made the deepest impression on the minds of the distressed inhabitants. The peasant discontinued his toil, the ox rested from the plough; all nature seemed to sympathise with their loss, and the muffled bells rang a peal of bob-majors.' In short, those 'distressed inhabitants' who had forgotten Beau Nash in his old age and misery, were only too willing to remember him now. The whole country echoed with his praises, both in the coffee-houses, and in the news-sheets. One of these news-sheets, according to Goldsmith, 'concluded with gravely declaiming that "impotent posterity would in vain fumble to produce his fellow". Another, equally sorrowful, gave us to know, "that he was indeed a man"; an assertion which I fancy none will be so hardy as to contradict. But the grandest of all the lamentations made upon this occasion was that in which he was called "a constellation of the heavenly sphere".' The dead Beau was not only flattered in the news-sheets, but posthumous honours of every kind were paid him by that city which had done so little to help him while he lived. The Corporation of Bath agreed—unanimously this time, as the question of money did not arise—that 'the offer of Mr. William Hoare of a portrait of Mr. Nash's picture, to be set up in the Town Hall, be accepted, with the thanks of the Corporation for the same'.

Doctor William Oliver, that kind, good and celebrated physician whose conversation and literary talents, according to Goldsmith, were well known, and who died at Bath three years after Beau Nash, and Doctor King, were among others who wrote eulogies of the Beau, and they were well fitted to do so, since they had been his friends during his lifetime. Doctor Oliver's eulogy was the first to appear, and ran thus:

A FAINT SKETCH OF THE LIFE, CHARACTER,
AND MANNERS OF THE LATE MR. NASH

Imperium in Imperio.—
De mortuis nil nisi bonum.

Bath, February 13, 1761.

This morning died
RICHARD NASH, ESQ.,
Aged eighty-eight.
He was by birth a gentleman, an ancient Briton;
By education, a student of Jesus College in Oxford;
By profession
His natural genius was too volatile for any.
He tried the army and the law;
But soon found his mind superior to both.
He was born to govern,
Nor was his dominion, like that of other legislators,
Over the servility of the vulgar,
But over the pride of the noble and the opulent.
His public character was great,
As it was self-built and self-maintained:
His private amiable,
As it was grateful, beneficent, and generous.
By the force of genius
He erected the city of Bath into a province of pleasure,
And became, by universal consent,
Its legislator and ruler.
He plann'd, improv'd, and regulated all the amusements of
the place;
His fundamental law was that of good breeding;
Hold sacred decency and decorum,
His constant maxim:

The Old Age of Beau Nash

Nobody, howsoever exalted
By beauty, blood, titles, or riches,
Could be guilty of a breach of it, unpunished—
The penalty, his disapprobation and public shame.
To maintain the sovereignty he had established,
He published Rules of Behaviour,
Which from their propriety, acquired the force of laws;
And which the highest never infring'd, without immediately
undergoing the public censure.
He kept the Men in order; most wisely,
By prohibiting the wearing swords in his dominions;
By which means
He prevented sudden passion from causing
The bitterness of unavailing repentance.
In all quarrels he was chosen Umpire—
And so just were his decisions,
That peace generally triumphed,
Crowned with the mutual thanks of both parties.
He kept the ladies in good-humour; most effectually,
By a nice observance of the rules of place and
precedence;
By ordaining scandals to be the infallible mark
Of a foolish head and a malicious heart,
Always rendering more suspicious
The reputation of her who propagated it,
Than that of the person abused.
Of the young, the gay, the heedless fair,
Just launching into the dangerous sea of pleasure,
He was ever, unsolicited (sometimes unregarded)
The kind protector:
Humanely correcting even their mistakes in dress,
As well as improprieties in conduct:
Nay, often warning them,
Though at the hazard of his life,
Against the artful snares of designing men,

The Old Age of Beau Nash

Or an improper acquaintance with women of doubtful
characters.
Thus did he establish his government on pillars
Of honour and politeness,
Which could never be shaken:
And maintained it, for full half a century,
With reputation, honour and undisputed authority.
Beloved, respected, and revered.
Of his private character, be it the first praise,
That while, by his conduct, the highest ranks became his
subjects,
He himself became
The servant of the poor and the distressed:
Whose cause he ever pleaded amongst the rich,
And enforced with all the eloquence of a good example:
They were ashamed not to relieve those wants
To which they saw him administer with
So noble an heart, and so liberal an hand.
Nor was his munificence confined to particulars,
He being, to all the public charities of this city,
A liberal benefactor;
Not only by his own most generous subscriptions,
But, by always assuming, in their behalf, the character of
A sturdy beggar;
Which he performed with such an authorative address
To all ranks without distinction,
That few of the worst hearts had courage to refuse,
What their own inclinations would not have prompted them
to bestow.
Of a noble spirit
And
A warm grateful heart,
The obelisk in the grove,
And
The beautiful needle in the square,

The Old Age of Beau Nash

Are magnificent testimonies.
The One
Erected to preserve the memory of a
Most interesting event to his country,
The restitution of health, by the healing waters of this place,
To the illustrious Prince of Orange,
Who came hither in a most languishing condition:
The Other,
A noble offering of thanks
To the late Prince of Wales, and his royal Consort,
For favours bestowed,
And honours by them conferred, on this city.
His long and peaceful reign, of
Absolute power,
Was so tempered by his
Excessive good-nature,
That no instance can be given either of his own cruelty,
Or of his suffering that of others to escape
Its proper reward.
Example unprecedented amongst absolute monarchs.

READER.

This monarch was a man,
And his foibles and his faults,
Which we would wish covered with the veil of good-nature,
Made of the same piece with his own:
But, truth forceth us unwillingly to confess,
His passions were strong;
Which, as they fired him to act strenuously in good,
Hurried him to some excesses of evil.

His fire, not used to be kept under by an early restraint,
Burst out too often into flaming acts,
Without waiting for the cool approbation of his judgment.
His generosity was so great,
That prudence often whispered him, in vain,

The Old Age of Beau Nash

That she feared it would enter the neighbouring confines of
profusion:
His charity so unbounded,
That the severe might suspect it sometimes to be
The offspring of folly, or ostentation.
With all these,
Be they foibles, follies, faults, or frailties,
It will be difficult to point out,
Amongst his temporary Kings of the whole earth,
More than One
Who hath fewer, or less pernicious to mankind.

His existence
(for life it scarcely might be called)
Was spun out to so great an age, that
The man
Was sunk, like many former heroes, in
The weakness and infirmities of exhausted nature;
The unwilling tax all animals must pay
For multiplicity of days.
Over his closing scene,
Charity long spread her all-covering mantle,
And dropped the curtain,
Before the poor actor, though he had played his part,
Was permitted to quit the stage.

Now may she protect his memory!
Every friend of Bath,
Every lover of decency, decorum, and good breeding,
Must sincerely deplore
The loss of so excellent a governor;
And join in the most fervent wishes (would I could say
hopes!)
That there may soon be found a man
Able and worthy,
To succeed him.

The Old Age of Beau Nash

Dr. King's epitaph is as follows:

EPITAPHIUM RICHARDI NASH, ARMIGERI
H. S. E.

RICHARDUS NASH,
Obscuro loco natus,
Et nullis ortus majoribus:
Cui tamen
(O rem miram, et incredibilem!)
Regnum opulentissimum florentissimumque
Plebs, proceres, principes,
Liberis suis suffragiis
Ultro detulerunt,
Quod et ipse summa cum dignitate tenuit,
annos plus quinquaginta,
Universo populo consentiente, approbante, plaudente.

Una voce præterea, unoque omnium ordinum con-
sensu,
Ad imperium suum adjuncta est
Magni nominis[1] Provincia:
Quam admirabili consilio et ratione
Per se, non unquam per legatos, administravit;
Eam quotannis invisere dignatus,
Et apud provinciales, quoad necesse fuit,
Solitus manere.

In tanta fortuna
Neque fastu turgidus Rex incessu patuit,
Neque, tyrannorum more, se jussit coli,
Aut amplos honores, titulosque sibi arrogavit;
Sed cuncta insignia, etiam regium diadema rejiciens,
Caput contentus fuit ornare
Galero Albo
Manifesto animi sui candoris signo.

[1]Tunbridge.

The Old Age of Beau Nash

Legislator prudentissimus,
Vel Solone et Lycurgo illustrior,
Leges, quascunque voluit,
Statuit, fixit, promulgavit;
Omnes quidem cum civibus suis,
Tum vero hospitibus, advenis, peregrinis
Gratas, jucundas, utiles.

Voluptatem arbiter et minister,
Sed gravis, sed elegans, sed urbanus,
Et in summa comitate satis adhibens severitatis,
Imprimis curavit,
Ut in virorum et fœminarum cœtibus
Nequis impudentur faceret,
Neque in iis quod inesset
Impuritatis, clamoris, tumulti.

Civitatem hanc celeberrimam,
Delicias suas.
Non modo pulcherrimis ædificiis auxit,
Sed præclara disciplina et moribus ornavit:
Quippe nemo quisquam
To Prepon melius intellexit, excoluit, docuit.

Justus, liberalis, benignus, facetus,
Atque amicus omnibus, præcipue miseris et egenis,
Nullos habuit inimicos,
Præter magnos quosdam ardeliones,
Et declamatores eos tristes et fanaticos,
Qui generi humano sunt inimicissimi.

Pacis et patriæ amans,
Concordiam, felicem et perpetuam,
In regno suo constituit,
Usque adeo,
Ut nullus alteri petulanter maledicere,
Aut facto nocere auderet;

The Old Age of Beau Nash

Neque, tanquam sibi metuens,
In publicum armatus prodire.
Fuit quanquam potentissimus,
Omnia arbitrio suo gubernans:
Haud tamen ipsa libertas
Magis usquam floruit
Gratia, gloria, auctoritate.
Singulare enim temperamentum invenit,
(Rem magnæ cogitationis,
Et rerum omnium fortasse difficillimam)
Quo ignobiles cum nobilibus, pauperes cum
divitibus,
Indocti cum doctissimis, ignavi cum fortissimis
Æquari se putarent,

REX OMNIBUS IDEM.

QUICQUID PECCAVERIT,

(nam peccamus omnes)
In seipsum magis, quam in alios,
Et errore, aut imprudentia magis quam scelere, aut
improbitate.

Peccavit;
Nusquam vero ignoratione decori, aut honesti,
Neque ita quidem usquam,
Ut non veniam ab humanis omnibus,
Facile impetrarit.

Hujus vitæ morumque exemplar
Si cæteri reges, regulique,
Et quotquot sunt regnorum præfecti,
Imitarentur;
(Utinam! iterumque utinam!)
Et ipse essent beati,
Et cunctæ orbis regiones beatissimæ.

The Old Age of Beau Nash

Talem virum, tantumque ademptum
Lugeant musæ, charitesque!
Lugeant Verenes, Cupidinesque!
Lugeant omnes juvenum et nympharum chori!
Tu vero, O Bathonia,
Ne cesse tuum lugere
Principem, præceptorem, amicum, patronum;
Hcu, hcu, nunquam posthac
Habitura parem!

Goldsmith administered a reproof, which, though less severe and less awful in its majesty, seems to be modelled on those of Doctor Johnson, to the lack of moral instruction contained both in the epitaph by Dr. Oliver and of that by Dr. King; but the reproof which might, with advantage, have been administered to Dr. Oliver's free verse, was not forthcoming. 'The reader sees in what alluring colours Nash's character is drawn; but he must consider that an intimate friend held the pencil; but the Doctor professes to say nothing of the dead but what was good; and such a maxim, though it serves his departed friend, is but badly calculated to improve the living. Dr. King, in his epitaph, however, is still more indulgent; he produces him as an example to kings, and prefers his laws even to those of Solon or Lycurgus. . . . The following translation', he continues, 'will give the English reader an idea of its contents, though not of its elegance:

THE EPITAPH OF RICHARD NASH, ESQ.

Here lies
RICHARD NASH.
Born in an obscure village,
And from mean ancestors.
To whom, however,
Strange to relate,
Both the vulgar and the mighty,

The Old Age of Beau Nash

Without bribe or compulsion,
Unanimously gave
A kingdom, equally rich and flourishing.
A kingdom which he governed
More than fifty years,
With universal approbation and applause.
To his empire also was added,
By the consent of all orders,
A celebrated province[1]
Which he ever swayed with great prudence,
Not by delegated power, but in person.
He deigned to visit it every year,
And while the necessities of state demanded his
presence,
He usually continued there.
In such greatness of fortune
His pride discovered itself by no marks of dignity;
Nor did he ever claim the honours of prostration.
Despising at once titles of adulation,
And laying aside all royal splendour,
Wearing not even the diadem,
He was content with being distinguish'd
only by the ornamental design
Of a white hat;
A symbol of the candour of his mind.
He was a most prudent legislator,
And more remarkable even than Solon or Lycurgus.
He at once established and authorized
Whatever laws were thought convenient,
Which were equally serviceable to the city,
And grateful to strangers,
Who made it their abode.
He was at once a provider and a judge of pleasures,

[1]Tunbridge.

The Old Age of Beau Nash

But still conducted them with gravity and elegance,
And repressed licentiousness with severity.
His chief care was employed,
In preventing obscenity or impudence
From offending the modesty of the morals
Of the Fair Sex.
And in banishing them from their Assemblies
Tumult, clamour, and abuse.
He not only adorned this city,
Which he loved,
With beautiful structures,
But improved it by his example;
As no man knew, no man taught, what was becoming
Better than he.
He was just, liberal, kind and facetious;
A friend to all, but particularly to the poor.
He had no enemies,
Except some of the trifling great,
Or dull declaimers, foes to all mankind.
Equally a lover of peace and of his country;
He fix'd a happy and lasting concord
In his kingdom,
So that none dare convey scandal, or injure by open violence
the universal peace,
Or even by carrying arms appear prepar'd for war,
With impunity.

But though his power was boundless,
Yet never did liberty flourish more, which he promoted,
Both by his authority, and cultivated for his fame.
He found out the happy secret
(A thing not to be considered without surprise)
Of uniting the vulgar and the great,
The poor and the rich,
The learned and ignorant,

The Old Age of Beau Nash

The cowardly and the brave,
In the bonds of society, an equal king to all.

Whatever his faults were,
For we all have faults,
They were rather obnoxious to himself than others;
They arose neither from imprudence nor mistake,
Never from dishonesty or corrupt principle,
But so harmless were they,
That though they failed to create our esteem,
Yet can they not want our pardon.

Could other kings and governors
But learn to imitate his example,
(Would to heaven they could!)
Then might they see themselves happy,
And their people still enjoying more true felicity.

Ye Muses and Graces mourn
His death;
Ye powers of Love, ye choirs of youth and virgins,
But thou, O Bathonia! more than the rest,
Cease not to weep,
Your king, your teacher, patron, friend,
Never, ah, never, to behold
His equal.'

In this manner was the light, glittering and warm dust that had been Beau Nash, blown away, out of the memories of men, to the sound of trumpets, eulogies, and lamentations. Alas, the unhappy subject of these magnificent eulogies left but few possessions to be distributed among his relatives. A small library of well-chosen books, some trinkets, and pictures, were his only inheritance; and with the exception of an agate étui, with a diamond on the top, a present to the

Beau from the Dowager Princess of Wales, and a gold box with Lady Euston's picture in the lid, which had been given to him by a former Countess of Burlington, there was nothing of any great value. Gone was that magnificent collection of snuff-boxes which had been his pride and delight; gone were the rings, the pictures, and the watches, which he had bought, for he had been obliged to sell these in the days of his want. A few family pictures, however, still remained to him, and, after his death, these were sold, by advertisement, for five guineas each.

Mrs. Juliana Papjoy, or Lady Betty Besom, finding herself homeless and penniless, after the death of the Beau who had befriended her, did not take to the streets—from which the Beau may, or may not, have rescued her, long ago; but, according to Mr. Melville, 'Perhaps from remorse at her previous mode of life, or perhaps from grief, she vowed she would never again sleep in a bed.' For the rest of her life, therefore, she slept in a large hollow tree, and, in the early dawns, her strange pointed face, her black elf-locks, and bird-black eyes might be seen peering through the dreamy green branches of this. Her livelihood, such as it was, she earned by gathering herbs and simples and by carrying messages, and in this condition she remained until she felt her death approaching, when, feeling a longing to die in the cottage in which she was born, she returned there on foot, just as that lengthening shadow overtook her. No ghost haunts that hollow tree; and the house in Saw-Close is deserted in the day-time, though at night, so I was told by an unhappy unemployed youth who attached himself to our party, singing and dancing is to be heard. But that narrow house seems at once ghostly and inexpressibly silent; the white panelling reminded me of the fur of a dirty white cat; in a room on the first floor there were boxes of what seemed to be cast-off and tawdry theatrical dresses and masks, and in a room of the floor above, there was a photograph of people

185

dressed in finery of the year 1905, under which was written, 'The Company of Dorothy, 1905'. 'What do people sing there?' enquired my sister-in-law, who had not been inside the house—'hymns?' The unemployed boy gave her a strange look. . . . 'No,' he replied . . .'you hear people dancing and singing.'

CHAPTER X

Ralph Allen and Prior Park

IN THE YEAR 1715, A YOUNG MAN OF TWENTY-TWO
years of age, the son of the landlord of a roadside inn
at St. Blaize, came to Bath to make his fortune. This
young man, whose fine appearance and wide mouth and dark
and solemn-looking eyes, we have seen in his portrait-draw-
ing by William Hoare, was named Ralph Allen. He was
destined, not only to make his own fortune, but to help
Beau Nash and the architect Wood in making the fortune of
Bath.

'In the year 1715', we are told by his friend and admirer,
Mr. Graves, 'Mr Allen was one of the clerks of the post office
in this city. In this situation, having got intelligence of a
wagon-load of arms coming up from the West for the use
of the disaffected in this part of England (who were supposed to have projected an insurrection in order to co-
operate with that in Scotland and the North of England),
he communicated this to General Wade, who was then
quartered in Bath with troops, and who, finding him a sensible, prudent young man, got him advanced after the death
of Mr. Quash, who was then Postmaster, to that station, and
afterwards married him to Miss Earl, his natural daughter.'
(This lady, who was married to Allen in 1718, died in 1722,
in the year of her father's first election to Parliament.) This
story, according to Mr. Peach, in his *Life and Times of Ralph
Allen*, is, however, inaccurate, for, 'in the first place Marshal
Wade never was quartered with troops in Bath; in the second

place, no rising in the West was at any time imminent; and in 1715 a wagon was a vehicle unknown, and if it had been, there was not a road at that period on which it could have travelled at the rate of a mile a day; and lastly, from whence could arms have been procured in the West to have supplied the disaffected?'

However this may have been, Ralph Allen did become Postmaster, after the death of Mr. Quash, and until about 1727, surveyed the business of the post office in the old church nave. At this time the church was surrounded by slum houses of a particularly loathsome character, and the neighbourhood was terrorised by the 'post office hangers on', who were violent towards the honest, and friends of the dishonest, officials. Mr. Allen reformed, not only the dishonest officials, but the actual working of the mails, and in the latter task he was helped by his father-in-law Marshal Wade.

That benevolent, humane and generous man, had, in 1726, begun the laying down of 'Highland Roads',—employing five hundred soldiers at sixpence a day extra pay, and earning as much devotion from them as he earned from the city of Bath when, from 1722 until 1741, he represented the city in Parliament.

The father and son-in-law, the closest friends and colleagues that could be imagined, were untiring in their efforts to improve the condition of Bath. In his private capacity, Marshal Wade was one of the principal subscribers towards the building of St. Michael's Church (not the present one); he gave to all public charities, and, as well, he made a passage through the slum buildings at the North Front of the Abbey, and succeeded in cleaning up the worst offences in the neighbourhood, at his own expense. (The block of buildings in question was not, however, removed until 1823.)

The Marshal seems to have contracted, at about this time, a mania for commissioning portraits of himself and of the members of the Corporation, and these were hung in the council-chamber. He had, also, a mania for gambling, and, at moments, for frequenting houses of a rather dangerous character.

Horace Walpole tells a story of one of the Marshal's adventures at a house of this kind—a story which is very illustrative of his character. The Marshal, having, with his usual recklessness, brought his finest snuff-box with him, found, after a time, that it was missing. Everybody in the room submitted to be searched, excepting one man, who refused, unless the Marshal would go into the next room with him. Then he told the Marshal that he was a gentleman by birth, and that, having sunk into the most hopeless poverty, he lived only by what wretched bets he could pick up, and by scraps of food given him by the waiters out of charity. 'At this moment I have half a fowl in my pocket', he said. 'I was afraid of being exposed. There it is; now, sir, you may search me.' The Marshal was so much moved that he gave him a hundred pounds. The snuff box, meanwhile, had been lying during this interview in the Marshal's inner pocket, whence it was, in due course, retrieved, by the Marshal's servant.

This incident, naturally, occurred in one of the Marshal's unofficial moments. The unofficial moments enjoyed by his son-in-law, Mr. Allen, seem to have been fewer; and his official hours while he was Postmaster, were, to such an unbusinesslike observer as myself, such winding labyrinths of boredom, that if I try to enter into them I shall never extricate myself. The reader may say that this does not matter; but I do not agree; for what means boredom for me, means a worse boredom for the reader. I will, therefore, spare us both, and will confine myself, merely, to remarking that in 1727, the post office was removed from Bath Street, and that the business was, from that time, carried on in the house which Mr. Allen shared with his brother Philip in

Ralph Allen and Prior Park

Liliput Alley, the house having been enlarged by Killigrew in order that the postal business might be carried on there.

The house had a fine façade, and a sloping terraced walk led down from Liliput Alley, the scene of the labours of Sally Lunn, as well as of Mr. Allen, to Harrison's Walks, and from the post office could be seen Hampton Down, on which, some years later, Richard Jones erected the strange building which was afterwards called Sham Castle.

It is believed that Ralph Allen's second marriage to Elizabeth Holder, the daughter of Richard Holder, of Hampton Manor House, the sister of Charles Holder, and the enemy of Miss Martha Blount, took place in the same year as the removal of the post office to Liliput Alley. The family of the new Mrs. Allen were, it seems, even then, in pecuniary difficulties, and Mr. Peach remarks that 'It is evident from the numerous deeds relating to mortgages, etc., that . . . Allen, in respect of considerations not explained, had acquired the right of exercising the privileges of ownership for many years before he purchased the property in 1742'. Allen behaved with his usual generosity in the matter of Hampton, and of Claverton, which was also the property of a Holder, and which was bought by Allen in 1752; and Charles Holder, his brother-in-law, continued to live in the village of Bathampton, on an allowance made him by his brother-in-law, until he died in 1763, at the age of eighty-nine.

But enough of post offices and mortgages. Let us leave them as fast as we can, and drive to Prior Park. (I may say, at this point, that I *did* drive to Prior Park: but that the present occupants, who, it was evident, did not inherit Mr. Allen's interests, would not allow me to look over the house, pleading, as an excuse, that they are Christian Brothers.)

However, although the vigilance of the Christian Brothers prevented me from seeing anything excepting the wide and beautiful hall leading into the vast park beyond, blue and limpid as a lake in a dream, there is no reason, I imagine,

190

why, excluded though I was, I should not write about the plans for building the house, and Ralph Allen's hospitality.

'Three events', says Mr. Peach, 'were to happen in 1742; namely, the election of Allen to the Mayoralty; the opening of the General Mineral Water Hospital, and the completion of a portion of Prior Park.'

By the time that the plans for building Prior Park were laid out by the great architect Wood, the beauty of the long despised Bath stone, which is the colour of dark honey, and looks smooth and sweet as honey, was, owing to the joint efforts of Wood and Ralph Allen, acknowledged even by the London architects who had regarded it with suspicion.

Wood's huge conception of the house, inevitable yet strange, like music, was in the end, less grandiose and ornate than first enthusiasm had suggested; but the beauties were not less; and the modification of the original plans were the result, it seems, of Allen's own wish. For Wood, writing seven years after the house was completed, says: 'The warmth of this resolution at last abating, an humble simplicity took its place.' It is sad that, as a result of some dispute about a modification of Wood's design for the roof of the stables, the old friendship between Wood and Allen ceased. The eastern wing, indeed, the Palladian bridge, and the planting, also, were given into the hands of another architect, about a year before the death of Wood.

I think I cannot do better than quote Mr. Peach's elaborate description of the architecture of the house. Long as it is, I quote this passage for three reasons; the first is that I like to imagine the scene in which Pope, Gainsborough, Pitt, Walpole, Chesterfield, Fielding, Smollett, Garrick—indeed, nearly all the most important men of the time were to be found. My second reason is that I am determined to thwart the Christian Brothers—whilst admitting that their house is their own property, I submit that it is also the property of many beautiful and wise ghosts. And my third reason is that

Ralph Allen and Prior Park

I find the description pleasing. (My favourite passage is that relating to Gainsborough's portrait of Garrick.[1])

The only person who seems to have disapproved of Prior Park, and of Mr. Allen's hospitality, although he was only too willing to avail himself of the latter, was Captain Philip Thicknesse. It must be remembered, however, that he made a point of disapproving of everything and everybody.

Captain Thicknesse described the house, the hospitality, and his host, in these terms:

'A noble seat, which *sees all* Bath, and which was built, probably for all Bath to see. The Founder of this House and Family was Ralph Allen; of low Birth, but no mean Intellects. It is said, the Postmaster of *Exeter*, being caught in a Storm upon a dreary Heath, in *Cornwall*, took shelter in a poor Man's Hut, the property of ALLEN's Father, and being kindly received by the humble Host, and seeing some Marks of Genius in this Boy, proposed taking him under his Care and Protection; a Proposal very acceptable to all Parties. He was accordingly taught to read and write, and then employed in the Post-Office, to receive and deliver Letters; during his Residence there, Mr. ——, the Postmaster, had formed a Scheme in which young ALLEN's Pen and Head were employed, of establishing a Cross-Post all over *England*; but Mr. —— was unable to carry it into Execution. Mr. ALLEN, however, possessed of some Materials for so great an Undertaking, and a much better Head, leaving his Master soon after, carried this great National Convenience into Execution; and while he was supposed to be gaining a Princely Fortune by digging Stones from the Bowels of the Earth, he actually picked it off the Surface, by traversing the whole Kingdom with Post-Horses. He was said to bear his great Prosperity with Humility, and to conduct all Business with the utmost Probity. That he affected a Simplicity of Manners and Dress,

[1]See Appendix.

we can testify; but we can by no Means allow that he was not a Man deeply charged with Pride, and without address enough to conceal it. His plain *Quaker*-coloured suit of Cloaths, and Shirt Sleaves with only a Chitterlin up the Slit, might, and did deceive the vulgar Eye; but he could not bear to let POPE (who was often his Visitor) call him what was true (*low-born* ALLEN), but made him substitute in its Place, that which was false (*humble* ALLEN). He was not, however, mean, for we once ate a most magnificent Dinner at his Table, served to thirty Persons, off *Dresden* China, and he seemed to take infinite Pains to shew his Munificence in every Respect. He left behind him, however, a Nephew and Namesake, whom we lately followed to the Grave, amidst the unaffected Tears and Sorrows of all, but those who might profit by his untimely Death. For he was one of the noblest works of God!'

But however much Captain Thicknesse may have disapproved of Ralph Allen, and his house, and his origin, other guests did not share his views.

Fielding's portrait of him, masquerading under the name of Mr. Allworthy, in *Tom Jones*, will give us the real man, undistorted by Thicknesse's malice.

'Neither Mr. Allworthy's house nor his heart were shut against any part of mankind; but they were both more particularly open to men of merit. To say the truth, this was the only house in the kingdom where you were sure to gain a dinner by deserving it.

'Above all others, men of genius and learning shared the principal place in his favour; and in these he had much discernment; for though he had missed the advantage of a learned education, yet, being blessed with vast natural abilities, he had so well profited by a vigorous, though late application to letters, and by much conversation with men of eminence in this way, that he was himself a very competent judge in most kinds of literature.

Ralph Allen and Prior Park

'It is no wonder that, in an age when this kind of merit is so little in fashion and so slenderly provided for, persons possessed of it should very eagerly flock to a place where they were sure of being received with great complaisance, indeed, where they might employ almost the same advantages of a liberal fortune as if they were entitled to it in their own right; for Mr. Allworthy was not one of those generous persons who are ready most bountifully to bestow meat, drink, and lodging on men of wit and learning, for which they expect no other return but entertainment, instruction, and subserviency; in a word, that such persons should be enrolled in the number of domestics, without wearing their master's clothes or receiving wages.

'On the contrary, every person in this house was perfect master of his own time: and as he might at his pleasure satisfy all his appetites within the restrictions only of law, virtue and religion: so he might, if his health required, or his inclination prompted him to temperance, or even to abstinence, absent himself from any meals, or retire from them whenever he was so disposed, without even a solicitation to the contrary: for, indeed, such solicitations from superiors always savour very strongly of commands. But all here were free from such impertinence, not only those whose company is in all other places esteemed a favour from their equality of fortune, but even those whose indigent circumstances make such an eleemosynary abode convenient to them, and who are therefore less welcome to a great man's table because they stand in need of it.'[1]

From the year 1734 until 1740, another, and a greater, writer than Fielding was in the habit of spending not only weeks, but months, at Prior Park, where he completed the fourth book of the *Dunciad*. This friendship between Alexander Pope and Allen originated in Mr. Allen's deep admira-

[1]*Tom Jones*, Book I., Chap. X.

tion of the sincerity and beautiful nature exhibited in Mr. Pope's published correspondence; and it became so intimate that any friend of Mr. Pope's was a welcome guest at Prior Park. This led to Pope inviting the Reverend Mr. Warburton (who was then a stranger to Allen, but who became, in time, not only, to all intents and purposes, an inmate of Prior Park, but also the husband of Allen's niece) to Prior Park for a six weeks' visit. The letter of invitation, dated 12th November, 1741, ran thus:

'My third motive for now troubling you is my own proper interest and pleasure. I am here in more leisure then I can possibly enjoy, even in my own house, *vacare literis*. It is at this place that your exhortations may be most effectual to make me resume the studies I had almost laid aside by perpetual avocations and dissipations. If it were practicable for you to pass a month or six weeks from home, it is here I could wish to be with you; and if you would attend to the continuation of your own noble work, or unbend to the idle amusement of commenting upon a Poet who has no other merit than that of aiming, by his moral strokes, to merit some regard from such men as advance truth and virtue in a more effectual way; in either case this place and this house would be an inviolable asylum to you from all you would desire to avoid in so public a scene as Bath. The worthy man who is the master of it invites you in the strongest terms, and is one who would treat you with love and veneration, rather than with what the world calls civility and regard. He is sincerer and plainer than almost any man now in this world, *antiquis moribus*. If the waters of Bath may be serviceable to your complaints (as I believe, from what you have told me of them), no opportunity can ever be better. It is just the best season. We are told the Bishop of Salisbury [Dr. Sherlock] is expected here daily, who, I know, is your friend; at least, though a Bishop, is too much a man of learning to be your enemy. You see I omit nothing to add to the weight in the balance, in which, however, I will not think *myself* light, since I have known your partiality. You will want no servant here. Your room will be next to mine, and one man will serve us. Here is a library, and a gallery 90 feet long to walk in, and a coach whenever you would take the air with me. Mr. Allen tells me you might, on horseback, be here in three days. It is less than 100 miles from Newark, the road through Leicester, Stowe-in-the-Wolds, Gloucester, and Cirencester, by Lord Bathurst's. I could engage to carry you to London from hence, and I would accommodate my time and journey to your conveniency.' Again, 22nd November: 'Yours is very full and kind: it is a friendly and very satisfactory answer, and all I can desire. Do but instantly fulfil it. Only I hope this will find you before you set out. For I think, on all considerations, your best way will be to take London in your way. You will owe me a real obligation by being made acquainted with the master of this house, and by sharing with me what I think one of the chief satisfactions of my life—his friendship.' Of this invitation Warburton did not fail to avail himself. On the 3rd March, 1742, we find him writing as follows to Dr. Doddridge: 'In Nov. Mr. Pope sent me so pressing an invitation to come to him at Mr. Allen's, near Bath, seconded by so kind an invitation of that good man, that I could not decline a long, tedious winter journey by London. I stayed at Widcombe in the most agreeable retired society with two excellent persons, so very dear to me, till after the Christmas holidays.'

Alas, in the end, everybody, excepting Mr. Allen, his niece, and the admiring Mr. Richard Graves, regretted that pressing invitation; and Mr. Pope was constrained, at last, to announce that Mr. Warburton was a sneaking parson, and to tell him he flattered.

But this was on the occasion of a later visit to Ralph Allen, when Pope brought his friend Martha Blount with him, and a guerilla warfare began between that lady and her hostess.

Ralph Allen and Prior Park

Nobody knows the exact reasons for that warfare, one school of thought holding that it was the result of Miss Blount's proprietary airs toward Pope, another claiming that Mrs. Allen had heard some scandal in connection with the two friends, a third saying that it arose from Allen's refusal to allow one of his carriages to take Miss Blount to the Roman Catholic church. In short, the affair is wrapped in mystery.

Certainly, Miss Blount complained to Pope, who, after some wrangling, left the house in a hurry, afterwards facilitating Miss Blount's escape.

'They used Mr. Pope very rudely', Miss Blount told Spence, 'and Mr. Warburton with a double complaisance, and they used me very oddly in a stiff, over-civil manner. I asked Mr. Pope if he had noticed their usage of him . . . he said he had not, and that the people had got some odd thing or other in their heads.' After Pope's departure, matters became much worse, and Miss Blount wrote to Pope, complaining that 'Mr. and Mrs. Allen never said a word, not so much as asked me how I went, where or when. In short, from every one of them much greater inhumanity than I could conceive anybody could show. . . . They talk to one another without putting me at all in the conversation. . . . I do really think these people would shove me out if I did not go soon.' . . . Worse than all, 'Mr. Warburton took no notice of me. . . . 'tis most wonderful'.

Pope then formed the opinion that he wished the man well, but that 'the woman is a minx, and an impertinent one, and he will do what she will have him'. He intended, so he informed Miss Blount, never to set foot in Mr. Allen's house again.

Meanwhile, Miss Blount escaped from the inhumanity in question; but in the end, some time before the death of Pope, the quarrel was patched up, as far as Pope and Allen were concerned, although the patches were rather painfully visible.

Ralph Allen and Prior Park

Mr. Pope, with Dr. (afterwards Bishop) Warburton were amongst the most constant visitors to Prior Park; but the friendships made in the library, the reconciliations between old enemies, the guerilla warfares carried on in the dining-room, would fill a book of twice this size.

It was there, for instance, that Mr. Quin met his old rival Garrick, whose acquaintance with Allen had begun with Garrick's enquiries about a property he wished to buy, in the neighbourhood of Bath. Gainsborough met Garrick there, very frequently, and painted one of the portraits of the actor during a visit to Prior Park. Sarah Fielding, the author of *David Simple*, lived in a neighbouring house, called Yew Cottage, and was one of Mr. and Mrs. Allen's most constant visitors, and such a beloved and intimate friend that it was not until the death of Allen, in 1764, that she left Widcombe, and went to live, for the sake of econo-mising, at the village Wick, which is now Bathwick Street, until her death in 1768. It was Sarah Fielding who intro-duced Allen to her brother Henry, who became one of his most beloved friends; whilst another novelist who visited Prior Park frequently was Richardson, who, meeting Mr. Richard Graves one day, in the parlour of Leak the book-seller, and having told him that he was going to dine with Mr. Allen at Prior Park, added: 'Twenty years ago, I was the most obscure man in Great Britain; and now I am ad-mitted to the company of the first characters of the king-dom.'

Princess Amelia and the Duke of York, with their host the Duke of Bedford, paid a visit to Mr. and Mrs. Allen in 1752, and the visit ended by Mr. Allen offering to lend Prior Park to the Princess and her brother, whilst he and Mrs. Allen and the inevitable Warburton went to Weymouth.

The inevitable Warburton was not, it may be said at this point, universally popular. Among his most trying traits was the show he made of his humility, of which he was so proud that he made a point of choosing, very ostentatiously, to sit next to the stupidest guest, or the guest of least importance, and engaging that unfortunate in conversation. By this means he succeeded, invariably, in calling the attention of the whole room to the unimportance and dullness of the person in question, (since it was well known that he had this habit); the guest was made aware of his own stupidity and lowly position (for the same reason), whilst the more important guests were shown that to Warburton their importance was of no interest.

On the whole, James Quin was the guest who appears to have disliked him most, for he took every opportunity of snubbing him, whilst Warburton, on his side, never lost an opportunity of patronising Quin. On one occasion, 'the saucy priest', as Quin called him, having asked him, in a condescending manner, to recite, Quin replied by speaking a passage from Otway's *Venice Preserved*, emphasising, by looks and voice, the lines:

> 'Honest men
> Are the soft, easy cushions on which knaves
> Repose and fatten'.

The saucy priest did, however, find an admirer in the Reverend Richard Graves, the rector of Claverton, and the author of *The Spiritual Quixote*, who, according to Mr. Peach, presented a striking appearance, for he wore ultra-clerical black, and always carried a black baggy umbrella, which he held before him, hanging on his open hand. 'His features, *whilst pleasant and intellectual, wore an eager expression*' (the italics are mine); 'and he never walked, but trotted.'

I think Dr. Warburton must have had a low opinion of his fellow-clergyman's brain, or of his social position, for we find Graves writing of him, in *The Triflers*: . . . . 'I ventured to pronounce Dr. Warburton one of the politest men I had ever seen. Those who only know him as engaged in con-

troversy, may be surprised at this. But I found him so attentive to everyone who spoke, particularly to myself, who am
the worst of all possible speakers, setting everything that I
said in the clearest light, and, in short, paying such deference
to his inferiors, as most of the company were . . . that he had
certainly a claim to the character of polite man, if destitute
of superficial gentleness.'

It must be said for Bishop Warburton (as he became) that
in spite of his rather obtrusive humility and other irritating
characteristics, he was, genuinely, attached to Ralph Allen,
for whom he felt an admiration approaching reverence; he
was, too, a devoted husband, and a good father to his only
child, who died young. And Allen, on his side, returned
Warburton's attachment.

Allen seems, indeed, to have inspired an almost universal
devotion in his friends; the only people who disapproved of
him (to my knowledge) being Captain Thicknesse and Miss
Blount. He was respected and loved by such different characters as Warburton, Marshal Wade, and William Pitt, who
had been invited to become candidate for Bath mainly
through the instrumentality of Allen, who had known him
three years before, when Pitt was ill in that city, and Allen
had helped the Corporation to organise demonstrations in
his honour. During the years 1757-1766, in which Pitt represented Bath in Parliament, his friendship with Allen was
unbroken, and it remained so, even after Pitt's breach with
his constituents, because the Mayor, the Sheriffs and the
Corporation of that city had addressed a letter to the King,
expressing their delight at the 'adequate' peace of Paris, when
he, Pitt, had, in one of the most famous of his speeches,
described that peace as 'inadequate'.[1]

Lord Stanhope believed the word 'adequate' found its
way into the address without any particular significance

[1]Pitt's correspondence with Allen on this subject will be found
in Appendix II.

being attached to it. But Pitt was angered by the expression, since, by implication, the address reversed every judgment the Council had, till then, passed upon his policy. He believed that the whole address, with the use of the offending word, was the work of the humble Bishop Warburton, who owed him his Bishopric. But though Pitt blamed the Bishop, he did not blame the Bishop's uncle-by-marriage, and, in the course of a letter to Mrs. Allen, he wrote: 'I cannot conclude my letter without expressing my sensible concern at Mr. Allen's uneasiness. No incidents can make the least change in the honour and love I bear him, or in the justice my heart does to his humane virtues.'

Pitt sold his house in Bath, and although he represented the city in Parliament until 1766, when he was created Earl of Chatham, he did not, on the only occasion when he revisited it, to drink the waters, revive his dead friendships.

Ralph Allen, on the 18th of October, 1763, the year of his misunderstanding with Pitt, feeling himself grown old, feeble, and ill, wrote this letter to the Mayor of Bath:

'SIR,—My weak state of health and growing Infirmities obliges me to beg that you and the other Gentlemen of the Corporation will permit me at their Hall to resign my Station of one of your Aldermen.

'Upon this occasion give me leave to make my most hearty acknowledgments for the great attention and distinguishing regard which you and they during a long course of years have been pleased to show me, and to give the strongest assurance that in the remainder of my Life, one of my greatest pleasure on all proper occasions will be to testifie my utmost regard for the welfare of our City, and to show you and the other Gentlemen of the Community, every friendly act that may be in the power of them and of

Sir,

Your most humble and obedient Servant,

RALPH ALLEN.'

'To Samuel Bush, Esq.,

'Mayor of Bath, who is desired at the next Town Hall to lay this letter before the Aldermen and Common Council of that City.

'P.S.—Upon this Resignation. That the five hundred pounds which I sometime since desired your acceptance of towards the expence of Building a new Town Hall in our City shall be payed to any person for that purpose which you may be pleased to receive it whenever that useful and ornamental design shall be entered upon.

R. ALLEN.'

The life of this enlightened, generous, and humane man was, indeed, drawing to a close, and on the 29th June, 1764, he died, in the seventy-first year of his age.

His grave bears this epitaph:

'Beneath this monument lieth entomb'd the body of Ralph Allen, Esqre, of Prior Park, who departed this life the 29th day of June, 1764, in the 71st year of his age, in full hopes of everlasting happiness in another state, through the infinite merit and mediation of our blessed Redeemer, Jesus Christ. And of Elizabeth Holder, his second wife, who died 20th September, 1766, aged 68.'

But a greater epitaph is his friend Fielding's description of him in *Tom Jones*: 'Should I tell my reader that I had known a man whose penetrating genius had enabled him to raise a large fortune where no beginning was chalked out to him; that he had done this with the most perfect preservation of his integrity, and not only without the least injustice or injury to any particular person, but with the highest advantage to trade, and a vast increase of the public revenue; and that he had expended one part of the income of this fortune in discovering a taste superior to most, by works where the highest dignity was united with the purest simplicity, and another part in displaying a degree of goodness superior to all men, by acts of charity to objects whose only recommendation were their merits or their wants; that he was most industrious in searching after merit in distress, most eager to relieve it, and then as careful (perhaps too careful) to conceal what he had done; that his house, his furniture, his gardens, his table, his private hospitality, and his public beneficence, all denoted the mind from which they flowed, and were all intrinsically rich and noble, without tinsel or external ostentation; that he filled every relation in life with the most adequate virtue; that he was most piously religious to his Creator, most zealously loyal to his sovereign; a most tender husband to his wife, a kind relation, a munificent patron, a warm and firm friend, a knowing and cheerful companion, indulgent to his servants, hospitable to his neighbours, charitable to the poor, and benevolent to all mankind. Should I add to these the epithets of wise, brave, elegant, and indeed, every amiable epithet in our language, I might surely say:

> Quis credet? nemo Hercule! nemo
> Vel duo, vel nemo.

And yet I know a man who is all I have here described.'

The writer of this great epithet died ten years before the man whom it portrayed; and his beloved Squire Allworthy not only helped to educate his friend's orphan children, but left to each of them, and to their aunt, Sarah Fielding, the sum of one hundred pounds.

CHAPTER XI

Fashionable Intelligence

THE HANDS OF THE CLOCK MOVE SO SLOWLY through the drowsy day and the moonlit night, that years may pass, for us, in an hour, and the ghosts who came to visit us will not be surprised at seeing each other, though such a dusty empty space divides them.

Some of the ghosts have returned to the rooms which they knew well, to write letters to their old friends, while others are running from house to house gossiping.

But Princess Amelia, whose visit to the Duke and Duchess of Bedford is over, and who has, by now, removed, with her lords and ladies in waiting, to the royal residence in West Gate, is sitting alone, at an early hour in this dream-like summer morning, 'angling in the river', as Mr. Hutton Perkins told Lord Chancellor Hardwicke, 'in a summer-house by the river-side in the garden, formerly known as Harrison's Walks, which has two fire-places in it, and to secure herself against the cold, she has put on a riding-habit, and a black velvet postillion cap, tied under her chin'.

In spite of the fact that Princess Amelia was scarcely still for a moment (excepting when she was angling in the river, or playing cards, and particularly Commerce, with Beau Nash, who is, by now, almost mummified with age—the clock has struck 1752)—in spite of the fact that she enjoyed riding, very fast, dressed in a laced scarlet coat, and a hunting cap, and followed by her groom Spurrier—in spite of the fact that she rose from her bed very early, and went to bed very late, she had grown to an unwieldly size.

She was, too, in the habit of taking snuff, and of using language which, if not actually bad, was certainly surprising. But this last trait did not matter, because, as the Princess was, at moments, very deaf, she could not hear the language she was using, and it could not, therefore, disturb or shock her.

It was unsafe, however, for others to rely upon her deafness, which, at moments, left her when its presence might have been preferred. It had not, for instance, prevented her from hearing the answer made her by a certain foreign potentate when she had admired the size and brilliance of his diamonds. The Prince accepted the compliment, and said, in a thoughtful manner, 'Yours are very small'. The Princess did not enjoy the reply; but speech deserted her, and the Prince won the battle.

But now she was fishing in the river, from the shelter of the summer-house, and was undisturbed either by the memory of the strange behaviour of the citizens of Richmond, in refusing to break their necks in climbing down the broken ladders which Princess Amelia had ordered to be placed against the walls of Richmond Park, or by the aspersions cast by the foreign Prince upon her diamonds.

As the long morning drifted away, the warmth shining from the two fire-places made Princess Amelia sleepy. She nodded her head, while the shining fish, who looked like a knight in a coat of mail, as he glittered among the blue leaves of the little river-waves, tugged, chivalrously, at the line and tackle. In the end, he pulled Princess Amelia's fishing-rod after him into the river, and the Princess awoke with a start.

A little later in that long summer morning (in 1771) the ghosts of the Duke and Duchess of Northumberland were sitting down to breakfast in their house at No. 10 North Parade, when, to their great surprise, the door opened and in came a gentleman who was a complete stranger to them, a shambling fashionably-dressed gentleman with a slightly bald head fringed with hair like feathers, rather goggling eyes, and a runaway chin. The gentleman, without taking the slightest notice of their presence, or of the fact that they had been speaking until they noticed his entrance, flung himself, unconcernedly, upon a sofa. After a few moments blank astonishment, the Duke and Duchess, according to Bishop Percy's account, recognised him, and, 'as he was then perfectly known to them both, they enquired of him the Bath news of the day; and imagining there was some mistake, endeavoured by easy and cheerful conversation to prevent his being too much embarrassed, till, breakfast being served, they invited him to stay and partake of it'. Fortunately or unfortunately, this invitation recalled Mr. Oliver Goldsmith—for it was he—to a realisation of his surroundings, and blushing to his eyes, he explained that he thought he was in the house of his friend Lord Clare (who lived next door to the Duke and Duchess, at No. 11), and withdrew from the room in a state of great confusion and flurry, pursued by invitations to dine with the Duke and Duchess.

But though, at this late hour, Mr. Oliver Goldsmith was still in a dreamland of his own, another ghost had been up betimes, and, hours before Mr. Goldsmith's embarrassing adventure, was writing a letter full of gossip from her house in Batheaston, two miles from Bath.

'Those who deal in the small wares of scandal', wrote Mrs. Scott, the sister of Elizabeth Montagu, 'will not want subjects.

'Miss Hunter, daughter to Orby Hunter, has lately furnished a copious topic. . . . She and Lord Pembroke, in spite of winds, waves, and war, left this kingdom for one where they imagined they may love with less molestation, where they cannot see a wife weep nor hear a father rage. They set off in a storm better suited to travelling witches than

flying lovers, but were so impeded by the weather, that a
captain sent out a boat and took the lady prisoner; but after
he had set her on shore, he found that, as she was of age, it
was difficult to assume any lawful authority over her, and,
having spent a night in tears and lamentations, she was
restored to Lord Pembroke. . . . His lordship resigned his
commission to his place of lord of the bedchamber, and
wrote a letter to Lady Pembroke, acknowledging her charms
and virtues and his own baseness (an unnecessary thing,
since the latter she must long have known, and was probably not absolutely ignorant of the former), but assuring
her Miss Hunter was irresistible; that he never intended to
return to England, and had taken care that £5,000 should be
paid her yearly. As Lady Pembroke is so handsome and
amiable, perhaps his conduct will be seen by the world in a
true light without any fashionable palliations. A report was
spread, that they were taken by a privateer, but I can hear of
none but of a very different capture—the clay-cold corpses of
Lord and Lady Kingstone, which were on their way to England for interment.'

Subsequently, to everybody's surprise and disgust, after
Miss Hunter had, actually, been captured and returned to
her father, who refused to receive her (with the result that
she went abroad, once more, with Lord Pembroke), that
gentleman wrote and asked Lady Pembroke to join them in
their retreat. And, wrote Horace Walpole, who was much
shocked, 'she, who is all gentleness and tenderness, was
with difficulty withheld from acting as mad a part from goodness as he had acted from madness and folly'. As for Mrs.
Scott, she, more interested than ever (and in possession of
more details), explained in another letter that 'Lord Pembroke, after he got to Holland, wrote to his lady to desire
her to come to them, assuring her that Miss Hunter would
be assiduous in her endeavours to oblige her, and that they
should form a very happy society, if she would bring over

her guitar, two servants who play on the French horn, and his dog Rover. This polite invitation she, Emma-like, was exceedingly ready to comply with, but the Duke of Marlborough had rather too much sense to permit it. His lordship has since written her word, he shall never be happy till he lives with her again. Absurd as all this is, it is certainly fact, and some add, that he has advised Miss Hunter to turn nun! To be sure he best knows how fit she is to take a vow of chastity! That he may by this time wish that she would take any vow that might separate her from him, is, I think, very probable.'

Eventually, and, I imagine, to the disappointment of everybody, Miss Hunter took vows, not as a nun, but as a wife, marrying a very respectable general and dying in the odour of sanctity.

Meanwhile, Horace Walpole—that strange, shrivelled, kind-hearted creature, with his acrid wit and his hatred of cruelty, his powers of affection and his talent for insincerity, his love of objects of virtu, and his terrible taste in architecture (he thought Hardwicke Hall ugly), his belief that Reynolds could not paint women, and that Mr. Anstey was as fine a poet as Dryden, his habit of entering a room as though he were stepping on a wet floor, and with his hat crushed between his knees—was complaining passionately to the Honourable Henry Seymour Conway (the clock has struck 1766) about Bath and the inhabitants thereof. He had, it seemed, a headache, and the waters had made him giddy. He disliked the place extremely, and was disappointed in it.

'Their new buildings that are so much admired, look like a collection of little hospitals; the rest is detestable; and all crammed together, and surrounded with perpendicular hills that have no beauty. The river is paltry enough to be the Seine or Tiber, Oh, how unlike my lovely Thames'. But these were not Mr. Walpole's only troubles, for he had met Lord

Chatham's coach, only the day before, full of such 'Grenville-looking children' that he had determined not to go to see him 'this day or two'. (According to Miss Berry, 'he disliked being in company with children, to whom he was little accustomed'). Nor was this all. For in the lodging next to Mr. Walpole there was a gentleman 'whom Mr. Walpole had not seen for some years; and he is grown either mad or superannuated, and talks without cessation or coherence; you would think all the articles in a dictionary were prating together at once'. And Mr. Walpole told George Montagu, the husband of Elizabeth Montagu, that he was tired to death of the place, and that he sat down by the waters of Babylon and wept whenever he thought 'of thee oh Strawberry'. Also he could not imagine what he would do when Mr. Chute, who was to stay with him till Tuesday, had gone, 'for I cannot play at cribbage by myself and the alternative is to see my Lady Vane open the ball, and glimmer at fifty-four'. Then he was afraid of Mr. Montagu's 'noble cousins at Badminton', and as for Prior Park, he could not go there either, because Mrs. Allen was just dead, and Warburton entered upon the premises.

'Adieu', he exclaimed in despair. 'These watering-places, that mimic a capital, and add vulgarisms and familiarities of their own, seem to me like abigails in cast gowns, and I am not young enough to take up with either.'

A short time afterwards, Mr. Walpole took great exception to the hills round Bath, and complained to Mr. Montagu that 'they run against one's nose'. He had been, however, to dine with 'an agreeable family, two miles from Bath, a Captain Miller and his wife, and her mother, Mrs. Riggs'. (This was at the village of Batheaston, which was the home, also, of Mrs. Scott.) 'They have', said Walpole, 'a small new-built house, with a bow window, directly opposite to which the Avon falls in a wide cascade, a church behind it in a vale, into which two mountains descend, leaving an opening into the distant country. A large village, with houses of gentry, is on one of the hills to the left. Their garden is little, but pretty, and watered with several small rivulets among the bushes. Meadows fall down to the road, and above the garden is terminated by another view of the river, the city, and the mountains. 'Tis a very diminutive principality, with large pretensions.'

Eventually, it transpired, Mr. Walpole found there was something wrong with Captain and Mrs. Miller too, like everything in or near Bath, for after they had travelled on the Continent: 'Alas!' complained Mr. Walpole, 'Mrs. Miller is returned a beauty, a genius, a Sappho, a tenth muse, as romantic as Mademoiselle de Scudéry, and as sophisticated as Mrs. Vesey. The Captain's fingers are loaded with cameos, his tongue runs over with virtue; and that both may contribute to the improvement of their country, they have introduced *bouts rimés* as a new discovery. They hold a Parnassus fair every Thursday, give out rhymes and themes, and all the flux and quality of Bath contend for the prizes. A Roman vase decked with pink ribbons and myrtle, receives the poetry, which is drawn out every festival. Six judges of these Olympian games retire and select the brightest compositions, which the respective successful acknowledge, kneel to Mrs. Calliope Miller, kiss her fair hand and are crowned by it with myrtle. The collection is printed, published—yes; on my faith, there are *bouts rimés* on a buttered muffin, by her grace the Duchess of Northumberland, receipts to make them by Corydon the Venerable alias George Pitt, others, very pretty, by Lord Palmerston, some by Lord Carlisle; many by Mrs. Miller herself, that have no fault but wanting metre. . . . There never was anything so entertaining or so dull.' . . . It must be said, however, that Miss Seward declares that the proceeds of the books were applied to the 'benefit of a charity at Bath, so that Lady Miller's institute' (Captain Miller had been knighted) 'was not only calculated to awaken and cultivate ingenuity, but to serve the purposes of benevolence and charity'.

The cultivation of ingenuity had not, however, fortunate results, as a rule; for the growth of Miss Seward's poetic powers, for instance, were 'awakened' at Batheaston. Not only this: but 'On one occasion', says Dr. Doran, in his book about Elizabeth Montagu (*A Lady of the Last Century*), 'some scandalous verses were dropped into the vase, the reading of which in the very first lines called up blushes on the cheeks of the modest, and caused suspicion to rest on the rather audacious Christopher Anstey. "An enemy hath done this", was the sum of the general comment.' Dr. Doran adds, gloomily, 'Lady Miller's death soon followed'.

Opinions about Lady Miller seem to have been divided, for Madame d'Arblay, some years later (in 1780), complained in her Diary and Letters that she was 'a round, plump, coarse-looking dame of about forty, and while all her aim is to appear an elegant woman of fashion, all her success is to seem an ordinary woman in very common life, with fine clothes on. Her movements are bustling, her air is mock-important, and her manners inelegant.' Madame d'Arblay does, however, give her credit for good-nature and a wish to be civil. But neither of these qualities could appease Dr. Johnson, who disapproved of the poetic contests, and said so, with his usual firmness. Mr. Boswell tried to stand up to the Doctor in this matter, but with the usual results:

'*Bouts rimés*', said Dr. Johnson, 'is a mere conceit, and an *old* conceit now, I wonder how people were persuaded to write in that manner for this lady.' 'I named', said Boswell, 'a gentleman of his acquaintance who wrote for the Vase.'

Johnson. 'He was a blockhead for his pains.'

Boswell. 'The Duchess of Northumberland wrote.'

Johnson. 'Sir, the Duchess of Northumberland may do as she pleases; nobody will say anything to a lady of her high rank. But I should be apt to throw ——'s verses in his face.'

Fashionable Intelligence

No wonder that Horace Walpole, who was accustomed, as a rule, to a very different type of blue-stocking from Lady Miller—such enchantresses, for instance, as Elizabeth Montagu (whom even Doctor Johnson tolerated and admired)— was vexed and bored by the literary pretensions of Batheaston. For nothing pleased him, either at Bath or in the neighbourhood of Bath, excepting Mr. Anstey's *New Bath Guide*, about which immortal work Mr. Walpole assured George Montagu that 'so much wit, so much humour, fun and poetry, so much originality, never met together before. Then the man has a better ear than Dryden or Handel. *A propos* to Dryden, he has burlesqued his Saint Cæcilia, that you will never read it again without laughing. There is a description of a milliner's box in all the terms of landscape, *painted lawns and chequered shades*, a moravian ode, and a methodist ditty, that are incomparable, and the best names that ever were composed. I can say it by heart, though a quarto; and if I had time, would write it you down, for it is not yet reprinted, and not one to be had.'

We can see, from this letter, that, although Mr. Walpole was difficult to please in some matters, nobody was more easy to please in others. The man who had a better ear than Dryden or Handel, at the time of the publication of this masterpiece, was a country squire of the age of forty-two, and had spent the last few years of his life in roaming between the House of Commons (he had been elected to this, but I do not know that he ever said or did anything noteworthy within its portals), his estate at Trumpington, and his house at Bath. The date of his arrival is not known with any certainty, but Mr. Peach believes it to have been the year 1764. The house which he occupied first, was near St. James's Square, but in 1770, years after his genius had dazzled Mr. Walpole, he bought No. 5 Royal Crescent, and lived there, in patriarchal style, with his wife (of whom Mrs. Montagu remarked that she was a very sensible, amiable woman, and

did not deal in the gossip of the place), and his thirteen
children. Mr. Anstey was, according to Mrs. Montagu, very
droll and amusing; he was, as well, much occupied in teach-
ing his sons Greek and Latin, so that they should be fitted
for the upper forms of Eton school, where their education
was to be finished.

The *New Bath Guide*, Mr. Anstey's masterpiece, is composed with the most complete artlessness. It has been claimed
for Mr. Anstey, that his use of this measure influenced
Moore, Hood, and Barham. I can see no reason why it
should have influenced anybody with the smallest gift for
verse, and it is inconceivable that Barham, who was, compared with Anstey, what a circus-rider is compared with an
elderly lady riding a donkey on the sands, should have been,
in any way, affected by this verse. It is fairly amusing to
read—once—but is quite incompetent. His parody of Milton
is particularly unfortunate.

> 'Whether thou in Lace and Ribbons
> Choose the Form of Mrs. Gibbons,
> Or the Nymph of smiling Look,
> At Bath yclept Janetta Cook.
> Bring, O bring the Essence Pot,
> Amber, Musk and Bergamot,
> Eau de Chypre, Eau de Luce,
> Sans Pareil, and Citron Juice.
> Nor thy Bandbox leave behind,
> Fill'd with Stores of ev'ry kind;
> All the enraptur'd Bard supposes,
> Who to Fancy Odes composes;
> All that Fancy's self has feign'd
> In a Band-box is contain'd:
> Painted Lawns, and chequer'd Shades,
> Crape, that's worn by love-lorn Maids,
> Water'd Tabbies, flow'r'd Brocades,

Vi'lets, Pinks, Italian Posies,
Myrtles, Jessamin, and Roses,
Aprons, Caps, and Kerchiefs clean,
Straw-built Hats, and Bonnets Green,
Catgut, Gauzes, Tippets, Ruffs,
Fans and Hoods, and feather'd Muffs,
Stomachers, and Paris nets,
Ear-Rings, Necklaces, Aigrets,
Fringes, Blonds, and Mignionets;
Fine Vermillion for the Cheek,
Velvet Patches a la Grecque.
Come, but don't forget the Gloves,
Which, with all the smiling Loves,
Venus caught young Cupid picking
From the tender Breast of Chicken;
Little Chicken, worthier far
Than the Birds of Juno's Car;
Soft Cythereas' Dove,
Let thy Skin my Skin improve;
Thou by Night shalt grace my Arm,
And by Day shalt teach to charm.'

These verses have such a strange and jaded flavour now,
that it is scarcely possible to believe that they were once a
record of life. Mr. Anstey had, however, some talent for in-
venting names for persons; he is the creator, for instance, of
Lady Pandora MacScurvey, of General Sulphur, of Master
Marmozet, and, above all, of Captain Cormorant, whose
name might have been an *alias* for the remarkable Captain
Thicknesse, whom we shall meet in the next chapter.

CHAPTER XII

Society in Bath

THE FLYING, DARTING SUN-MOTES, HAPPY AND quick as the moments that are passing, the moments that cast shadows cold as the leaves on the youngest and loveliest face, are tired of the deep shadows of the room where Marshall Wade is lying dead—shades that are dark as those cast by a magnolia tree. They are flying away, and are playing upon the faces of the young ladies who are riding on horseback, away into the green distance.

The bright, light glancing forms, the polished speed of the horses, brush aside the dark and glittering branches, till showers of trilling dew fall upon them, from the thickly feathered leaves. The young ladies' hair seems like the white clouds of spring, beneath the happy darkness of the branches. Soon, those young forms, those young faces, that bright hair, will be rendered immortal, for ever youthful, beyond old age, beyond death, by a young man who will come to live in the room where Marshall Wade is lying.

Ten years later—in 1758—Captain Philip Thicknesse, who, according to his own later description of himself, was 'late Governor-General of Landguard Fort, and unfortunately the father of Lord Audley', was in a bustling state of self-importance. For had he not persuaded his young friend Mr. Thomas Gainsborough, whom he had met at Ipswich, to live in Bath (at No. 14 the Churchyard, the house in which Marshall Wade had died), and had he not offered Mr. Gainsborough his own head 'to be held up as the decoy duck', so that other sitters might be induced to buy portraits.

Captain Thicknesse claimed to be 'the first man who perceived, through clouds of bad colouring, what an accurate eye he, Gainsborough, possessed, and the truth of his drawings'; he therefore had 'dragged him from the obscurity of a country town at a time when all his neighbours were as ignorant of his great talent as himself'. When Captain Thicknesse had performed this feat, and had held his own head up as a decoy-duck, he found that 'the first sitting (not above fifteen minutes) is all that has ever been done to it . . . business came in so fast'.

Thomas Gainsborough's charges for portraits can scarcely be said to have been exorbitant; at first, that charge was five guineas, then so swift was his fame, and so many the demands, it became eight guineas—then forty guineas for a half-length, and one hundred for a full length.

During the sixteen years which Gainsborough spent in Bath, he painted Lady Spencer and her daughter (afterwards the Duchess of Devonshire), Lord and Lady Ligonier, Lord Campden, the Duke of Argyll, Lady Grosvenor, Lady Sussex, the Duke of Cumberland and, perhaps (but this is not certain), Lord Chesterfield and the Duke of Bedford. He painted as well, the odd Mrs. Macaulay, several portraits of Garrick and of his friend Henderson, Foote, Quin, the Misses Linley, and Graves; also (it is believed by Sir Walter Armstrong), the Blue Boy, but this, again, is not certain.[1]

It is sad to think that Mrs. Delany disapproved of his portraits, and said as much, in her Autobiography: 'This morning went with Lady Westmoreland to see Mr. Gains-

[1]He was not engaged in portrait-painting only; but with some of his loveliest landscapes. He enjoyed, for instance, painting Hampton Rocks, just outside Bath, and an elm tree, near the road from Bath to London, which was known, from that time, as Gainsborough's Elm.

borough's pictures (the man that painted Mr. Wise and Mr. Lucy), and they may well be called what Mr. Webb unjustly says of Rubens—they are splendid impositions.'[1]

The man who painted splendid impositions, was, though given to shyness with people he did not know well, of a very friendly nature, and had, like most painters, a gay disposition. He was, therefore, much liked by his sitters, and became on terms of great friendship with several of these, and especially with Garrick, Henderson, and old Mr. Quin, who left him fifty pounds in his will. The fussy and querulous Captain Thicknesse, who was not a favourite with Mrs. Gainsborough, spent as much time as he could spare from quarrelling, in Gainsborough's company, and was never tired of boasting about this, and of telling anecdotes to prove it. For instance: 'After returning from the Concert at Bath near twenty years ago', (this was written in 1788), 'where we had been charmed by Miss Linley's voice, I went home to supper with my friend, who sent his servant for a bit of clay from the small beer barrel, with which he first modelled, and then coloured her head, and that, too, in a quarter of an hour, in such a manner that I protest it appeared to me even superior to his paintings. The next day I took a friend or two to his house to see it, but it was *not* to be seen; the servant had thrown it down from the mantelpiece and broke it.' (*A Sketch of the Life of Thomas Gainsborough.*)

In the end, however, Captain Thicknesse was, according to his version of the story, very badly treated by Mr. Gainsborough, whom he accused of having promised to make a present of a portrait of Capt. Thicknesse, to that gentleman's wife, on the lines of exchange and barter—she having sent him a valuable musical instrument in expectation of receiving the portrait.

What, then, can have been Capt. Thicknesse's feelings when, after a great deal of fussing and a great many importunities on his part, and after many delays, his friend sent her no more than a hasty sketch? Captain Thicknesse very naturally returned this, with 'a few reproachful lines'. Gainsborough's family declared that the instrument had been paid for, and that Gainsborough had never promised to paint Captain Thicknesse. Knowing Capt. Thicknesse, one can form some kind of idea of what 'the few reproachful lines' were like; in any case, on receiving them, Gainsborough was so enraged that he left Bath for London immediately, only returning to Bath in order to shut up his house, pack up his belongings, and inform Captain Thicknesse that he had no intention of living in Bath any longer. Whereupon that 'persistent patron' (as Monsieur Barbeau called him) succeeded in persuading himself that all Gainsborough's future success in London was due to his recommendations. 'I was much alarmed lest with all his merit or genius he might be in London a long time before he was properly known to that class of people who could *essentially* serve him. . . . I therefore wrote to Lord Bateman, who knew him, and who admired his talents, stating the above particulars, and urging him, at the same time, for both our sakes, to give him countenance and make him known. His Lordship, for me, or both our sakes, did so, and his remove from Bath to London proved as good a move as it was from Ipswich to Bath.'

Monsieur Barbeau remarks, rather unkindly, that 'If this service was really rendered, it was probably unknown to Gainsborough; he had, indeed, little need of such a passport; his fame, which had spread from Bath throughout the United Kingdom, was already a national boast'.

Captain Thicknesse seems to me, at this safe distance, to have been a fascinating character, but Mr. E. Peach[1] cannot believe that he had one single redeeming trait, unless he was sincere in his professions of love for his brother Ralph, who

[1]Cf. *Historic Houses in Bath*, Simpkin, Marshall & Co.

'died suddenly while performing some of his own music at a Concert in Bath'.

Captain Thicknesse, who was born in 1719, and was the third son of the Reverend Ralph Thicknesse, of Farthinghoe, Northamptonshire, began by joining the Marines, in which he rose to the rank of Captain. He was then in about the year 1750 made Governor of Landguard Fort, on the coast of Suffolk, through the influence of his family, and proceeded to quarrel with everybody. He began by quarrelling with Colonel Vernon, who commanded a regiment of Volunteers in the district. Having won this battle, and drawn the Secretary of War, Charles Townshend, into his campaign—(it seems that, originally, the Captain was in the right)—he showed Townshend's private letter to everybody concerned (or unconcerned) in order to prove his victory. Then, having the advantage of living exactly opposite to the Colonel, at Landguard, he erected a wooden gun crowned by lines reflecting upon the Colonel's bravery, facing the Colonel's house, in order that that gentleman could not look out of window without seeing it. Finally, when the Colonel stood for Parliament, Captain Thicknesse uttered such libels upon him, contained in handbills, that the long-suffering Colonel sued him, and Captain Thicknesse was not only fined, but imprisoned for a year. This encounter with the law does not seem, however, to have damped his ardour in the least. In the end (the year was 1763) he retired from his position as Governor of Landguard Fort, with, as he explained, 'a recompense of two thousand four hundred pounds from the present possessor, Captain Singleton'.

During Captain Thicknesse's Governorship of Landguard Fort, he had divided his time between his charge and Bath, where, at that time, he occupied No. 6 Walcot Terrace; and afterwards 9 Royal Crescent; from there he moved to The Lodge, Bathampton, and finally to a house named The Hermitage. Now, having resigned his charge, he could give his undivided attention to Bath, where he stirred up a considerable amount of excitement, and unending quarrels.

Captain Thicknesse married often, and, for the most part, under remarkable circumstances. His first wife, whom he met when he was forty-two years old (one year before he left Landguard Fort), was a rich young lady of the name of Lanove. And Captain Thicknesse, being wise in his generation, and realising that her family would never allow her to marry him (and obtain possession of her money) unless he first involved her in a scandal, entered into a feigned marriage with her, so that her parents were only too glad to hurry on a real marriage at whatever cost. This lady bore him three daughters, and then died (with two of her daughters) of a disease called 'Pelham sore throat'.

Captain Thicknesse, soon afterwards, met a rich widow named Concanen, whose husband, Matthew Concanen, had been impertinent to Pope in a paper called the *Speculatist*, and had met with his reward, for he was immortalised in the lines:

> 'Cook shall be Prior, and Concanen Swift,'

and

> 'True to the bottom see Concanen creep
> A cold, long-winded native of the deep.'

Mrs. Concanen was very rich, but Captain Thicknesse could, at the moment, think of no plan by which he might induce her to share her fortune with him. At last, however, one of His Majesty's Judges, anxious to help the cause of virtue, suggested to him that, should he insinuate himself into the widow's house, which was in South Parade, at night time, and then, putting on his nightcap, look out of the widow's bedroom window when the walks were full of company, the widow would, without a doubt, accept his proposal of marriage with alacrity. Captain Thicknesse lost no time in following the Judge's suggestion, which would, no doubt, have met with the desired results, had not Captain

Thicknesse, immediately afterwards, met Lady Elizabeth
Touchet (sister of the Earl of Castlehaven and Baron Audley,
and heiress to the latter title), and decided to marry her
instead. But he thought the story of the widow too good a
joke to be lost, and took every opportunity of telling it: 'So I
left the widow to finish her second mourning', he explained
with his usual delicacy, 'and was soon after married to Lady
Elizabeth Touchet.'

No wonder that the virtuous Captain Thicknesse, shocked
by the cynicism of the world in which he lived, wrote (in
The New Prose Guide) . . . 'The very actions which youth and
innocence naturally lead the honest, unsuspicious, often the
best-hearted women into, are construed into vices of the
deepest dye. The most wicked insinuations are thrown out,
under the specious appearance of friendship; and when the
subject is prepared to receive the variolous matter, it is
poured forth with such torrents, that the contagion spreads
far and wide; the domestic happiness of whole families is
disturbed, to give place, and fortune, to these hellish gamblers, who by one infernal coup de main break through the
bonds of all faith, honour and honesty.'

Lady Elizabeth Touchet provided her husband with two
sons, George and Philip (who became, as soon as they were
of an age capable of quarrelling or of being quarrelled with,
a source of constant interest to their father), and two daughters, both of whom were sent to nunneries in France.

Captain Thicknesse, as soon as the younger son had
attained his seventeenth year, arranged and staged a highly
satisfactory quarrel between the two brothers, and, in the
interests of virtue, took the younger son before magistrates
to swear that his elder brother had set him upon a runaway
horse with the intention of killing him and inheriting his
fortune—a wicked story, which had, quite undoubtedly,
originated in the mind of Captain Thicknesse, and which
was proved, afterwards, to be a lie. Then, after a while, to the

Captain's great discomfiture, the brothers became friends; and from that time their indignant father could think of nothing bad enough to say about either of them. He was, in addition, grieved that he could not possess himself of their fortunes. For years, a guerilla warfare was carried on. Eventually, Captain Thicknesse brought off a master coup of strategy. He was, by now, living at 'The Hermitage', a property which was situated between the west wing of Lansdown Crescent and Somerset Place, and rendered cheerful by the fact that he had buried his last surviving daughter by his first marriage, in the grounds. His younger son, hearing that his father intended to live abroad, offered to buy the property for £500; but, being only eighteen years old, he was not, as yet, in possession of his fortune, and so gave his father an acceptance for this sum. A short while after, having obtained the money in question, he paid Captain Thicknesse the £500, but presented him with an extra £100. He must, therefore, have been a little surprised when, some years after, having spent large sums of money upon the house, and having offered to allow his father to rebuy the house on the repayment of the £500, that old gentleman produced the original acceptance, with a flourish, and denied that he had ever been paid.

Captain Thicknesse was, however, not content with being a man of action. He was, as well, a man of letters, and wrote not only a *Sketch of the Life of Thomas Gainsborough*, but also a *Bath Guide*, in which he was painfully frank on the subject of Mrs. Catherine Macauley, the author of a *History of England*. In the end, being harassed by debt, he left Bath, to the relief of most of the inhabitants, and went to live in Boulogne with his third wife (she was a niece of Sir Richard Ford). This lady had the happiness of surviving her husband for thirty-two years; since in 1792, just as he was about to start on a journey to Italy, this remarkable old gentleman died, leaving a will which began thus:

Society in Bath

'I leave my right hand, to be cut off after my death, to my son Lord Audley; I desire it may be sent to him, in hopes that such a sight may remind him of his duty to God, after having so long abandoned the duty he owed to a father, *who once so affectionately* loved him.'

I do not know what Mrs. Catherine Macauley thought of Captain Thicknesse's attack upon her, but it is, at least, certain that she left Bath in the year in which it was written. Perhaps the 'extraordinary ovations from enthusiastic admirers' to which, according to Monsieur Barbeau, she was accustomed, may have enabled her to bear Captain Thicknesse's disapproval with fortitude. We hear, for instance, of her being paid 'a tribute of six odes and a gold medal in the presence of a brilliant and select company', on April the 2nd, 1777, the anniversary of her birth; and tributes of all kinds seem to have been not only accustomed but expected. Mrs. Macauley seems, for instance, to have received endless tributes from the Reverend Dr. Wilson (the son of Bishop Wilson). 'Here' (in No. 2 Alfred Street) 'they resided together', says Markland, 'and so enthusiastic was the divine's admiration of the authoress, that he actually placed her statue, adorned as the Goddess of Liberty, within the altar railing of the church of St. Stephen's, Walbrook, of which parish he was rector.' Alas, in the end Mrs. Macauley grew tired of this fervent admirer, and, at the age of fifty, married a young gentleman named Graham, aged twenty-one. Markland adds gloomily: 'The statue did not remain long, as it was taken down again by the statuary who erected it, at the doctor's instigation; whether from motives of revenge, on account of her marriage with Graham, or from fear, because the vestry was about to cite him before the tribunals, it is hard to say. Be it as it may, the Doctor, very soon after this transaction, sold the vault that he had built with the intention of there depositing her remains.'

Mr. Graham, the supplanter of Dr. Wilson in the affections

of Mrs. Macauley, was the younger brother of the notorious quack 'Dr. Graham', who treated his patients in the modern manner, by plunging them into mud baths, and who was in the habit of exhibiting Emma Lyons, afterwards Lady Hamilton, upon his invention 'the celestial bed', in the character of the Goddess of Health and Beauty, whilst the Doctor lectured to the large and enthusiastic audience on the virtues of both these desirable qualities.

It is sad to think that poor Mrs. Macauley's marriage with the younger Mr. Graham diminished her popularity. So much so, indeed, that what with Captain Thicknesse's attack upon her, and what with the ridicule passed upon her because of this untimely marriage, she was obliged to leave Bath, in 1778. Even kind Mrs. Elizabeth Montagu told her sister-in-law that 'had she married a great-great-grandson of one of the regicides'—this refers to Mrs. Macauley's splutterings about Liberty—'however youthful he had been, it would have been pardonable; but the second mate of a surgeon to an Indian man-of-war, of twenty-two, seems no way accountable. If ye Minerva she carried on the outside of her coach had been consulted, no doubt but the sage goddess, even in effigy, would have given signs of disapprobation.' As for Mr. Anstey, he wrote some verses on the subject, and put them into the vase at Batheaston; where they met with so great a success, that not only were they read to the Batheaston company twice, but Mrs. Montagu copied them out, and sent them to Mrs. Robinson.

Two years before Mrs. Macauley's hasty departure from Bath, a lady who was, five years afterwards, to fall into the same disgrace as Mrs. Macauley, made a long stay in the city, with her first husband. Mr. and Mrs. Thrale were in the habit of visiting Bath; and on this occasion, a stout, elderly gentleman (whose costume, as a rule, consisted of a stock and wristbands, a wig called a Busby, but often wanting powder, a three-cornered hat, and a coat which was either of

dark mulberry colour or brown, 'inclining to the colour of
Scotch snuff'; large brass or gilt buttons, a black waistcoat,
and small-clothes which were sometimes of corduroy, black
stockings, and large easy shoes with buckles) might have
been seen rolling upon the conversation in Mrs. Thrale's
drawing-room, like a porpoise upon waves. Mrs. Thrale's
front door was as likely as not opened to visitors by the
black but learned Mr. Francis Barber, Doctor Johnson's negro
servant, who was born in Jamaica, and whom the Doctor
had contracted in some mysterious manner—largely because
his original master did not know how to dispose of him.

Doctor Johnson, on being made a present of the un-
wanted Mr. Barber, freed him immediately from his condition as slave, and made him his personal servant, though
nobody ever discovered in what Mr. Barber's services consisted, for, according to Hawkins:

'The great busby wig which, throughout his life, he
affected to wear, by that closeness of texture which it had
contracted and suffered to retain, was ever nearly as impene-
trable by a comb as a quickset hedge, and little of the dust
that had once settled on his outer garment was ever known
to have been disturbed by the brush.'

Mr. Francis Barber, when twenty-three years of age, was
sent by Doctor Johnson to a school in Northamptonshire,
with the recommendation to 'be a good boy', and in order
also that he might learn Latin and the fact that there was,
fundamentally, no difference between himself and the other
scholars excepting in the pigmentation of the skin. Unfortunately, the moment that Mr. Barber had received this
desirable education it worked havoc with his nervous system, his sense of injustice at being of a different colour to the
other scholars increased, and he contracted, as well, curious
ideas of freedom, so that he ran away from the Doctor twice,
in spite of their devotion to each other—once to serve in
an apothecary's shop, and once to sea. The Doctor was, on

this second occasion, obliged to spend a great deal of time and money in buying Mr. Barber out of the Navy, and restoring him to that 'nest of people in his house, where the lame, the blind, the rich, and the sorrowful, found a sure refuge from all the evils whence his little income could secure him'.

At Bath, however, Mr. Barber seemed fairly contented, and peace reigned, whilst even Mr. Boswell, who had followed the travellers, and was staying at the same tavern— 'The Pelican'—was snubbed very rarely.

The conversations at Mrs. Thrale's house in Bath must have astonished the more fashionable visitors a good deal, and the astonishment may have added to the awe in which they held the great man; for, as Boswell tells us, 'while talking, or even musing, as he sat in his chair, he commonly held his head to one side towards his right shoulder, and shook it in a tremulous manner, moving his body backwards, and rubbing his left knee in the same direction with the palm of his hand. In the intervals of calculating he made various sounds with his mouth, sometimes as if ruminating or what is called chewing the cud, sometimes giving a half whistle, sometimes making his tongue play backwards from the roof of his mouth, as if clucking like a hen, and sometimes protruding it against his upper gums in front, as if pronouncing quickly, under his breath, 'too, too, too'; all this accompanied sometimes with a thoughtful look, but more frequently with a smile. Generally, when he had concluded a period, in the course of a dispute, by which time he was a good deal exhausted by violence and vociferation, he used to blow out his breath like a whale. This, I suppose, was a relief to his lungs, and seemed in him to be a contemptuous mode of expression, as if he had made the arguments of the opponent fly like chaff before the wind.'

During the Doctor's walks to and from Mr. and Mrs. Thrale's house, which must have been as full of incident as were his visits to Mrs. Thrale's drawing-room, he, Mr.

Society in Bath

Boswell, and Mr. Barber were pursued by clouds of beggars, for the Doctor could never resist giving away every coin he found in his pocket. 'He loved the poor', said Piozzi, 'as I never yet saw anyone else do, with an earnest desire to make them happy. What signifies, says someone, giving half-pence to common beggars? They only lay it out in gin and tobacco. "And why", says Johnson, "should they be denied such sweetness of their existence? It is surely very savage to refuse them every possible avenue to pleasure, reckoned too coarse for our own acceptance. Life is a pill which none of us can bear to swallow without gilding; yet for the poor we delight in stuffing it still barer; and are not ashamed to show even visible displeasure, if ever the bitter taste is taken from their mouths."

'Doctor Johnson and his retinue came and went. Four years after their visit, Miss Frances Burney, fresh from the labours and the glories brought upon her by *Evelina*, spent the season in Bath, in Mr. and Mrs. Thrale's house, and surrounded by a constant stream of admirers. The household, indeed, can rarely have known an hour's quiet. (This was one of three visits made by Miss Burney to the city; long afterwards, when she was Madame d'Arblay, she lived there—from the end of 1815 to the middle of 1818; and it was in Bath that she died, in the year 1840).'

So great had been Mrs. Thrale's pleasure in the beauties of Bath that, after Mr. Thrale's death, a year after the visit paid by them to Mrs. Burney, she decided to live there, in No. 8 Gay Street, which had floral decorations, and had been built for Mr. Gay, who was member of Parliament for the city in 1727. Alas, there it was that she, no longer young, met youthful Mr. Piozzi, and shocked the city of Bath and called down on herself the condemnation of Doctor Johnson by marrying him. After this marriage the house in Gay Street seems to have been buzzing with parties from morning to night, and old Mrs. Piozzi was, according to one writer 'in a perpetual state of rampant senility'. Unfortunately, like many gay, good-natured, pleasure-loving and energetic people, she could not remember that her youth had passed, and we find her (in 1819) giving a grand ball in the Lower Rooms in honour of her eightieth birthday, and leading the dance with her nephew, Sir John Salusbury. I think this a charming incident, but it has met with much disapproval, like her marriage with poor Mr. Piozzi, against whom nothing could, with justice, be said. He was amiable, he had no designs upon his wife's money, and Mrs. Piozzi exercised an affectionate domination over him.

These ladies, then, were residents, but there were others, some with more beauty, others with more sense and greater wits, who arrived, in a flash of brilliance, like a humming-bird, and were gone again. There was, for instance, Mrs. Elizabeth Montagu, of whom even Doctor Johnson approved, although she quarrelled with him. 'Mrs. Montagu, sir, does not make a trade of her wit; but Mrs. Montagu is a very extraordinary woman; she has a constant stream of conversation, and it is always impregnated—it has always meaning.' . . . 'That lady exerts more *mind* in conversation than any person I ever met with. Sir, she displays such powers of ratiocination, such radiations of intellectual eminence, as are amazing.' Nor did Doctor Johnson stop at this, for, on one occasion, when he, accompanied by Mr. Boswell, had attended one of Mrs. Montagu's parties in London, when 'a splendid company had assembled, consisting of the most eminent literary characters', Mr. Boswell thought the Doctor 'seemed highly pleased with the respect and attention that was shown him, and asked him on our return home if he were not highly *gratified* by his visit. "No, sir", said he; "not highly *gratified*, yet I do not recollect to have passed many evenings with fewer objections".'

Mrs. Montagu, the friend of Horace Walpole, of Mrs. Garrick, of Burke—the lady who defied Voltaire when he delivered his notorious attack on Shakespeare—the lady who was called 'Fidget' by her intimates, who had a room, in her house in London, hung with tapestries made of feathers, and who gave an annual feast to the chimney-sweeps of London, found Bath pleasing but not exciting. Writing to her sister-in-law, Mrs. Robinson, after a visit to Bath, in June, 1779, she said: 'As I had not been to Bath since the Circus was finished and the Crescent begun, I was much struck with the beauty of the town. In point of society and amusement, it comes next, but after a long interval, to London. . . . I should dislike Bath much less, if the houses were larger. I always take the largest that can be got in the Circus or Crescent. On the outside it appears a good stone edifice; in the inside, it is a nest of boxes, in which I should be stifled, if the masonry were not so bad as to admit winds at many places. The society and mode of life are infinitely preferable to what one can find in any other country town, but much less agreeable than London. I believe if I were to act the part of Minos in this world, I should use it as a kind of purgatory to which I should send those who had not the taste or qualifications which deserved to be put into the capital city, nor were yet so disagreeably unsociable as to merit suffering the terrors and horrors of a long winter in this country.'

A year later, Mrs. Montagu had come to the conclusion that 'I consider, really life here as a mere dream. Some walk very gracefully, and talk very agreeably in their sleep; but a young man should not begin life by acting Le Sonambule. It is very well to do so between the acts of a busy drama, or, alas! as a farce, when the chief catastrophe is over, and the curtain is dropped between the *busy* world and us.'

Mrs. Montagu, though kindly, was rendered impatient both of stupidity and sluggishness, and sloppy morals irritated her to an equal degree; her wit was equalled by her perception, and she must have been, for shams of any kind, a terrifying companion. For instance, speaking of party politics, she remarked that they were 'pursued for the benefit of individuals, not for the good of the country. . . . the heads of politicians are very full of powder, and very empty of thought'. Her comments on acquaintances she made at the watering-places were as amusing as they were alarming. 'I think the Miss Allens sensible, and I believe them good: but I do not think the Graces assisted Lucina at her birth.' . . . And 'Lady Parker and her daughters make a very remarkable figure. One of the ladies looks like a state-bed running upon castors. She has robbed the valance and tester of a bed for a trimming.'

When at Bath, Mrs. Montagu seems to have spent most of her time in the company of the Primate, and the charming and good-natured Mr. and Mrs. Anstey. Mr. Anstey, in spite of his robust look, his rather rich-blooded, lively face, and his full figure, was just recovering from a shock, for Mrs. Montagu told her sister-in-law that 'he had arrived in London first to behold the horrors of the conflagration, and on his return back, his countenance bore the expression of horror, from the dreadful things he had beheld. He got back to Bath just in time to be present at the riots there.'

I imagine, too, that Mrs. Montagu occupied any time that was left vacant, with her 'great piece of feather-work', for which she had begged her sister-in-law, Mrs. Robinson's help: 'If you have an opportunity of getting me any feathers, they will be very acceptable. The brown tails of partridges are very useful, tho' not so brilliant as some others.' And Mrs. Scott, that lady whose wits were brighter than any feathers of partridge, or golden pheasant, or peacock, or parrot, floated in and out of her sister's lodging. But it was no unusual proceeding for Mrs. Scott to drive into Bath, since she lived at Batheaston, the Parnassus of Mrs. Calliope Miller, only two miles from that city.

On one occasion, rather earlier than this date (in 1777), Mrs. Scott had noticed, from time to time, a little lame child,

Scottish by birth, and aged between four and five years. Sometimes she saw him leaving his dame's school near the South Parade, where he had lodgings with his uncle (at No. 6), or driving over the Downs with Mrs. Home and the author of *Douglas*. Once, indeed, she saw him at the old Orchard Street theatre. *As You Like It* was being performed, and the innocent infant, in the course of the wrestling scene in the first act, shouted: 'Why! An't they brothers?' Alas, he was soon to be disillusioned on the subject of brotherly love, by 'a few weeks' residence at home' which convinced him, as he assured his readers in his Autobiography (he had, till then, lived, as an only child, in the house of his grandfather), 'that a quarrel between brothers was a very natural event'.

This melancholy knowledge did not, however, prevent Sir Walter Scott from remembering this first visit to the theatre with what seems to me a rather exaggerated, though touching, wonder; and, in his *Reviewal of the Life of John Kemble*, he records that wonder, very fully:

'There are few things', wrote Sir Walter, 'which those gifted with any degree of imagination recollect with a sense of more anxious and mysterious delight than the first dramatic representation which they have witnessed. The unusual form of the house, filled with such groups of crowded spectators, themselves forming an extraordinary spectacle to the eye which had never witnessed it before; yet all intent upon that wide and mystic curtain, whose dusky undulations permit us now and then to discern the momentary glitter of some gaudy form, or the spangles of some sandalled foot, which trips lightly within; then the light, brilliant as that of day; then the music, which, in itself, a treat sufficient in every other situation, an inexperience mistakes for the very play we have come to witness; then the slow rise of the shadowy curtain, disclosing, as if by actual magic, a new land, with woods, and mountains, and lakes, lighted, it seems to us, by another sun, and inhabited by a race of beings different from ourselves, whose language is poetry—whose dress, demeanour, and sentiments seem something supernatural—and whose whole actions and discourse are calculated not for the ordinary tone of every-day life, but to excite the stronger and more powerful faculties—to melt with sorrow, overpower with terror, astonish with the marvellous, or convulse with irresistible laughter:—all these wonders stamp indelible impressions on the memory. Those mixed feelings, also, which perplex us between a sense that the scene is but a plaything, and an interest which ever and anon surprises us into a transient belief that that which so strangely affects us cannot be fictitious; those mixed and puzzled feelings, also, are exciting in the highest degree. Then there are the bursts of applause, like distant thunder, and the permission afforded to clap our little hands, and add our own scream of delight to a sound so commanding. All this, and much, much more, is fresh in our memory, although, when we felt these sensations, we looked on the stage which Garrick had not yet left. It is now a long while since; yet we have not passed many hours of such unmixed delight, and we still remember the sinking lights, the dispersing crowd, with the vain longings which we felt that the music would again sound, the magic curtain once more arise, and the enchanting dream recommence; and the astonishment with which we look upon the elder part of our company, who, having the means, did not spend every evening in the theatre.'

Mr. Peach, who quotes this passage in his *Historic Houses in Bath and their Associations*, adds, with commendable restraint, that the infant was 'particularly struck with the stone figure of Neptune, which stood at that time near the South Parade ferry'.

CHAPTER XIII

The Theatre in Bath

AT THE END OF JANUARY, 1766, MR. JAMES
Quin, the famous actor, lay on his death-bed, in a
lodging-house in Pierrepont Street (the house, in
fact, which had once been occupied by Lord Chesterfield).
Mr. Quin was enfeebled by age, but in spite of this, and of
his irregular and forgetful habits, his last Will and Testa-
ment had been drawn up with the greatest care, and included
the following legacies: 'I give and bequeath unto Mr.
Thomas Gainsborough, Limner, now living at Bath, fifty
pounds'; it included, as well, a legacy to the kind landlady
who had looked after him with so much care: 'I give and
bequeath unto Mrs. Mary Simpson, landlady of the Centre
House, in Pierpont Street, in Bath, one hundred pounds; to
be paid by my executors into her own hands, independant of
all her creditors whatsoever'.

The seventy-three-year-old Mr. Quin had found his life in
Bath a quiet and peaceful ending to years of turmoil, excitement and splendour, wherein he had been hailed as the
greatest Falstaff of his age, had fought a duel and undergone
a trial for manslaughter, had been a friend of Pope and of
Swift, had (according to his biographer), 'during the course
of his acting, from his judgment in the English language,
and the knowledge of the history of Great Britain, corrected
many mistakes which our immortal bard Shakespeare had by
oversight, or by the volatileness of his genius, suffered to
creep into his works; he also changed many obsolete

phrases in his favourite poet'. . . . These corrections of the volatileness of Shakespeare's genius had produced the happiest results, inasmuch as (according to *The Life of James Quin*, published in 1766) 'The Prince of Wales, father to his present Majesty', chose that gentleman to instruct his children in the proper pronunciation of the English language; and, in the course of this instruction, they became so enthusiastic that 'His Majesty, with his brothers and sisters, represented several plays under Mr. Quin's tuition at Leicester House'. The narrative continues thus: 'Nothing could surpass the joy he felt, when he was from time to time informed of the virtuous and gracious disposition of his royal pupil, contemplating with pleasure the felicity of the nation under so good and just a prince; and upon being informed with what elegance and noble propriety His Majesty delivered his first gracious speech from the throne, he cried out in a kind of ecstasy, "Ay—I taught the boy to speak".' His Majesty, on his side, never forgot these lessons in elocution, and gave his old friend a pension.

Mr. Quin was not, however, so easily pleased on every occasion; for once, being called upon to announce the non-appearance of a certain actress and dancer, 'because she had dislocated her ankle', he added, thoughtfully: 'I wish it had been her neck'.

Mr. Quin was, apparently, a fine actor, although—and perhaps he can scarcely be blamed for this—when he was obliged to speak verse which has since, for more than one reason, been forgotten, the impressive nature of the verse was added to by a 'visible tear trickling down his cheek'. But these occasions were rare, for his gifts were, as a rule, confined to the work of Shakespeare; his speaking of Milton's verse was also, it appears, remarkable and impressive: 'A man of strong common sense, with an equal good humour and bad temper, fair and honest in his dealings, with too much sense of his own importance to prevent him from becoming, at moments, ridiculous, he walked, as well as talked, in blank verse' (according to his biographer). He was capable of great generosity and of a fine friendship. On hearing, for instance, that James Thomson, author of *The Seasons*, was imprisoned in a spunging-house for a debt of seventy pounds, Mr. Quin swaggered into his room, much to the discomfiture of poor Thomson, who had tried to conceal his wants, and informed his friend that he had come to sup with him, knowing perfectly well that Mr. Thomson had not enough money in his pocket to pay for a supper. After Mr. Thomson had endured a few moments' anguish on this score, Mr. Quin informed him that he had ordered the supper, and half a dozen bottles of claret, to be brought from a neighbouring inn. And, finally, when Mr. Quin and Mr. Thomson had finished the last glass to be drained from the half-dozen bottles of claret, Mr. Quin said, very gravely: 'It is time now we should balance accounts'. When the unhappy Mr. Thomson showed signs of returning apprehension Mr. Quin added: 'Mr. Thomson, the pleasure I have had in perusing your works, I cannot estimate at less than a hundred pounds, and I insist upon now acquitting my debt.' On saying this, he put down a note for that amount, and left the house without waiting for a reply.

This, then, was the kind of irascible, good-hearted old gentleman who, in order to hurt his friend, Beau Nash, was accused by the Beau's enemies of treachery towards him. During the sixteen years which Quin spent in Bath, he was, according to his biographer, 'without any interruption to his ease, contentment, pleasantry, and humour; though he was not without his calumniators, his satirists, and even his murderers; for he was many times put to death, even in the public papers, long before he really departed this life. . . . The witlings of Bath constantly buzzing about him, to catch each accent falling from his tongue, in order to pass it current for their own, were not content with robbing him of his wit, but more than once attacked his reputation; for not to mention the ridiculous reports of his marriage at church, where they would insinuate he had not been for many years, what but the highest pitch of malice could have framed the report which was spread of his design to supplant Beau Nash, during his life, as Master of the Ceremonies?'

Mr. Quin's loss to the stage was irreparable. That loss was occasioned by a quarrel with his old friend, Rich; and because of this, Mr. Quin, in spite of his contract with that gentleman, retired to Bath; but, after a time, his anger fading, he sent Mr. Rich the following letter:

'I am at Bath. Quin.'

The answer he received was:

'Stay there and be d—d. Rich.'

This cost the stage one of its greatest actors; but, in spite of his quarrel with Rich, Quin came to London from Bath, in 1749, to play the part of Othello in Covent Garden theatre, for the benefit of the sufferers from the fire in Cornhill. He returned, too, on other occasions, and especially to act the part of Falstaff for his old friend, Ryan; but, in 1754, having lost two of his front teeth, he refused to perform this yearly task, with firmness and propriety:

'My dear Friend', he wrote, 'There is no person on earth whom I would rather serve than Ryan, but, by G——, I will whistle Falstaff for no man.'

When Mr. Quin was in his earliest youth, the splendours to which he, and his fellow-actors, were accustomed in their performances at Drury Lane, were very great, as can be seen from this list of the properties of that theatre, published in *The Tatler* in 1709 (nine years before Mr. Quin's first appearance in public):

'Three Bottles and a half of lightning.

One Shower of Snow in the finest French Paper.

Two showers of a browner sort.

The Theatre in Bath

A Sea, consisting of a dozen large waves; the tenth bigger
  than ordinary, and a little damaged.
A dozen and a half of Clouds, trimmed with black, and
  well conditioned.
A Mustard bowl to make Thunder with.
The Complexion of a Murderer in a Bandbox; consisting
  of a large piece of burnt Cork, and a Coal black
  Peruke.'

Whilst Rowe tells us, but this time in verse, of other glories
to be found there:

'Hung on the self-same Peg, in union rest
Young Tarquin's Trowsers, and Lucretia's Vest,
Whilst without pulling Quoives Roxana lays
Close by Statira's Petticoat her Stays.

. . . .

Near these sets up a Dragon-drawn Calash,
There a Ghost's Doublet delicately slash'd,
Bleeds from the mangled Breast, and gapes a frightful
  Gash.
In crimson wrought the sanguine Floods abound,
And seem to gutter from the streaming Wound.
Here Iris bends her various painted Arch,
There artificial Clouds in sullen Order march,
Here stands a Crown upon a Rack, and there
A Witch's Broomstick by great Hector's Spear;
Here stands a Throne, and there the Cynick's Tub,
Here Bullock's Cudgel, there Alcidas' Club:
Beads, Plumes, and Spangles in Confusion rise,
Whilst Rocks of Cornish Diamonds reach the Skies.
Crests, Corslets, all the Pomp of Battle join,
In one Effulgence, one promiscuous shine.'

But in Bath, at the beginning of the century, no such
splendours as these were to be found; and the misery of the
strolling players that visited the town was very great.

The Theatre in Bath

The first theatre in Bath was built in 1705, on the site of the Mineral Water Hospital, at the top of Parsonage Lane. The cost of this building was £1,300, and was subscribed by various people of rank, whose coats-of-arms were, in consequence, painted on the interior walls. It was a small and wretched building, containing only one box, and this with accommodation for only four persons.

According to Fleming, the manager, in 1730, was a man named Hornby. People wishing to entertain their acquaintances would, very often, hire the theatre, and order the performance; and Lord Chesterfield in one of his letters speaks of one of these gala-performances, ordered by the Countess of Burlington, in which the audience consisted of seventeen persons. But a few days later, Mrs. Hamilton 'bespoke the play at night, which we all interested ourselves so much to fill, that there were as many people turned back as let in'. Beyond knowing that Farquhar's *Recruiting Officer*, Gay's *The Beggars' Opera*, and (according to *The Tatler*, 17th May, 1709) a play named *Alexander the Great* (probably Lee's *Rival Queens*, which bears this sub-title), there are no records of the plays performed in this dreary theatre.

At last the theatre was sold, and, for some time after this, the plays were acted in a room under the ball-room at Simpson's, at the Globe, or the George, Inns, or at a 'theatre' in Kingsmead Street, which, in the playbills, was called 'The New Theatre'. This consisted of a room about 25 feet wide and 50 feet long, with a gallery opposite the stage. But the attendance, though sparse, was magnificent in quality.

On the 16th July, 1750, we hear that on 'Thursday in the evening their Royal Highnesses (the Prince and Princess of Wales) drank tea at Ralph Allen's, Esqre., and afterwards went to the play, and saw *The Tragedy of Tamerlane* performed by Mr. Sinnett's Company, at the command of Lady Augusta'.

The play in question must have been performed at the New Theatre, for the Orchard Street Theatre was not opened

The Theatre in Bath

until July, 1750, and Simpson's Rooms were not used for theatrical performances until the beginning of that season. However, the list of plays performed in this theatre and in these rooms, included *Othello*, *The Merchant of Venice*, *Richard the Third*, *Romeo and Juliet*, Otway's *The Orphan*, Farquhar's *The Constant Couple*, Mrs. Centlivre's *The Gamester*, Steele's *The Conscious Lovers*, Addison's *Cato*, Gay's *Beggars' Opera*, Lee's *Theodosius*, and Southern's *Oronooko*. But as time went on the performances grew rarer and rarer, for the actors had drifted away, starved into nothingness.

Thirty pounds was the receipt of the fullest house, and the avaricious Lady Hawley, who was at that time in possession of Simpson's Rooms, was entitled to a third share of the profits, and one-fourth for the use of scenes and dresses. 'The standing expense [we are told by Mainwaring, in his *Annals of Bath*] was £2 10s. a night, which included music, attendants, bills, and tallow candles! The remainder was divided among twelve performers.' We may imagine the miserable character of the acting, and the wretchedness of the unhappy performers. But this misery and want was typical of the strolling players of this time, and Steele, in *The Spectator*, describes how 'Alexander the Great was acted in a paper Cravat; the next day the Earl of Essex seemed to have no Distress but his Poverty: and my Lord Foppington the same morning wanted any better means to shew himself a Fop than by wearing Stockings of different Colours'.

We may imagine the character of the acting in Bath, at this early time, from the reports remaining to us of celebrated actors in London. Verbruggen, for instance, who was the original Oronooko, was 'a fellow with a crackt voice, he clangs his words as if he spoke out of a broken drum'. Davies says of him that 'He was a little inkneed, which gave him a shambling gait', and he adds, in an ecstasy of admiration, 'Verbruggen was Nature without Extravagance—Freedom without Licentiousness, and Vociferous without bellowing'.

The Theatre in Bath

As for Mr. Betterton, another famous London actor of the time, *his* voice was 'low and grumbling, yet he could tune it by an artful climax, which enforc'd universal attention, even from the Fops and Orange Girls'.

The attractions offered in the Bath theatrical performances were not to be compared with these. But at last, in 1747, a London actor named Hippisley was seized with the wish to build a theatre in Bath, and an advertisement was sent to the Nobility and Gentry of Bath, informing them that:

> 'Plays are like mirrors made for men to see
> How B A D they are, how G O O D they ought to be.'

And announcing, furthermore, that:

'In all ages, and in all Countries, where Liberty and Learning flourish'd, the Stage never fail'd of receiving Sanction and Protection from the Great and Noble.

'Theatrical Performances, when conducted with Decency and Learning, have always been esteem'd the most rational Amusements, by the Polite and Thinking Part of Mankind. Strangers, therefore, must be greatly surpris'd to find at Bath Entertainments of this Sort in no better Perfection than they are, as it is a Place during its Seasons, honour'd with so great a Number of Persons, eminent for Politeness, Judgement and Taste; and where might reasonably be expected (next to London) the best Theatre in England.

'The present Play-House, or rather Play room, is so small and incommodious, that 'tis almost impossible to have Things done better in it than they are. The Profits arising from the Performance, as now conducted, will not support a larger, or better, Company of Actors. . . . And nothing can be more disagreeable than for Persons of the *first Quality*, and those of the *lowest Rank*, to be seated on the same bench together, which must be the Case here, *if the Former will Honour*, and the Latter have an Inclination, to see a Play.' (These italics are mine.)

240

The Theatre in Bath

'To remedy this, and for the better Entertainment of the quality it is humbly proposed to erect a Regular, commodious THEATRE, on the most convenient Spot of Ground that can be got; to be managed by Mr. *Hippisley* (who for many years has been a Performer in *London*) and Others; and to add such a sufficient Number of Good Performers to the present Company as will (it is hoped) never fail of giving Pleasure and Satisfaction to the most judicious Audience and greatly contribute towards making Bath the most agreeable Place in the Kingdom.'

Nothing could have been more tactfully worded, and the 'Persons of the First Quality who Honoured the Play' were pleased and gratified by the proposal, whatever 'Those who had an Inclination to see it' may have felt.

Unfortunately, Wood, who seems to have been interested in the building of the theatre, tells us that, less than a year after the idea sprang into being, Mr. Hippisley died. However, a certain brewer and chandler, John Palmer, inherited the idea, and built the theatre, which was opened in 1750, with the first part of Shakespeare's *Henry IV*. The theatre was called the Orchard Street Theatre, and was the scene of many triumphs, and much great acting, before, in time, it was changed from being a theatre into being the Masonic Hall.

The New Theatre, meanwhile, rivalled the Orchard Street Theatre as fiercely as possible, and, indeed, was able to show among the names of patrons, in the December preceding the opening of the Orchard Street Theatre, those of 'ten peers, nine peeresses, five earls' daughters, and fifteen baronets and knights'. (This information was culled from Mr. Beville S. Penley's *The Bath Stage*.)

The names of Mr. Dancer, Mr. Palmer, Mr. Morgan, Mr. Castle, Mr. Furnival, Mr. Brown, Mr. Brookes, Mr. Barrington, Mr. Fitzmaurice, Mr. Martin, Mr. Green, and Mr.

Falkner may be found among the play-bills of this time, as well as the names of Mrs. Green, Mrs. Clayton, Mrs. Mozeen, Mrs. Cowper, Mrs. Bishop, Miss Ibbott, Miss Lowe, Miss Hippisley, Miss Roche, Miss Goring, and Miss Helme—names which have drifted out of men's memories like the sounds of the music in the ball-rooms, names which are faded like the little dry leaves that drift over the ball-rooms' floors, after this long century.

The indefatigable Mr. Palmer (aided by his son) met with such success in his theatrical venture, that he enlarged the theatre in the year 1774 (or 1775) and added pillars of the Ionic and Doric orders, which, according to one enthusiastic admirer, were 'expressive of and bore analogy to the ornaments of the place'. In addition to these activities, the two Palmers were in the habit of visiting London in order to discover new actors for their theatre, and these visits produced an important result; for, struck with the slowness and inconvenience of the journey and of the postal communications—the latter were dependent on a cart with a single horse and a single driver, and formed an urgent invitation to highwaymen—so much so that the equipage rarely arrived in the state in which it started—the younger Mr. Palmer was seized with the idea of replacing this melancholy and useless vehicle by the system of post carriages which were used for transporting his theatrical companies from Bath to Bristol —in which last-named town he had acquired a theatre also. Mr. Palmer, therefore, proposed the use of mail-coaches, with a new system of relays; and, after having had some communications with the Government, he succeeded, after a great deal of difficulty, in seeing Pitt, and converting him to his plan. Upon the Government accepting this, Mr. Palmer became Superintendent and Comptroller-General of Posts, with a salary of £1,500 a year, and a percentage on the profits raised; and from this post he became Member of Parliament for Bath.

The Theatre in Bath

In October, 1722, Mr. Palmer was able to announce that a new young actor, appearing under the assumed name of Courtney, and introduced to him by Mr. Garrick, would take the part of Hamlet. 'When it was buzzed about in the Rooms, in the walks, and all over the city of Bath' (wrote Davies, in his *Genuine Narrative*) 'that a new actor was arrived from London under the patronage of the great Roscius, all people of whatever rank were eager to see the phenomenon. The house was soon filled, and he had the satisfaction to act Hamlet to a very brilliant audience.'

Thomas Gainsborough was amongst the audience that welcomed Courtney (whose real name was Henderson, and who became one of the greatest actors of the age) to Bath; and so much struck was he by the new actor's performance that he invited the young man to his house, painted his portrait, and they became intimate and lifelong friends.

Mr. Courtney's (or Henderson's) début as Hamlet met with such applause that, a few days later, it was decided that he should play in *Richard III.*; and after this, as Benedict, Macbeth, Bobadil, Bayes, Essex, etc., etc., until at last, in December, he decided to appear under his own name, in the character of Hotspur in *Henry IV*.

Mr. Henderson was sent to Bath by Mr. Garrick because the latter believed his voice would not carry in a large London theatre, and because (according to an undated letter from Cumberland to Garrick, written, probably, about the year 1774): 'Nature has not been beneficent to him in figure or in face; a prominent forehead, corpulent habit, inactive features, and not a quick eye'; nevertheless, Cumberland was bound to admit that 'He has great sensibility, just elocution, a perfect ear, good sense, and the most marking pauses (next to your own) I ever heard; in the latter respect it stands next to you' [Garrick], 'very near you. His memory is ready to a surprising degree.'

From 1772, the year of Henderson's appearance, until

1782, apart from the various plays by Shakespeare that were acted, we may find in the Play-bills the names of Ben Jonson's *Every Man in His Humour*, Beaumont and Fletcher's *Rule a Wife and Have a Wife*, and *Philaster*, an adaptation of Milton's *Comus*, Dryden's *The Spanish Friar*, Otway's *Venice Preserved* and *The Orphan*, Buckingham's *The Rehearsal*, Wycherley's *The Country Wife* and *The Plain Dealer*, Congreve's *Love for Love*, Farquhar's *The Beaux' Stratagem*, Vanbrugh's *The Provoked Wife* and *The Provoked Husband*, as well as Goldsmith's *She Stoops to Conquer*, young Mr. Sheridan's *The Rivals*, *A Trip to Scarborough*, *The School for Scandal*, *The Duenna* and *The Critic*.

The actual appearance of the stage (with the scenery, the management of stage crowds, the dresses, etc.) was, throughout the eighteenth century, remarkable. A pamphlet called *The Taste of the Town, or a Guide to all Public Diversions*, which was printed in 1731, announces that: 'I have known a tragedy succeed by the irresistible force of a squadron of Turkish turbans and scimitars, and another owe the whole of its merit to the graceful procession of a Mufti and a tribe of priests'. In 1757, the preface to a work named *Jeffery's Collection of Dresses*, proclaims that 'as to the stage dresses it is only necessary to remark that they are at once elegant and characteristic; and amongst many other regulations of more importance for which the public is obliged to the genius and judgment of the present manager of our principal theatre' (David Garrick) 'is that of the dresses, which are no longer the heterogeneous and absurd mixtures of foreign and ancient modes which formerly debased our tragedies by representing a Roman general in a full-bottomed peruke, and the sovereign of an Eastern Empire in trunk hose'.

The genius and judgment in question, resulted in David Garrick appearing (with some persistence) as Macbeth in a court suit of sky-blue and scarlet; another result, too, was that he was scolded by pamphleteers for 'disguising himself

The Theatre in Bath

[in John Home's *Tragedy of Douglas*] for a Grecian chief in the dress of a modern Venetian gondolier', and for introducing 'a Polish procession made up of white friars, with some other moveables, like a bishop, *des enfants de chœur*, nuns, etc.' into a play about ancient Sparta. Not content with these defiances of the Time Spirit, Garrick appeared as Othello (in 1765) in a full suit of gold-laced scarlet, a small cocked hat, knee breeches, and silk stockings which rendered a pair of gouty legs especially prominent. On another occasion, he acted the same part in a regimental suit of King George the II.'s bodyguard, with a flowing wig; whilst our old friend, Mr. James Quin, when *he* appeared as Othello, crowned his black face with a large powdered major wig. John Kemble acted the part of Hamlet 'suitably attired in a modern court dress of rich black velvet, with a star on his breast, the garter and pendant, riband of an order, mourning sword and buckles, with deep ruffles; the hair in powder, which in the scenes of feigned distraction flowed dishevelled in front over the shoulders'. The ladies were dressed in the same striking manner: Perdita, on one occasion, wore a pink lutestring dress covered with a white mignonet, a long stomacher, and a hoop festooned with flowers, whilst Mrs. Cibber, in 1753, attired herself for the part of Juliet in a full white satin dress with an enormous hoop.

These splendours were in existence in London; but we may feel sure that under Mr. Palmer's able management, the Bath theatre did not lose by comparison.

Henderson remained at Bath until 1777, appearing in most of the great rôles, both tragic and comic, and being greeted, invariably, with the same admiration. 'The continual practice I am in here', he wrote, on 24th October, 1772, 'is of great advantage to me—I once thought it a hardship to be forced upon so many characters. I think so now no longer, being convinced that every part I play, however unsuited to me, does me good. In London it would do me harm for this reason: there are computed to be thirty different audiences in London, here there are but two; and those who see me at a disadvantage one night, see me at an advantage the next.'

At last, in 1777, Henderson was invited to the Haymarket Theatre, where the enthusiasm he aroused was such that his manager gained £4,500 by the engagement, which lasted a little over a month.

There was, however, one person who was not pleased by Henderson's success, and that was David Garrick, who had written, in 1775: 'I have seen the great Henderson, who has something, and is nothing—he might be made to figure among the puppets of these times. His Don John is a comic Cato, and his Hamlet a mixture of tragedy, comedy, pastoral, farce, and nonsense. However, though my wife is outrageous, I am in the secret; and see sparks of fire which must be blown to warm even a London audience at Christmas—he is a dramatic phenomenon, and his friends, but more particularly Cumberland, has [*sic*] ruined him; he has a manner of pairing when he would be emphatic; that is ridiculous, and must be changed or he would not be suffered at the Bedford Coffee-house.'

In spite of Garrick's disapproval, however, it appears that Henderson was a really great actor. It was said of him that 'In the variety of Shakespeare's soliloquies, where more is meant than meets the eye, he has no equal'. He was finest, apparently, in the parts of Shylock and Falstaff, in which latter rôle he was believed, by contemporaries, to rank next to James Quin.

There may, perhaps, have been some personal reason for Garrick's disapproval of Henderson, although it is difficult to believe him capable of a petty resentment; for, although Henderson certainly does not connect Garrick's distaste for his acting with this event, he relates, in one of his letters, that Garrick, who one day heard him mimic certain contemporary actors—among them Barry, Woodward and Love—insisted that Henderson should imitate him also—which Henderson did at last with some reluctance, reproducing certain faults of Garrick's so minutely that the latter fell into a passion.

A year before Henderson's departure from Bath, he happened, for one reason or another, to find himself in Birmingham, and, after visiting the local theatre, wrote to Palmer, in a state of great excitement, that he had discovered 'an actress who never had had an equal, nor would she have a superior'. Unfortunately, Mr. Palmer's company was completed, for that season; but two years afterwards, he remembered Henderson's enthusiasm, and engaged the lady who had aroused it. This young actress had passed a few unhappy and unsuccessful months at Drury Lane Theatre, and had, at last, been dismissed by Garrick, whom she accused, afterwards, of malice towards her: 'Instead of doing me common justice . . . he rather depreciated my talents'. . . . And Horace Walpole explained to the Countess of Ossory, a little later, when Mrs. Siddons was famous, that she had complained that 'He did nothing but put her out; that he told her she moved her right hand when it should have been her left. In short, said she, I found I must not shade the tip of his nose.'

It was, therefore, in Bath that Mr. Henderson's discovery, the twenty-three-year-old Mrs. Siddons, gained her first success, free from the fear of casting a shadow upon Mr. Garrick's nose; and that success was gained by her début in Vanbrugh's *The Provoked Husband*. She tells us, in her Memoranda: 'I now made an engagement at Bath. There my talents and industry were encouraged by the greatest indulgence, and I may say, with some admiration. Tragedies, which had been almost banished, again resumed their proper interest; but still I had the mortification of being obliged to personate many subordinate characters in comedy, the first being by contract, in the possession of another lady. To this I was obliged to submit, or to forfeit a part of my salary, which was only three pounds a week. Tragedies were now becoming more and more fashionable. This was favourable to my cast of powers; and whilst I laboured hard I began to earn a distinct and flattering reputation. Hard labour indeed it was, for, after the rehearsal at Bath, and on a Monday evening, I had to go and act at Bristol [where Mr. Palmer owned a theatre, as we have seen already] on the evening of the same day, and reaching Bath again, after a drive of twelve miles, I was obliged to represent some fatiguing part there on the Tuesday evening. Meanwhile I was gaining private friends as well as public favour; and my industry and perseverance were indefatigable. When I recollect all this labour of mind and body, I wonder that I had strength and courage to support it, interrupted as I was by the cares of a mother, and by the childish sports of my little ones, who were often most unwillingly hushed to silence, from interrupting their mother's studies.'

Among Mrs. Siddons' new friends, Mr. Thomas Sheridan was to be found. This chameleon like old gentleman, who had started life as an actor, had then become manager of a theatre in Dublin, and after this a fashionable teacher of elocution in London, which latter profession was interrupted, from time to time, by Mr. Sheridan's need to live cheaply in France, or to seek the benefit of the law for the relief of insolvent debtors. His life was rendered exciting, too, by his quarrels with his old friend Doctor Johnson. Now at last, tired by all these occupations, he had come to settle in Bath, with his four children. Doctor Johnson's judgment of his friend was severe, but just. It is true that the Doctor, on hearing that Lord Bute had given Sheridan a pension of £200 a year, so that he might have leisure in which to compile his dictionary, had exclaimed: 'What! Have they given *him* a pension? Then it's time for me to give up mine!' But, relenting after a while, he added, 'However, I am glad that Mr. Sheridan has a pension, for he is a very good man'. Mr.

The Theatre in Bath

Sheridan furnished, too, an admirable opportunity for the Doctor to snub David Garrick, for when the latter advanced the theory that 'Sheridan has too much vanity to be a good man', Doctor Johnson countered it with: 'No, Sir, there is, to be sure, in Sheridan, something to reprehend and everything to laugh at; but, Sir, he is a good man. No, Sir, were mankind to be divided into good and bad, he would stand considerably within the ranks of the good.'

I do not know if this enthusiastic tribute was repeated to old Mr. Sheridan, but a great many of the same kind indubitably reached him, and produced a depressing effect; so that he was not, on the whole, sorry to leave London for Bath, in the year 1770—two years before the time when that strange, impetuous, hot-headed young man, his son Richard, eloped with the young and beautiful Elizabeth Linley to France. But that runaway, secret marriage, and the duels which followed, were far from the thoughts of old Mr. Sheridan when, 'Whilst at Bath for his health', Miss Lefanu tells us in her *Memoirs of the Life and Writings of Mrs. F. Sheridan*, 'he was strongly solicited to go to the play to witness the performance of a young actress who was said to distance all competition in tragedy. . . . He found, to his astonishment, that it was the lady who had made so little impression on him some years before in the *Runaway*, but who, as Garrick had secretly declared, was possessed of tragic powers sufficient to delight and electrify an audience. There prevailed at that time and long afterwards a very disagreeable clause in the articles of the Bath company, by which they were obliged to perform also at Bristol, and in consequence, by some mistake in their frequent and hurried journeys, the stage clothes of this admired actress were not arrived on the night Mr. Sheridan saw her, and she was obliged to perform in one of the dresses she usually wore in private life. But no disadvantage of dress could conceal her transcendental merit from an eye so penetrating as that of Mr. Sheridan, and after the play was over he went behind the scenes to get introduced to her, in order to compliment her. . . . Mr. Sheridan said, "I am surprised, Madam, that with such talents you should confine yourself to the country; talents that would be sure of commanding in London fame and success." The actress modestly replied that she had already tried London, but without the success that had been anticipated; and that she was advised by her friends to be content with the fame and profit she obtained at Bath, particularly as her voice was deemed unequal to the extent of a London theatre.' Immediately on his return to London, he spoke to the acting manager of Drury Lane, strenuously recommending her to him.

Years afterwards (in 1782) she was invited to return to Drury Lane Theatre, which was then under the management of the younger Sheridan. 'After my former dismissal from thence, it may be imagined', she wrote, 'that this was a triumphal moment.'

A benefit performance was arranged for Mrs. Siddons in the Bath theatre, on the night of the 21st May, 1782, and the tragedy performed (not without reason) was called *The Distressed Mother*, whilst Mrs. Sheridan declared her intention of reciting, at the end of the play, *A Poetical Address*, written by herself, in which she would explain to the audience her reasons for leaving Bath. The poem began as follows:

MRS. SIDDONS'S THREE REASONS

Have I not raised some expectation here?—
Wrote by herself?—What! authoress and player?—
True, we have heard her—thus I guess'd you'd say,
With decency recite another's lay;
But never heard, nor ever could we dream
Herself had sipp'd the Heliconian stream.
Perhaps you farther said—Excuse me pray,
For thus supposing all that you might say—
What will she treat of in this same address,

The Theatre in Bath

Is it to show her learning?—Can you guess?
Here let me answer—No: far different views
Possess'd my soul, and fir'd my virgin Muse;
'Twas honest gratitude, at whose request
Shamed be the heart that will not do its best.
The time draws nigh when I must bid adieu
To this delightful spot—nay ev'n to you—
To you, whose fost'ring kindness rear'd my name,
O'erlooked my faults, but magnified my fame.
How shall I bear the parting? Well I know
Anticipation here is daily woe.
Oh! could kind Fortune, where I next am thrown,
Bestow but half the candour you have shewn.
Envy o'ercome, will hurl her pointless dart,
And critic gall be shed without its smart,
The numerous doubts and fears I entertain,
Be idle all—as all possess'd in vain.—
But to my promise. If I thus am blessed,
In friendship link'd, beyond my worth caress'd—
Why don't I here, you'll say, content remain,
Nor seek uncertainties for certain gain?
What can compensate for the risks you run;
And what your reasons?—Surely you have none.
To argue here would but your time abuse:
I keep my word—my reason I produce—

Half-way through the Tragic Muse's recitation, therefore,
Master Henry, Miss Sally, and Miss Maria Siddons, who had
been hidden in their mother's dressing-room, were led on to
the stage, and Mrs. Siddons declaimed these lines:

These are the moles that bear me from your side;
Where I was rooted—where I could have died.
Stand forth, ye elves, and plead your mother's cause;
Ye little magnets, whose soft influence draws
Me from a point where every gentle breeze

The Theatre in Bath

Wafted my bark to happiness and ease—
Sends me adventurous on a larger main,
In hopes that you may profit by my gain.
Have I been hasty?—am I then to blame;
Answer, all ye who own a parent's name?
Thus have I tried you with an untaught Muse,
Who for your favour still most humbly sues,
That you, for classic learning, will receive
My soul's best wishes, which I freely give—
For polished periods round, and touched with art—
The fervent offering of my grateful heart.

These polished periods round, and touched with art, were received with enthusiasm, and the benefit performance yielded £145 18s.

On October the 10th she made her appearance at Drury Lane Theatre, at the salary of ten guineas a week; and in 1784, the weekly sum paid to this actress of whom Henderson had said 'she never had had an equal, nor would ever have a superior', was raised to twenty-three guineas and seven shillings.

And at this point we may leave Mrs. Siddons.

CHAPTER XIV

Some Men of War

AFTER THE DEATH OF BEAU NASH, A CERTAIN amiable kindly gentleman named Collett succeeded him, but, incapable of keeping order or of enforcing decent behaviour, he was only too glad, after two years of insubordination on the part of his subjects, to resign in favour of Mr. Derrick, who was a gentleman, an Irishman, the means of introducing Mr. Boswell to London, and the recipient, alternately, of the approval and disapproval of Doctor Johnson.

Mr. Derrick was, apparently, raised to the post of Master of the Ceremonies quite by chance—and that chance was not, for him, a fortunate one. It seems (according to the *Life of James Quin*) that Mr. Derrick, who was paying a haphazard visit to Bath, happened to compliment 'a certain noble lord in a poem'—for he had literary pretensions. The noble lord, on being praised in this manner, said, half-seriously, half-jokingly, 'Suppose we make D—— King of Bath'; whereupon two or three ladies who had been praised in the same poem, decided to take the proposal seriously, and, as a result of their efforts, Mr. Derrick became the King of Bath.

Unfortunately, although the new Master of the Ceremonies did his uttermost to be agreeable, he did not possess Beau Nash's gift for pleasing everybody; and matters went from bad to worse, until at last, when a certain party was given, a woman of fashion was omitted—because Mr.

Derrick had forgotten her existence. The wrath aroused by this forgetfulness was so extreme that the lady's partisans urged that Mr. Derrick was unfit for his duties and should be deposed. But, even in the midst of their wrath, his would-be deposers could not forget the beauty of their own manners, and called together a meeting in order to discuss the most elegant way in which to administer thanks for his services when dismissing him. Mr. Quin, who was an arbiter of good manners, and who understood the art of quarrelling politely better than anybody, was, very naturally, consulted, and remembering poor Mr. Derrick's minute stature—one of the characters in *Humphrey Clinker* compares him to Tom Thumb—replied, 'My lord, if you have a mind to put him out, do it at once, and clap an extinguisher over him!'

Mr. Derrick was, therefore, dethroned, and was supplanted for a time (according to the *Life of Quin*) by 'Monsieur ——, who, with all the abject servility and *outrée politesse* for which his countrymen are so celebrated, could not give so much satisfaction as his poetical predecessor'.

Mr. Derrick, meanwhile, occupied the time of his banishment in canvassing his former supporters, who had not forgotten the poem written in their praise; he produced, as well (being unable to forgive the use of the word 'extinguisher'), this melancholy verse:

AN EPIGRAM CORRECTED

'When Quin of all grace and all dignity void
Murdered Cato the Censor, and Brutus destroyed,
He strutted, he mouth'd; you no passion could trace
In his action, delivery or plum-pudding face;
When he massacred Comus the gay god of mirth
He was suffered because we of actors had dearth.
But when Foote with strong judgement and true genuine wit
Upon all his peculiar absurdities hit;

When Garrick arose, with those talents and fire,
Which nature and all the nine Muses inspire,
Poor Guts was neglected, or laughed off the stage.
So bursting with envy and tortured with rage;
He damned the whole town in a fury and fled,
Little Bayes an extinguisher clapp'd on his head.

· · · · · · · ·

Yet we never shall Falstaff behold so well done,
With such character, human, such spirit, such fun,
So great that we knew not which most to admire,
Glutton, parasite, pandar, pimp, letcher, or liar;
When he acted the part, his own picture he drew.'

It was now the turn of Mr. Quin to become violently angry—so much so, indeed, that Mr. Derrick grew frightened, and thought it better to placate him. This, however, was a difficult matter, and Mr. Derrick was beginning to despair, when he remarked, suddenly, old Mr. Quin's passion for the fish John Dory—(he was extremely gluttonous). John Dorys were not, at this time, in season, but, by some happy chance, Mr. Derrick had an acquaintance at Plymouth—a sailor. He wrote, therefore, to this sea officer imploring him 'not to fail upon his return to bring up as many John Dorys as he could possibly cram in the postchaise; to take particular care to have them of the best kind that could be got'; adding that he, Derrick, would 'make him any possible return in his power, as his future welfare entirely depended upon it'.

The story ends happily, for the 'sea-officer who was Mr. Derrick's correspondent, executed his commission so completely and arrived so critically at Bath with his cargo, at a time when there were no John Dorys to be had at any price in that part of the country, that Quin upon receiving the present, was perfectly reconciled to Mr. Derrick, and entirely forgave him for his satirical attempt in rhyme'.

Quin's biographer adds: 'Quin, having once professed a friendship for a person, never withdrew it, unless he had the most cogent reasons for his conduct; so that Derrick was now extremely elated with the prospect of Quin's protection, and therefore renewed with additional assiduity his application to the leading nobility of Bath, in order to be reinstated in his former office. Nor were his hopes groundless, for from the moment it was known that Quin had given him his suffrage, every one eagerly endeavoured to follow his example; and the little Monarch of Bath once more regained his throne.'

For five years, peace, or comparative peace, reigned, and nobody made fun of the uncrowned King's stature, or took inordinate liberties with his good-nature.

At the end of that time, however, he fell ill, and the war broke out afresh and with a new violence. Rival candidates, and their supporters, quarrelled openly across the dying man's bed; circulars, pamphlets, and letters urging the claims of one or the other would-be successor to Derrick, fell from the skies into every street, on to every gathering of fashionable people. The battles were public and undisguised, and when Derrick lay dead, they became even more indecent. One party urged the claims of a Major Brereton, the Vice-President during Derrick's illness; the other party supported Mr. Plomer, who was Manager of the Bristol balls. Mr. Plomer's supporters, practical in all things, raised seventy recruits, whose names were listed at the Assembly Rooms, and this annoyed Major Brereton's supporters, who, at first, protested, and then, in a fit of fright, tried to bribe Mr. Plomer to renounce his candidature. In the midst of these squabbles, a third gentleman named Jones, who, whilst being a professional gambler, was eager to advance his prospects by abjuring gambling, if that would ensure his election as Master of the Ceremonies, appeared as their rival, amidst clouds of glory and floods of repentance. The contest became more and more violent, urged on by broadsheets, meetings, addresses, epigrams, pamphlets and poems. Even Mr. Garrick joined in, and wrote 'a satirical piece'. But these persuasions were not believed to be forcible enough, and when Mr. Plomer made his appearance in one of the Assembly Rooms, he was dragged out by the nose! This remarkable expression of opinion led to others; and in the end, a fortnight after this event, a riot of such violence took place that the Mayor was obliged to read the Riot Act three times before due attention was paid to him. Before his arrival (the occasion was a public speech, made by one of Mr. Plomer's supporters), shrieks, yells, blows and abuse were followed by a general fight—all against all—in which the women were even more violent than the men. 'Among the ladies' (according to the *Bath and Bristol Chronicle*, 13th April, 1769) *'who began the fray'*, the spirit of opposition afforded work for the milliners, hairdressers, and mantua makers. At last the Mayor appeared.'

In the end, neither of the gentlemen whose claims were so hotly contested, won: for instead, the more peaceable Captain Wade—a nephew of Marshal Wade—was elected, and received, in token of that election, a gold medal, bearing on one side a figure of Venus, with the words *Venus decens*, and on the reverse a laurel branch, with the words *Arbiter elegantiæ, communi consensu.*

A few years later, however, the martial Captain Brereton *did* succeed in becoming Master of the Ceremonies; but, by that time, other Assembly Rooms had been opened in the Upper Town, under the rule of another Master of the Ceremonies—and from then onwards, the city was in a state of constant warfare.

Mars, Venus, and Mercury were the planets in the ascendant. In 1788, Chantreau, in his *Voyage dans les Trois Royaumes*, announced that 'There are more loose women in the spring; there are, in fact, hardly any in London, except such as walk the streets, who have not been to Bath at least four or five times in their lives'. The disreputable Lady Vane was accepted everywhere, and bad manners caused but little surprise, excepting in a few rare cases.

Cross Mr. Tobias Smollett, however, must be reckoned as one objector. Seventeen years before Monsieur Chantreau's denunciation of Bath, Mr. Smollett, unable, even now, to forgive that city for not accepting him as a doctor, was busy finishing his novel *Humphrey Clinker*, and Mathew Bramble, that strangely living puppet of human flesh and blood through whose mouth Smollett's dying voice, his dying petulant anger, sounded, could find nothing right in the city.

'Every upstart of fortune, harnessed in the trappings of the mode, presents himself at Bath, as in the very focus of observation. Clerks and factors from the East Indies, loaded with the spoil of plundered provinces; planters, negro drivers, and hucksters from our American plantations, enriched they know not how; agents, commissaries, and contractors, who have fattened in two successive wars on the blood of the nation; usurers, brokers, and jobbers of every kind; men of low birth and no breeding, have found themselves suddenly translated into a state of affluence, unknown to former ages; and no wonder that their brains should be intoxicated with pride, vanity, and presumption. Knowing no other criterion of greatness but the ostentation of wealth, they discharge their affluence, without taste or conduct, through every channel of the most absurd extravagance; and all of them hurry to Bath because here without any further qualification they can mingle with the princes and nobles of the land.'— 'Even the wives and daughters of low tradesmen', continued Mr. Bramble, in the same muttering, grumbling tone, 'who, like shovel-nosed sharks, prey on the blubber of those uncouth whales of fortune, are infected with the same rage of displaying their importance, and the slightest indisposition serves them for a pretext to insist on being conveyed to

Bath, where they may hobble country dances and cotillons among lordlings, squires, counsellors and clergy.'

When it came to the routs, the balls, and the assemblies, in spite of the elegance of the 'Jessamies', and of those gentlemen whose principal accompaniment was that of whistling airs through their toothpicks, Mr. Bramble's nephew Jeremy Melford found these as amusing as they were shocking. 'I was extremely diverted last ball night', he wrote, 'to see the Master of the Ceremonies leading, with great solemnity, to the upper end of the room, an antiquated abigail, dressed in her lady's cast clothes, whom he, I suppose, mistook for some Countess lately arrived at the Bath. The ball was opened by a Scotch lord, with a mulatto heiress from St. Christopher's; and the gay Colonel Tinsel danced all the evening with the daughter of an eminent tinman from the borough of Southwark. Yesterday morning at the pump-room, I saw a broken-winded Wapping landlady squeeze through a circle of peers to salute her brandy-merchant, who stood by the window, propped on crutches; and a paralytic attorney of Shoe Lane, in shuffling up to the bar, kicked the shins of the Chancellor of England, while his lordship in a cut bob drank a glass of water at the pump.'

As for the tea parties! 'There was nothing but jostling, scrambling, pulling, snatching, struggling, scolding and screaming. The nosegays were torn from one another's hands and bosoms; the glasses and china went to wreck; the tables and floors were strewn with comfits. Some cried, some swore, and the tropes and figures of Billingsgate were used without reserve in all their native zest and flavour, nor were those flowers of rhetoric unattended with significant gesticulation. Some snapped their fingers, some forked them out, some clapped their hands, and some their backsides; at length they fairly proceeded to pulling caps, and everything seemed to presage battle.' In the end, to Jeremy Melford's surprise, it was discovered that one of the principal amazons was a baroness, and the other the widow of a wealthy knight.

But the mulatto heiresses and the shovel-nosed sharks, the baronesses and the clerks and factors from the East Indies, loaded with the spoil of plundered provinces, the planters, the negro drivers, and the hucksters from our American plantations—all these were eclipsed in splendour by a new visitor—Colonel Clive.

Mrs. Scott, writing to her sister-in-law at Naples, had explained: 'This place [Bath] is by no means full, but it contains much wealth. Colonel Clive, the nabob-maker [is not that almost as great a title as the famous Earl of Warwick's?], lives at Westgate House, with all the Clives about him. He has sold his possessions in India to the East Indian Company for £30,000 per annum, a trifling sum, which he dedicates to the buying of land. In a time when property is so fluctuating, I think he may see himself possessor of the whole kingdom, should his distempers allow him a long life; but his health is bad. . . . He lives in little pomp; moderate in his table, and still more in his equipage and retinue.'

Fourteen years before Mr. Smollett's outburst on the subject of factors 'loaded with the spoil of plundered provinces', Colonel Clive had brought a fresh and fantastic note into fashionable life. Horace Walpole, writing to Sir Horace Mann (in 1760), said: 'There are some big news from the East Indies. I don't know what, except that the hero Clive has taken Mazulipatan and the Great Mogul's grandmother. I suppose she will be brought over and put in the Tower with the Shahgoest, the strange Indian beast that Mr. Pitt gave to the King this winter.'

According to the *Annual Register*, the beast was 'a very beautiful and uncommon animal, lately arrived from the East Indies, presented by Jaffier Alby Cann, Nabob of Bengal, to General Clive, who sent it to the Right Honourable William Pitt, Esqʳᵉ, and of which that gentleman had the honour to obtain His Majesty's acceptance, is lodged in the Tower. It is called in the Indostan language a Shah Goest, and is even in that country esteemed an extraordinary rarity.'

The Shah Goest, and the Great Mogul's grandmother, having been taken, Colonel Clive was now obliged by his health to make a short stay at Bath (in 1774). He lived at No. 14 the Circus, and it was supposed that he stayed in Bath in order to take the waters. But this was not possible, owing to the epileptic fits from which he suffered—the result of over-work, overstrain, and his long exposure to the Indian climate.

A few years later, from the autumn of 1780 until August, 1781, Captain Horatio Nelson stayed in Bath, during his convalescence from a long illness, at No. 2 Pierrepoint Street, the house of Mr. Spry, the father of Dr. Spry. Captain Nelson was, at the time of his stay in Bath, aged twenty-two, and had, earlier in the year, been chosen to command the sea part of the expedition against Fort Juan, on the Rio San Juan, which runs into the Atlantic from the huge American lake Nicaragua. The appalling climate and the ceaseless exertion told on his health to such an extent that, on his return to Europe, he was sent to Bath to recuperate. 'My health, thank God', he wrote on 15th February, 1781, 'is very near perfectly restored, and I have very near the perfect use of my limbs, except my left arm.'

Though Captain Nelson's stay in Bath lasted only till August, when he was put in command of the *Albemarle*, he returned to Bath again and again, in order to visit his father. In 1784, the father and son were together, and in September, 1797, and January, 1798, Captain, now Lord, Nelson, visited Bath, being anxious about his father's health, which was failing fast.

On the 24th April, 1802, Lord Nelson, too ill to travel, received this letter from Bath, written by the husband of his niece Kitty:

'My dear Lord,

Your good old father is very ill, and I have directions from Dr. Parry and Mr. Spry to say to you that he is certainly in great danger. Whatever orders you send me shall be executed.

Believe me, my dear Lord,
Yours affectionately,
G. Matcham.'

Two days later, on the 26th of April, 1802, Mr. Nelson died.

But that death occurred twenty-two years after the time when young Captain Nelson recovered his health in Bath, and three years after the time when Lord Nelson, no longer so young, looked out of the window and watched the tall feathers of the ladies (feathers so tall that they swayed in the wind like palm-trees blown by a sirocco—for, according to *The Times*, 'The Ladies now wear feathers of exactly their own length, so that a woman of fashion is twice as long upon her feet as in her bed') surrounding the equipage of Sir Robert Mackworth, who, we are assured by *The Times* (21st January, 1794), appeared to be 'no otherwise distinguished than by the particularity of his equipage'. Sir Robert Mackworth, it seems, drove 'four horses of different colours in his phaeton, which has four wheels painted to correspond with the colours of the horses; in the midst of his badge of his distinction, the bloody hand, is the figure of 4, which he explains in this way, four in hand. The motto "This is the Tippy". If anything', *The Times* adds, severely, 'can add to the folly of the whole it is that he intends to crop four opposite ears of his horses, to make room for four monstrous roses, of different colours, to match.'

Sometimes this cortège of monstrous fools, roses, and feathers, or mulatto heiresses and invalid nabobs, would fly, as if blown by a tropical wind, past a house which seemed shadowed, even in the highest sunlight.

Some Men of War

In this house, No. 23 The Circus, lived the mother and sisters of young Major John André, whose life was short and whose death was tragic.

'The execution of Major André is, indeed, one of the saddest episodes of the American war, and in the judgment of many it left a deep stain on the reputation of Washington. The victim was well fitted to attract to himself a halo of romantic interest. Though only twenty-nine, he had already shown the promise of a brilliant career. He was a skilful artist; and the singular charm of his conversation, and the singular beauty of his frank, generous, and amiable character, endeared him to all with whom he came in contact, and was acknowledged by no one more fully than by those American officers with whom he spent the last sad days of his life. Nothing could be more dignified, more courageous, more candid, and at the same time more free from everything like boasting or ostentation, than his conduct under the terrible trial that had fallen upon him, and it is even now impossible to read without emotion those last letters in which he commended to his country and his old commander the care of his widowed mother, and asked Washington to grant him a single favour—that he might die the death of a soldier and not of a spy. At the same time it is but justice to remember that he suffered under the unanimous sentence of a board consisting of fourteen general officers, and that two of these —Steuben and Lafayette—were not Americans. Nor can the justice of the sentence, in my opinion, be reasonably impugned. As a matter of strict right, the American sentence against André appears to me unassailable, and it is only on grounds of mercy and magnanimity that it can be questioned.'[1]

The event which led to his death is recorded in Mackenzie's *America*, as follows:

'The Americans had a strong fortress at West Point, on

[1]Lecky's *History of the Eighteenth Century*, Vol. IV.

the Hudson River. It was one of the most important places in the country, and its acquisition was anxiously desired by the English. Possession of West Point would have given them command of the Hudson, up which their ships of war could have sailed for more than a hundred miles. But that fort, sitting impregnably on rocks, two hundred feet above the level of the river, was hard to win; and the Americans were careful to garrison effectively a position so vitally important.

'In the American army was an officer named Arnold, who had served, not without distinction, from the beginning of the war. He had fought in Canada when the Americans unsuccessfully invaded that province. His courage and skill had been conspicuous in the engagements which led to the surrender of Burgoyne. He was, however, a vain, reckless, unscrupulous person. He had by extravagance in living involved himself in debt, which he aggravated hopelessly by ill-judged mercantile speculations. He had influence with Washington to obtain the command of West Point. There is little doubt that when he sought the appointment it was with the full intention of selling that important fortress to the enemy. He opened negotiations at once with Sir Henry Clinton, then in command of the English army at New York.

'At midnight Major André landed from the boat of a British ship of war, at a lonely place where Arnold waited him. The conference lasted so long that it was deemed unsafe for André to return to the ship. He was conducted to a place of concealment within the American lines, to await the return of darkness. He completed his arrangement with Arnold, and received drawings of the betrayed fortress. His mission was now accomplished. The ship from which he had come lay full in view. Would that he could reach her! But difficulties arose, and it was resolved that he must ride to New York, a distance of fifty miles. Disguising himself as he best could, André reluctantly accepted this very doubtful method of escape from his fearful jeopardy.

'Within the American lines he had some narrow escapes, but the pass given by Arnold carried him through. He was at length beyond the lines. His danger might now be considered at an end, and he rode cheerfully on his lonely journey. He was crossing a small stream—thick woods on his right hand and his left enhanced the darkness of the night. Three armed men stepped suddenly from among the trees and ordered him to stand. From the dress of one of them, André thought he was among friends. He hastened to tell them he was a British officer, on very special business, and he must not be detained. Alas for poor Major André, they were not friends; and the dress which deceived him had been given to the man who wore it when he was a prisoner with the English, in place of a better garment of which his captors had stripped him.

'André was searched; but at first nothing was found. It seemed as if he might yet be allowed to proceed, when one of the three exclaimed, "Boys, I am not satisfied. His boots must come off." André's countenance fell. His boots were searched, and Arnold's drawings of West Point were discovered. The men knew then that he was a spy. He vainly offered them money; they were incorruptible. He was taken to the nearest military station, and the tidings were at once sent to Washington, who chanced to be then at West Point. Arnold had timely intimation of the disaster, and fled for refuge to a British ship of war.

'André was tried by a court formed of officers of the American army. He gave a frank and truthful account of his part in the unhappy transaction—bringing into due prominence the circumstance that he was brought, without intention or knowledge on his part, within the American lines. The court judged him on his own statement, and condemned him to be hanged as a spy.

'His capture and sentence caused deep sensation in the English army, and every effort was made to save him. But Washington was resolute that he should die. The danger to the patriot cause had been too great to leave any place for relenting. There were dark intimations of other treasons yet unrevealed. It was needful to give emphatic warning of the perils which waited on such unlawful negotiations. André begged that he might be allowed to die a soldier's death. Even this poor boon was refused to the unhappy man. Since the awful lesson must be given, Washington considered that no circumstance fitted to enhance its terrors should be withheld. But this was mercifully concealed from André to the very last.

'Ten days after his arrest, André was led forth to die. He was under the impression that his last request had been granted, and that he would die by the bullet. It was a fresh pang when the gibbet, with its ghastly preparations, stood before him. "How hard is my fate," he said; "but it will soon be over." He bandaged his own eyes; with his own hands adjusted the noose to his neck. The cart on which he stood moved away, and poor Major André was no longer in the world of living men. Forty years afterwards his remains were brought home to England and laid in Westminster Abbey.'

But a little cold wind is scattering those ghosts—the nabobs and the mulatto heiresses, and the ladies crowned with feathers as tall as themselves; the slave-drivers and the odd-looking men from our southern plantations. The wind is blowing them past the house from which Captain Nelson is watching them, and past the house where the great Lord Clive had lived for a while, and past that darkened and strange house in the Circus where Major André's mother and sisters move from shadowed room to shadowed room, in an eternal silence. The foolish laughing crowd is being blown over the edge of the century, into a world of plantations where they will meet Miss Austen, and Dr. Caraboo and the Princess Caraboo, and William Beckford, the owner of the Abbey of Fonthill, which was built by torchlight.

These new ghosts are strange to those of our last hundred years, and perhaps this light and glittering dust, blown by a remembered wind, will not be sad to sink into dust again, in the empire of the eternal shade.

The Stables and Pavilion of Prior Park

IN PURSUANCE OF THE MODIFIED DESIGN, THE west wing was begun, but again some deviation from the design was made before its completion. This wing consisted of a principal and half-storey, extending 172 ft. 8 in. in front by 34 ft. 4 in. in depth on the plinth course of stone. In the centre there was the hay-house, 20 ft. high, with a pigeon-house over it of the same altitude, four six-horse stables, three coach-houses, and harness-rooms. The stables and hay-houses were arched or vaulted over with stone, which was so intended from the first by the architect, who borrowed the idea from the stables of Mr. Hanbury of Pontypool. The rest of the floorings and roof of the whole were intended to have been of timber, covered with Cornish slate. But in the execution of the building Allen resolved to make use of nothing but stone for a covering for this wing of offices. This substitution of stone for timber disarranged the architect's plan, and the changing of the material for the roof not only interfered with the altitude of some of the offices, but also greatly interfered with the essential characteristics of the building itself. Of the external walls, only that which fronts the south was faced with wrought free-stone; and this was to have exhibited the Doric order in its plainest dress, but so high as to include a principal and a half-storey above it, separated by a fascia or band. A tetra-style frontispiece in the middle of the whole line, before such an advanced part of the building, was to have contained two of the staircases, one on each end of the hay-house, and at the same time appear as a proper basement of the pigeon-house, which was to have crowned the edifice with magnificence and beauty; for the basement extends 50 ft., and a square of that size in the middle of the building was to have been covered with a pyramidal roof, divided into two parts, and to have discovered the body of the crowning ornament. It will be seen, therefore, in what respect the change affected the edifice. The joists intended for the timber roof had such a projection given them in the design as would have afforded protection in wet weather to persons walking from one part of this wing of offices to the other. When, however, the ends of the joists came to be represented in stone, they were contracted to small corbels, of little use and less beauty, when considered as part of the crowning ornament to columns of the Doric order.

The stables were divided into six recessed stalls on every side, arched, and lined with dressed stone. Allen treated his horses like gentlemen. They were richly caparisoned, and he always had four to his coach, in which his guests drove out with much state. Wood was not quite satisfied, however, with the stables; he wanted a little more magnitude, and would have preferred a recess at each stall to contain a bin for a horse. This wing was finished about 1736 or 1737.

After the completion of the west wing, the pavilion was to serve as an arch for coaches to drive under, and as a poultry- and pigeon-house. This structure was built and finished with wrought freestone. The lower part of it was composed of four hollow legs, each 9 ft. square by 13½ ft. in length, every front containing an aperture of 16 ft. in breadth, all arched over. The body of the building was crowned at the altitude of 22½ ft. with a cornice, surmounted by a plain attic, 6 ft. in height, supporting a pyramidal design, terminating in an octagonal pedestal turret, 10 ft. in diameter, covered with a dome, the whole being finished with an ornament, consisting of a base, ball, baluster, and vane, making the extreme height 59 ft., or 39 ft. above the vaulted arch for coaches. The cells for pigeons were made of wrought freestone. The poultry were similarly provided for in the low building by which the west wing was united with the pavilion. It consisted of three rooms, facing southward, with three apertures to every room, arched over.

CENTRAL MANSION

Some deviation from the general plan was rendered necessary by the addition of a closet, which destroyed the continuity of the original basement lines of the central mansion, from the necessity it involved of placing the pavilion lower than was intended. Another consequence was that the line having thus been broken, the architect felt no scruple in laying the foundation of the main central structure higher than was originally intended; and the bottom of the plinth was, therefore, 15 in. higher than that of the west wing. The building thus elevated stood upon the plinth course of stone, 147 ft. in length by 80 ft. in breadth, inclusive of the projections in front and rear, and consisted of basement, principal and chamber stories, with garrets taken out of the altitude of some of the rooms of the latter.

The mansion was constructed of solid blocks of very large dimensions, in equal courses both within and without, with a course of brick between; so that the walls were equally strong on both sides, and were able to bear the superincumbent masonry without being liable to 'buckle' under the weight. The rooms in the basement storey were 12 ft. high, but a narrow passage, running through the middle of the house from end to end, was lower by 1 foot. The chimneys in the several rooms were dressed with architraves, some of which were crowned with their proper friezes and cornices, all in freestone; and with the same material the door-cases next the passage were made, architraves being worked upon the external faces as the proper dress for the apertures. This passage being divided into five equal parts, regularly finished with freestone ornaments, became the beauty of the inside of the basement storey, the rooms of which received their light from square windows in the north front, but those on the south from oblong windows. It should be added that not only were the walls of the entire house outside and inside built of Bath stone of the best quality, carefully wrought in the sheds, every stone for its place, but the floors of the basement rooms were laid with the hard, calcined, shelly ragstone, which is the first bed or stratum, or as Wood further says, 'the roof of the subterraneous quarries', the next stratum being the 'picking bed', which is not so hard and durable. On this basement storey were a servants' hall, a housekeeper's room, a butler's pantry, and a room for the footmen, a small beer cellar, a strong-beer cellar, wine vault, laundry, bakehouse, kitchen, scullery, larder, and pantry. There were also a dairy and milk-room, with scullery, and an apartment set aside for w.c.'s should 'any such conveniences be wanted within the body of the house'. The several rooms were arched, or vaulted over by stone, and the stairs also made of stone, so that the defects peculiar to plaster were effectually avoided in this almost uniquely-constructed house.

On the first floor the hall extended from the front to the rear of the house, and to the eastward of the hall there were a parlour, study, store-rooms, chapel, and back staircase; and to the northward a portico or grand pavilion. The altitude of this pavilion, as well as that of the chapel, was determined by the base of the roof; but all the other rooms were covered over at 16 ft. of height, the whole of the architectural ornamentations being of Bath stone, though these were afterwards removed from the parlour and dining-room, which, to the disgust of Wood, were then lined with oak, the irate architect denouncing it as a 'depredation'.

Some compensation, however, was vouchsafed to him by his being permitted to finish the whole of the upper stories, passages, and gallery (20 ft. high), as well as the chapel, with dressed stone. The chapel was of the Ionic order, sustaining the Corinthian. The parlour was finished in the Ionic order, and the dining-room, hall, principal staircase, and gallery were completed in the Corinthian order.

The portico, already mentioned, on the north front was a hexastyle; and it seems that, although divested of some of its beauty for the convenience of the garret windows, it was designed by Wood to excel in grandeur that which had been just executed at Wanstead by his old rival, Colin Campbell. The portico consisted of Ionic columns supporting a Corinthian entablature. The columns were 3ft. $1\frac{1}{2}$ in. in diameter, which exceeds the Wanstead column by $1\frac{1}{2}$ in.; the intercolumnation being what is called a *systylos* or systyle—*i.e.* the space between the columns equalling two diameters of the shaft at the bottom, whilst the distance between each of the plinths on which the column or shaft rests is equivalent to its own diameter. The entablature was carried all round the house, with the exception of the west end, where it was sacrificed to the exigencies of the windows. Each front was crowned by a handsome balustrade.

The east wing was designed by Richard Jones, and the object was chiefly to provide bedroom accommodation. It contains a hall and a picture-gallery; and this wing is connected with the centre by an open corridor. In the midst of the grove was a fine lawn, sloping down from the house; near the summit of this lawn rose a plentiful spring, gushing out of a rock covered with firs, and forming a constant cascade of about thirty feet, not carried down a regular flight of steps, but tumbling in a natural fall over the broken and mossy stones till it came to the bottom of the rock, then running off in a pebbly channel, that, with many lesser falls, winded along till it fell into a lake at the foot of a hill, about a quarter of a mile or less below the house on the south side (facing north-west).

The lake was, and still is, in the midst of a grove, and the cascade gushed out of a rock; but we have shown that the site of the mansion was a watershed of the south-east branch of the Lyn; and after issuing from the rock, the water passed through the culverts constructed under the foundations, then formed the cascade, passed into the small lake in the grove, then entered an open channel, and passed into the pretty lake at the bottom of the park. Richard Jones designed the exquisite Palladian bridge by which it is spanned, and of which Allen, in 1751, laid the foundation stone. There is a full-length portrait of Garrick, painted by Gainsborough, one of that master's greatest works, done at Prior Park. We wish we could give a more circumstantial account of the local associations which connect it with Prior Park. The figure of Garrick is very characteristic, and the attitude seems intended to represent *Genius*; the right arm is carelessly thrown round the base of a bust of Shakespeare resting on a plinth, whilst in the distance, to the left, the Palladian bridge is the conspicuous object.

Besides the east wing, Jones erected near it a small but very pretty cottage for the gardener. After Allen's death this cottage was called *The Priory*, and has recently been enlarged and transformed into a lovely residence.

Within a few yards westward of the upper lodge gate is the entrance to what once was a very pretty and well-kept private walk, traditionally known as *Pope's Walk*. This walk runs parallel with the carriage road, and leads down to a picturesque old arch, which forms a roadway over a narrow chasm, and was manifestly intended in former times for, and used as, a path for the use of the shepherds to cross with their flocks. This walk was not laid out until ten years after Pope's death. On each side is a quickset hedge, and at intervals there are lovely peeps of the distant scenery to right and left.

Pitt-Allen Correspondence

To the King's Most Excellent Majesty.

'*We, the Mayor, Aldermen, and Common Council of the ancient and loyal city of Bath, do beg leave to congratulate, and most humbly to thank your Majesty for an* ADEQUATE *and advantageous peace, which you have graciously procured for your people, after a long and very expensive, though necessary and glorious war, which your Majesty, upon your accession to the throne, found your kingdom engaged in.*

'*And we take the liberty to assure your Majesty, that upon all occasions we shall be ready to give the most evident proofs of the truest zeal and duty, which the most dutiful subjects can testify to the most gracious and best of princes.*

'*In testimony whereof we have hereunto affixed our Common Seal, the 28th day of May, 1763.*'

To Ralph Allen, Esq.

HAYES, *June 2, 1763.*

'DEAR SIR,—Having declined accompanying Sir John Seabright in presenting the address from Bath, transmitted to us jointly by the Town Clerk, I think it, on all accounts, indispensably necessary that I should inform you of the reason of my conduct. The epithet of *adequate* given to the peace contains a description of the conditions of it, so repugnant to my unalterable opinion concerning many of them, and fully declared by me in Parliament, that it was as impossible for me to obey the Corporation's commands in presenting their address, as it was unexpected to receive such a commission. As to my opinion of the peace, I will only say, that I formed it with sincerity according to such lights as my little experience and small portion of my understanding could afford me. This conviction must remain to myself the constant rule of my conduct; and I leave to others, with much deference to their better information, to follow their own judgment. Give me leave, my dear, good sir, to desire to convey, through you, to Mr. Mayor, and to the gentlemen of the Corporation, these my free sentiments; and with the justest sense of their past goodness towards me, plainly to confess that I perceive I am but ill qualified to form pretensions to the future favour of gentlemen, who are come to think so differently from me, on matters of the highest importance to the national welfare.

'I am ever, with respectful and affectionate esteem, my dear sir,

'Your faithful friend and obliged humble Servant,

'(Signed) W. PITT.

'Lady Chatham joins with me in all compliments to the family of Prior Park.'

To the Right Hon. Mr. Pitt.

'PRIOR PARK, *June* 4, 1763.

'MY DEAREST SIR,—It is extremely painful to me to find by the letter which you was pleased to send to me the 2nd of this month, that the word *adequate*, in the Bath address, has been so very offensive to you, as to hinder the sincerest and most zealous of your friends in the Corporation from testifying for the future their great attachment to you.

'Upon this occasion, in justice to them, it is incumbent on me to acquaint you, that the unexceptionable word does not rest with them, but myself; who suddenly drew up that address, to prevent their sending of another, which the Mayor brought to me, in terms that I could not concur in;

copies of the two forms I have taken the liberty to send to you in the enclosed paper, for your private perusal; and Sir John Seabright having, in his letter to Mr. Clutterbuck, only acquainted him, that in your absence in the country he delivered the address, I shall decline executing of your commands to the Corporation on this delicate point, unless you renew them, upon your perusal of this letter, which for safety I have sent by a messenger, and I beg your answer to it by him, who has orders to wait for it.

'Permit me to say that I have not the least objection to, but the highest regard and even veneration for, your whole conduct; neither have I any apology to make for the expression in which I am so unfortunate to differ from you. And with the utmost respect, affection, and gratitude, you will always find me to be, my dearest sir, your most humble and obedient servant,

'(Signed) R. ALLEN.

'The best wishes of this family always attend Lady Chatham.

'R. A.'

To Ralph Allen, Esquire.

'HAYES, *June* 5, 1763.

'MY DEAR SIR,—I am sorry that my letter of the 2nd inst. should give you uneasiness, and occasion to you the trouble of sending a messenger to Hayes. I desire you to be assured, that few things can give me more real concern, than to find that my notions of the public good differ so widely from those of the man whose goodness of heart and private views I shall ever respect and love. I am not insensible to your kind motives for wishing to interpose time for second thoughts; but knowing how much you approve an open and ingenuous proceeding, I trust that you will see the unfitness of my concealing from my constituents the insurmountable reasons which prevent my obeying their commands in presenting an address, containing a disavowal of my opinion delivered in Parliament relating to the peace. As their servant, I owe to these gentlemen an explanation of my conduct on this occasion, and as a man not forgetful of the distinguished honour of having been invited to represent them, I owe it, in gratitude, to them, not to think of embarrassing and encumbering, for the future, friends to whom I have such obligations; and who now view with approbation measures of an administration, founded on the subversion of that system which once procured me the countenance and favour of the city of Bath. On these plain grounds, very coolly weighed, I will venture to beg again that my equitable good friend will be so good to convey to Mr. Mayor and the gentlemen of the Corporation my sentiments, as contained in my letter of the 2nd instant.

'I am ever, with unchanging sentiments of respect and affection,

'My dear sir, most faithfully yours,

'W. PITT.'

Letter to Mrs. Allen, accompanying the last addressed to Ralph Allen, June 5th, 1763.

'I cannot conclude my letter without expressing my sensible concern at Mr. Allen's uneasiness. No incidents can make the least change in the honour and love I bear him, or in the justice my heart does to his humane and benevolent virtues.'

(The context of this letter to Mrs. Allen is missing.)

To the Right Hon. Mr. Pitt.

'PRIOR PARK, *June 9th.*

'MY DEAREST SIR,—With the greatest anxiety and concern, I have in obedience to your positive and repeated commands executed the most painful commission that I ever received.

'Upon this disagreeable occasion, give me leave just to say that, however different our abilities may be, it is the duty of every honest man, after he has made the strictest enquiry, to act pursuant to the light which the Supreme Being has been pleased to dispense to him; and this being the rule that I am persuaded we both govern ourselves by, I shall take the liberty, not only to add, that it is impossible for any person to retain higher sentiments of your late glorious administration than I do, nor can be with truer fidelity, zeal, affection, and respect than I have been, still am, and always shall be, my dearest sir,

'Your most humble and most obedient servant,

'(Signed) R. ALLEN.

'The best wishes of this family wait upon Lady Chatham.'

The Bath Address-Book

THE PRINCESS AMELIA	*The Royal Residence, West Gate.*
MAJOR ANDRÉ	*23 Circus.*
CHRISTOPHER ANSTEY, ESQRE.	*5 Royal Crescent.*
MISS JANE AUSTEN	*4 Sydney Place,* from the spring of 1801 till 1805, when she removed to *1 Gay Street* and afterwards to *Green Park Buildings.*
WILLIAM BECKFORD, ESQRE.	*Beckford House, Lansdown Crescent.*
JOHN, DUKE OF BEDFORD	*15 Circus.*
JAMES BOSWELL, ESQRE.	*The Pelican Inn, Walcot Street.*
MISS FRANCES BURNEY	
EDMUND BURKE, ESQRE.	*11 North Parade.*
WILLIAM PITT, EARL OF CHATHAM	*7 Circus*
EARL OF CHESTERFIELD	*Pierrepont Street* (opposite the Doric Portico. The house was designed by Wood).
LORD CLIVE	*14 Circus.*
EARL OF CORK AND BURLINGTON	*Nassau House, The Orange Grove* (designed and built by himself, about 1730).

The Bath Address-Book

MRS. DELANY — The house in *St. John's Court*, built by Thomas Greenway and previously occupied by Beau Nash.

THOMAS GAINSBOROUGH — 14 *Abbey Churchyard*, then 8 *Ainslie's Belvedere*, then 24 *Circus*.

OLIVER GOLDSMITH — (as a visitor to Viscount Clare) 11 *North Parade*.

SELINA, COUNTESS OF HUNTINGDON — 4 *Edgar Buildings*.

DOCTOR JOHNSON — *The Pelican Inn*.

THE DUKE AND DUCHESS OF KINGSTON (ELIZABETH CHUDLEIGH) — *Kingston House* (south-west of the Abbey in Kingston Buildings).

SIR THOMAS LAWRENCE — 2 *Alfred Street* (during boyhood).

THOMAS LINLEY AND HIS DAUGHTER ELIZA (afterwards MRS. RICHARD SHERIDAN) — 5 *Pierrepont Street* (Mrs. Sheridan was born in this house).

SALLY LUNN — *Liliput Alley* (afterwards called North Parade Passage).

MRS. CATHERINE MACAULEY — 2 *Alfred Street* (formerly called Alfred House).

BEAU NASH — *Saint John's Court* (the house became, afterwards, the 'Garrick's Head'), afterwards *The Saw-Close*.

ADMIRAL VISCOUNT NELSON (then Captain Nelson) — 2 *Pierrepont Street*.

MRS. PIOZZI	8 *Gay Street.*
JAMES QUIN	House in *Pierrepont Street* (formerly occupied by Chesterfield).
SIR WALTER SCOTT (as a child)	6 *South Parade.*
CAPTAIN PHILIP THICKNESSE	6 *Walcot Terrace,* 9 *Royal Crescent, The Lodge, Bathampton, The Hermitage.*
MARSHAL WADE	14 *Abbey Churchyard.*
HORACE WALPOLE	*Chapel Court.*
JOSIAH WEDGWOOD	*Show-Rooms in Westgate Buildings*
GENERAL WOLFE	5 *Trim Street,* near St. John's Gate or Trim Bridge.
JOHN WOOD THE ELDER	The centre house on the North side of *Queen Square, A Villa at Batheaston,* and 41 *Gay Street* (at the corner of Old King Street, forms, in reality, a portion of Queen Square).
JOHN WOOD THE YOUNGER	His father's house, 41 *Gay Street,* and his father's *Villa at Batheaston.*

Index

282

Index

Index

Index

Index

Index

Index